# I LOVE LISTS!

**Written by Linda Schwartz**
**Illustrated by Beverly Armstrong**

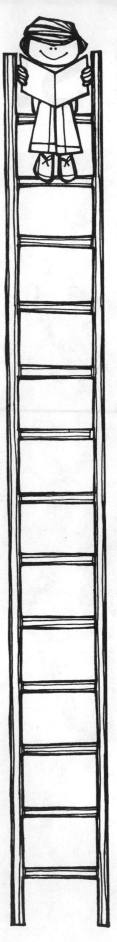

# The Learning Works

*Dedicated with love
to
Stan, Stephen, Michael,
and
Mom and Dad —
special people at the top
of my list.*

*Special thanks to Beverly Armstrong for her outstanding
artistic ability and creativity and to Sherri Butterfield for
her meticulous editing and consistent concern for quality.*

## Edited by Sherri M. Butterfield

Copyright © 1988
**The Learning Works, Inc.**
Santa Barbara, California 93160
All rights reserved.
Printed in the United States of America.

# Introduction

***I Love Lists!*** is a remarkable collection of nearly two hundred separate lists drawn from all major subject areas. This book includes lists related to art, astronomy, careers, chemistry, computers, dance, geography, geology, health, history, hobbies, law, literature, measurement, medicine, metrics, music, numerals, nutrition, phonics, politics, space, sports, theater, and more. There are lists of architects, artists, and authors; lists of careers, codes, and comets; lists of flowers, phobias, and firsts; lists of people, places, and palindromes; lists of similes, suffixes, and synonyms. And there are lists of things—things to celebrate, things to collect, things to eat, things to wear, and things to write about. At the end of many lists are instructions for follow-up activities tailored to the actual list content.

Within this book, the lists are arranged in six major sections entitled **Language Arts**, **Social Studies**, **Science**, **Math**, **The Arts and Sports**, and **Just for Fun**. In each section, closely related lists are grouped in subsections and alphabetized by title or topic. For example, a two-page list of Prehistoric Animals appears near the end of the Animals subsection within the Science section. And a two-page list of Astronauts opens the Space subsection of the Science section. In addition to an amazing array of lists, many of the six sections contain a page of Bonus Ideas for using the lists within that section in interesting and creative ways and a page that offers readers an opportunity to add to the section by creating their own special lists.

The lists in this book can be used in a variety of ways. Not only do they make ideal resources for reference, but they can also serve as the bases for quiz and game questions and as topics for research. They may be used to develop skill in alphabetizing, chronologizing, classifying, and comparing. And they are guaranteed to inspire creative expression in the form of centers, charts, displays, graphs, illustrations, paintings, plays, poems, posters, stories, and time lines. They will help students explore word origins and meanings, increase their vocabularies, and expand their knowledge of the world around them. In short, **I Love Lists!** gives readers of all ages nearly two hundred reasons to do exactly that—love lists!

**Protoceratops yoga jack-in-the-box kunzite prestidigitation frogmouth all pewter chorizo duodecillion Zambezi nerd Kenya eucalyptus dancer Vizsla**

# Contents

# Contents
## (continued)

# Contents
## (continued)

# Language Arts

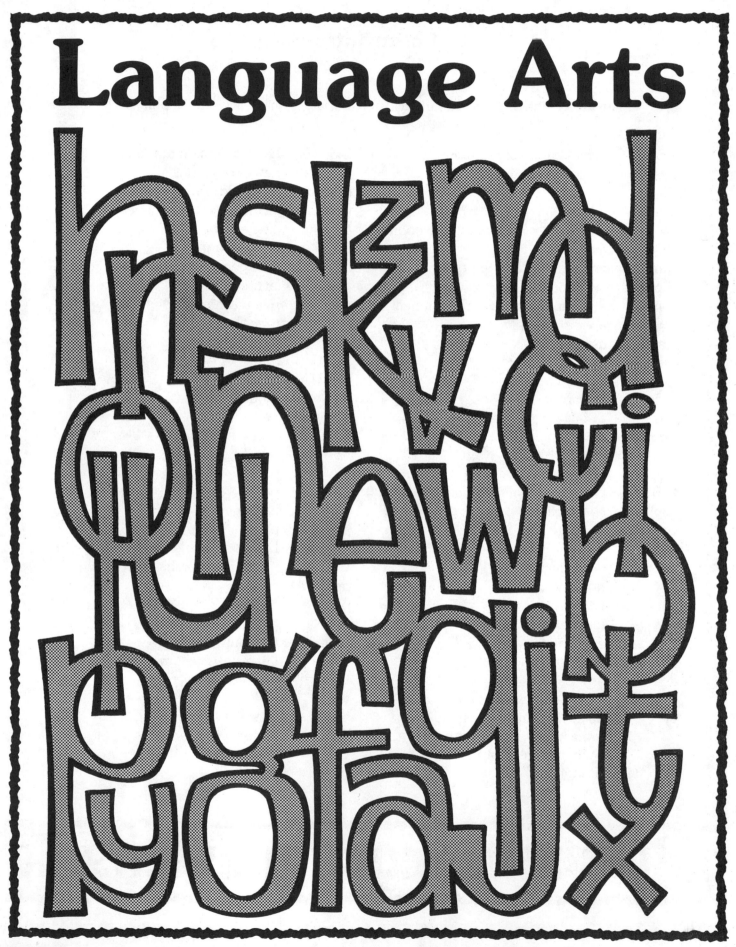

# Abbreviations

An **abbreviation** is a shortened or contracted form of a word or phrase.

| | | | | |
|---|---|---|---|---|
| abbr. | abbreviated, abbreviation | | ibid. | Latin *ibidem*, in the same place |
| acct. | account, accountant | | i.e. | Latin *id est*, that is |
| adj. | adjective | | illust. | illustrated, illustration |
| adv. | adverb | | inc. | incomplete, incorporated |
| A.M. | Latin *ante meridiem*, before noon | | interj. | interjection |
| amt. | amount | | I.O.U. | I owe you |
| anon. | anonymous, anonymously | | I.Q. | intelligence quotient |
| approx. | approximate, approximately | | lat. | latitude |
| appt. | appoint, appointed, appointment | | mfg. | manufacturing |
| apt. | apartment, aptitude | | misc. | miscellaneous |
| assn. | association | | mo. | month |
| assoc. | associate | | M.P.G. | miles per gallon |
| asst. | assistant | | M.P.H. | miles per hour |
| avdp. | avoirdupois | | mt. | mount, mountain |
| avg. | average | | n. | noun |
| bldg. | building | | no. | north, number |
| chap. | chapter | | nos. | numbers |
| co. | company | | p. | page |
| C.O.D. | cash on delivery, collect on delivery | | pd. | paid |
| conj. | conjunction | | pkg. | package |
| contd. | continued | | pl. | plural |
| corp. | corporation | | P.M. | Latin *post meridiem*, after noon |
| dept. | department | | P.O. | post office, purchase order |
| dist. | distance, district | | pp. | pages |
| ea. | each | | ppd. | postpaid, prepaid |
| e.g. | Latin *exempli gratia*, for example | | pr. | pair, price, printed |
| elem. | elementary | | pron. | pronoun |
| encyc. | encyclopedia | | P.S. | Latin *postscriptum*, postscript |
| esp. | especially | | univ. | universal, university |
| est. | established, estimate, estimated | | v. | verb |
| etc. | Latin *et cetera*, and others (of the same kind), and so forth | | v., vs. | versus |
| | | | vss. | verses, versions |
| fig. | figure, meaning picture or illustration | | wk. | week |
| govt. | government | | yr. | year |

# bldg.conj.encyc.fig.ibid.n.wk.

# Abbreviations
## (continued)

### Addresses and Directions

| | |
|---|---|
| Ave. | Avenue |
| Blvd. | Boulevard |
| E. | East |
| Frwy. | Freeway |
| Hwy. | Highway |
| Ln. | Lane |
| N., No. | North |
| Pkwy. | Parkway |
| Pl. | Place |
| Rd. | Road |
| Rte. | Route |
| S., So. | South |
| Sq. | Square |
| St. | Street |
| Terr. | Terrace |

### Days of the Week

| | |
|---|---|
| Sun. | Sunday |
| Mon. | Monday |
| Tues. | Tuesday |
| Wed. | Wednesday |
| Thurs. | Thursday |
| Fri. | Friday |
| Sat. | Saturday |

### Months of the Year

| | |
|---|---|
| Jan. | January |
| Feb. | February |
| Mar. | March |
| Apr. | April |
| May | May |
| June | June |
| July | July |
| Aug. | August |
| Sept. | September |
| Oct. | October |
| Nov. | November |
| Dec. | December |

### Titles

| | |
|---|---|
| Adm. | Admiral |
| atty. | attorney |
| dent. | dentist |
| Capt. | Captain |
| Col. | Colonel |
| Dr. | Doctor |
| Gen. | General |
| Gov. | Governor |
| Hon. | Honorable |
| Jr. | Junior |
| Lt. | Lieutenant |
| Maj. | Major |
| mgr. | manager |
| Miss | (unmarried woman) |
| Mr. | Mister |
| Mrs. | Mistress (married woman) |
| Pres. | President |
| Rep. | Representative |
| Rev. | Reverend |
| Secy. | Secretary |
| Sr. | Senior |
| Supt. | Superintendent |

### Units of Measure

| | | | |
|---|---|---|---|
| a. | acre | m | meter |
| bbl. | barrel | mg | milligram |
| bu. | bushel | mi. | mile |
| C. | Celsius, Centigrade | min. | minute |
| c. | cup | ml | milliliter |
| cm | centimeter | mm | millimeter |
| d. | day | mo. | month |
| deg. | degree | oz. | ounce |
| doz. | dozen | pk. | peck |
| F | Fahrenheit | pt. | pint |
| ft. | foot | qt. | quart |
| gal. | gallon | rd. | rod |
| gm | gram | sec. | second |
| hr. | hour | T. | tablespoon |
| ht. | height | t. | teaspoon |
| in. | inch | tbsp. | tablespoon |
| kg | kilogram | tsp. | teaspoon |
| kl | kiloliter | vol. | volume |
| l | liter | wt. | weight |
| lb. | pound | yd. | yard |
| | | yr. | year |

# Acronyms

An **acronym** is a word formed from the initial letter or letters of words in a phrase. It is often written entirely in capital letters and is usually pronounced as a word.

| | |
|---|---|
| **AIDS** | acquired immune deficiency syndrome |
| **ASAP** | as soon as possible |
| **AWOL** | absent without leave |
| **CAT** | computerized axial tomography |
| **CORE** | Congress of Racial Equality |
| **loran** | long-range navigation |
| **MADD** | Mothers Against Drunk Driving |
| **maser** | microwave amplification by stimulated emission of radiation |
| **NASA** | National Aeronautics and Space Administration |
| **NASCAR** | National Association of Stock Car Auto Racing |
| **NATO** | North Atlantic Treaty Organization |
| **NOW** | National Organization for Women |
| **OPEC** | Organization of Petroleum Exporting Countries |
| **OSHA** | Occupational Safety and Health Administration |
| **radar** | radio detecting and ranging |
| **RAM** | random access memory |
| **ROM** | read only memory |
| **SADD** | Students Against Drunk Driving |
| **SALT** | Strategic Arms Limitation Talks |
| **SAT** | Scholastic Aptitude Test |
| **scuba** | self-contained underwater breathing apparatus |
| **SEATO** | Southeast Asia Treaty Organization |
| **sonar** | sound navigation ranging |
| **STOL** | short takeoff and landing |
| **SWAT** | special weapons and tactics |
| **UNESCO** | United Nations Educational, Scientific, and Cultural Organization |
| **UNICEF** | United Nations International Children's Emergency Fund |
| **VISTA** | Volunteers in Service to America |
| **Wac** | Women's Army Corps; a member of the Women's Army Corps |
| **Waf** | Women in the Air Force; a member of the women's component of the Air Force formed after World War II |
| **WHO** | World Health Organization |
| **zip** | zone improvement plan |

# Adjectives

An **adjective** is a word that describes a noun or a pronoun. An adjective tells which one, what kind, or how many.

| | | |
|---|---|---|
| absent | jubilant | regal |
| absurd | juicy | resourceful |
| basic | keen | silky |
| belligerent | kindly | slender |
| casual | lazy | thick |
| crooked | lovely | tireless |
| damp | massive | unhappy |
| delightful | mellow | usual |
| eligible | nervous | versatile |
| enormous | nice | vivid |
| faithful | obscure | windy |
| fleshy | obvious | wiry |
| gaunt | poignant | xenolithic |
| gloomy | previous | xeric |
| healthy | quaint | young |
| helpful | queasy | youthful |
| icy | | zany |
| idle | | zestful |

lazy lovely lizard

# Adverbs

An **adverb** is a word that describes a verb, an adjective, or another adverb. An adverb tells how, when, where, or to what degree.

| | | |
|---|---|---|
| angrily | jointly | rather |
| away | justly | regularly |
| barely | keenly | sharply |
| boastfully | knowingly | slyly |
| casually | legally | thoughtfully |
| cheerfully | lustily | truthfully |
| daintily | merely | upstairs |
| deceptively | moderately | uselessly |
| excitedly | neglectfully | violently |
| expectantly | nowhere | visibly |
| falsely | obviously | weakly |
| fearfully | orderly | wishfully |
| gloomily | passively | xenially |
| guiltily | possibly | xenocentrically |
| hastily | quickly | yearly |
| humbly | quietly | yes |
| immediately | | zealously |
| inwardly | | zestfully |

The vulture
vaulted violently.

# Antonyms

**Antonyms** are words that are opposite in meaning.

| | | |
|---|---|---|
| abate-increase | comply-resist | inferior-superior |
| above-below | crooked-straight | join-separate |
| absent-present | dark-light | joy-grief |
| accept-refuse | day-night | kind-cruel |
| achieve-fail | decrease-increase | large-small |
| active-passive | deep-shallow | leave-stay |
| advance-retreat | defeat-victory | long-short |
| alike-different | difficult-easy | loose-tight |
| allow-forbid | down-up | lose-win |
| always-never | dry-wet | many-few |
| ambitious-lazy | early-late | maximum-minimum |
| appear-vanish | easy-hard | noisy-quiet |
| arrival-departure | empty-full | offense-defense |
| ascent-descent | evil-good | often-seldom |
| asleep-awake | exact-vague | on-off |
| attack-defend | exterior-interior | part-whole |
| back-front | fancy-plain | permanent-temporary |
| beautiful-ugly | far-near | plentiful-scarce |
| before-after | fast-slow | polite-rude |
| begin-end | first-last | pull-push |
| believe-doubt | flimsy-solid | regular-irregular |
| beneficial-harmful | foe-friend | rich-poor |
| best-worst | foolish-wise | rough-smooth |
| bold-timid | forget-remember | save-spend |
| bottom-top | fragile-sturdy | short-tall |
| bright-dull | fresh-stale | shrink-swell |
| busy-idle | give-take | start-stop |
| calm-excited | guilty-innocent | strong-weak |
| cheerful-somber | happy-sad | tame-wild |
| clean-dirty | hard-soft | thick-thin |
| close-open | healthy-sick | true-false |
| cold-hot | heavy-light | usual-unusual |
| common-rare | high-low | wide-narrow |
| complex-simple | include-omit | zenith-nadir |

# *Bi-* Words

The prefix **bi-** means "two, twice, coming or occurring every two, or coming or occurring twice." Below is a list of words that start with this prefix. How many words can you add to the list?

| | | |
|---|---|---|
| biangular | biennial | binomial |
| biannual | bifacial | binuclear |
| biarticulate | bifanged | bipartisan |
| biaxial | bifilar | bipartite |
| bicentennial | biflagellate | biped |
| bicephalous | bifocal | biplane |
| bicolor | bifoliate | bipolar |
| bicorn | bilabial | bipropellant |
| bicorporal | bilateral | biradiate |
| bicultural | bimolecular | bireme |
| bicuspid | binary | bisect |
| bicycle | | biweekly |

Here are some other prefixes that indicate numbers. Select one of these prefixes and list ten or more words in which it is used.

| | | | |
|---|---|---|---|
| *tri-* | three | *sept-, septi-* | seven |
| *quad-* | four | *octa-, octo-* | eight |
| *penta-, quint-* | five | *novem-* | nine |
| *hexa-, hex-, sext-* | six | *deca-, dec-, deka-* | ten |

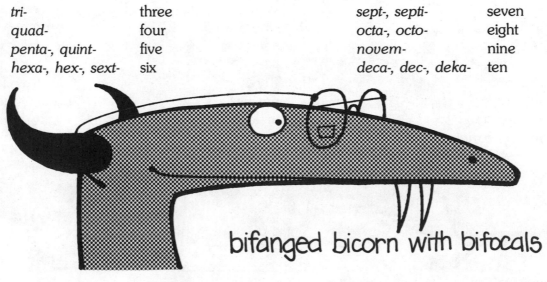

bifanged bicorn with bifocals

# Compound Words

| | | | | |
|---|---|---|---|---|
| absentminded | battleship | checkerboard | driftwood | football |
| aftermath | bedroom | cheeseburger | driveway | footnote |
| afternoon | bedspread | chessboard | drugstore | footprint |
| aircraft | bedtime | classroom | drumstick | forever |
| airfield | beehive | coastline | dugout | framework |
| airline | beside | coffeepot | earache | freshman |
| airmail | birthday | copyright | eardrum | frostbite |
| airplane | birthmark | countdown | earmark | fullback |
| airport | birthplace | courthouse | earthbound | gaslight |
| airstrip | blackberry | courtyard | earthquake | gatehouse |
| airtight | blackbird | cowboy | eggnog | gatekeeper |
| alongside | blackboard | crowbar | eggplant | getaway |
| angelfish | blackmail | cupcake | eggshell | gingerbread |
| another | blackout | daybreak | elsewhere | glassware |
| anybody | blindfold | daytime | evergreen | goldfish |
| anyone | bluebell | deckhand | everybody | grapefruit |
| anything | bluebird | deerskin | everyone | grapevine |
| applesauce | bluegrass | dewdrop | everything | hairbrush |
| armband | boathouse | dishpan | eyebrow | halfway |
| armchair | boldface | dodgeball | eyelash | handbook |
| armhole | brainstorm | dogcart | eyelid | handcuff |
| backbone | brakeman | doorbell | fairground | handshake |
| backfire | breakfast | doormat | fairway | hangnail |
| background | briefcase | doorway | farewell | headline |
| backhand | broomstick | doubleheader | farmhand | highway |
| bagpipe | buckskin | downhill | farmhouse | hilltop |
| bareback | bulldog | downpour | farmland | homework |
| barefoot | bullfight | downstairs | farmyard | horseback |
| barnyard | butterfly | downstream | fingernail | houseboat |
| baseball | buttermilk | downtown | fingerprint | housefly |
| baseman | campfire | dragonfly | fireplace | household |
| basketball | campground | drainpipe | fireworks | however |
| bathrobe | candlestick | drawback | flagpole | icebox |
| bathroom | catfish | drawbridge | flashlight | icecap |
| bathtub | cattleman | drawstring | flowerpot | inchworm |
| battlefield | chalkboard | dressmaker | foolproof | innkeeper |

# Compound Words
## (continued)

| | | | | |
|---|---|---|---|---|
| inside | mouthpiece | peanut | scarecrow | toothpick |
| into | necktie | peppercorn | scoutmaster | trademark |
| jackpot | newspaper | peppermint | seafood | tugboat |
| jaywalk | nightfall | pickpocket | seaport | turnpike |
| jellyfish | nightgown | pigtail | seashore | typewriter |
| junkyard | nobody | pillowcase | seesaw | undergo |
| kettledrum | notebook | pineapple | shipmate | underground |
| keyboard | oatmeal | pipeline | shipwreck | underline |
| keyhole | offshore | pitchfork | shortstop | underwater |
| kickoff | outboard | playground | skyline | upright |
| laborsaving | outdoors | popcorn | slipknot | vineyard |
| ladybug | outfit | postmark | smallpox | wallpaper |
| landmark | outguess | quicksand | snowball | wastebasket |
| landslide | outlaw | railroad | starboard | watermelon |
| lifeboat | outline | railway | steamboat | waterway |
| lifeline | outrage | rainbow | sunburn | weekend |
| lifetime | outside | raincoat | sunshine | whatever |
| liftoff | overdose | raindrop | supermarket | widespread |
| lighthouse | overdue | rainfall | surfboard | wildfire |
| limestone | overgrowth | rattlesnake | tablespoon | windmill |
| locksmith | overtime | roadblock | tadpole | within |
| lookout | overweight | roadside | tailbone | without |
| mailbox | paintbrush | roommate | takeoff | wolfhound |
| mainstream | pancake | rosebud | teaspoon | woodshed |
| masterpiece | paperback | rowboat | textbook | woodwork |
| moonlight | paperweight | runway | themselves | worldwide |
| motorboat | parkway | sailboat | tightrope | yardstick |
| motorcycle | password | sandbox | toenail | |

Select ten compound words from the list on pages 15 and 16. Illustrate each word on a separate page of a booklet. Do *not* write the word. Give your booklet to a friend to see if he or she can use the pictures you drew to identify the compound words you selected.

# Conjunctions

A **conjunction** is a word that joins together individual words or groups of words in a sentence.

| Coordinating | Correlative | Subordinating |
|---|---|---|
| and | either . . . or | after |
| but | neither . . . nor | as |
| for | not only . . . but also | because |
| nor | | if |
| or | | when |

# Interjections

An **interjection** is a word that expresses emotion and has no grammatical relation to other words in a sentence.

| | |
|---|---|
| Ah! | Ouch! |
| Alas! | Phooey! |
| Bah! | Pooh! |
| Dear me! | Pshaw! |
| Farewell! | Shoo! |
| Good-bye! | Shame! |
| Heavens! | Tut! |
| Help! | Ugh! |
| My goodness! | Well! |
| Oh! | Whew! |

Dear me!

Pshaw!

# Contractions

A **contraction** is a shortened form of a single word or of a word pair. An apostrophe is used to show where a letter or letters have been omitted to create the shortened form.

## Be

| | |
|---|---|
| I'm | I am |
| you're | you are |
| he's | he is |
| she's | she is |
| it's | it is |
| we're | we are |
| they're | they are |

## Have

| | |
|---|---|
| I've | I have |
| you've | you have |
| we've | we have |
| they've | they have |

## Not

| | |
|---|---|
| isn't | is not |
| aren't | are not |
| won't | will not |
| can't | cannot |
| wouldn't | would not |
| don't | do not |
| doesn't | does not |
| haven't | have not |
| hasn't | has not |
| hadn't | had not |
| shouldn't | should not |
| mightn't | might not |
| mustn't | must not |
| oughtn't | ought not |
| wasn't | was not |
| weren't | were not |

## Will

| | |
|---|---|
| I'll | I will |
| you'll | you will |
| he'll | he will |
| she'll | she will |
| it'll | it will |
| we'll | we will |
| they'll | they will |
| who'll | who will |

## Would

| | |
|---|---|
| I'd | I would |
| you'd | you would |
| he'd | he would |
| she'd | she would |
| we'd | we would |
| they'd | they would |

## And More

| | |
|---|---|
| I'd | I had |
| he'd | he had |
| let's | let us |
| that's | that is |
| | that has |
| what's | what is |
| | what has |
| where's | where is |
| | where has |
| who's | who is |
| | who has |

# Expressions

all gussied up

backseat driver

baker's dozen

bated breath

bed of roses

behind the eight ball

big cheese

bite the dust

bone to pick

bring down the house

castles in Spain

charley horse

cut the mustard

Davy Jones's locker

dead as a doornail

dead duck

the deep six

devil's advocate

diamond in the rough

dog days

duck soup

egg money

elbow grease

eleventh hour

face the music

fall in love

fast and loose

a feather in one's cap

feel one's oats

a fly in the ointment

fly off the handle

forty acres and a mule

four corners of the earth

full of beans

get one's fingers burned

get one's goat

handwriting on the wall

hit the road

humble pie

in a pickle

it's Greek to me

Johnny-come-lately

kit and caboodle

lame duck

let George do it

mad as a hatter

make hay while the sun shines

Monday-morning quarterback

month of Sundays

out of kilter

over the hill

play second fiddle

pretty kettle of fish

pull the wool over one's eyes

rain cats and dogs

Choose five of these expressions. For each one you choose, draw two pictures.
In one picture, show what the expression makes you think of. In the other picture, illustrate what the expression really means.

# Homophones

**Homophones** are words that sound alike but have different spellings and meanings.

| | | |
|---|---|---|
| acts, ax | capital, capitol | flea, flee |
| ad, add | carat (karat), carrot | flew, flu, flue |
| aerie, airy | cell, sell | floe, flow |
| aid, aide | cellar, seller | flour, flower |
| ail, ale | cent, scent, sent | for, fore, four |
| air, err, heir | cereal, serial | foreword, forward |
| aisle, isle | cheap, cheep | forth, fourth |
| all, awl | chews, choose | foul, fowl |
| allowed, aloud | chili, chilly | franc, frank |
| altar, alter | chord, cord | frays, phrase |
| ant, aunt | chute, shoot | friar, fryer |
| arc, ark | cite, sight, site | gait, gate |
| ate, eight | clause, claws | genes, jeans |
| auricle, oracle | close, clothes | gild, guild |
| aye, eye, I | coarse, course | gilt, guilt |
| bail, bale | colonel, kernel | gored, gourd |
| bald, balled, bawled | core, corps | gorilla, guerrilla |
| band, banned | counsel, council | grate, great |
| bare, bear | creak, creek | groan, grown |
| barren, baron | currant, current | guessed, guest |
| base, bass | cymbal, symbol | guise, guys |
| be, bee | dear, deer | hail, hale |
| beach, beech | descent, dissent | hair, hare |
| beat, beet | desert, dessert | hall, haul |
| been, bin | dew, do, due | halve, have |
| bell, belle | die, dye | hangar, hanger |
| berry, bury | doe, dough | hay, hey |
| berth, birth | dual, duel | heal, heel, he'll |
| better, bettor | ducked, duct | hear, here |
| billed, build | earn, urn | heard, herd |
| blew, blue | ewe, yew, you | he'd, heed |
| bloc, block | eyelet, islet | hew, hue |
| boar, bore | faint, feint | hi, high |
| board, bored | fair, fare | higher, hire |
| bold, bowled | faun, fawn | him, hymn |
| boll, bowl | faze, phase | hoard, horde |
| bough, bow | feat, feet | hoarse, horse |
| bread, bred | find, fined | hole, whole |
| bridal, bridle | fir, fur | hostel, hostile |
| buy, by | flair, flare | hour, our |

# Homophones
## (continued)

| | | |
|---|---|---|
| idle, idol | pail, pale | serf, surf |
| in, inn | pain, pane | sew, so, sow |
| jam, jamb | pair, pare, pear | shear, sheer |
| jinks, jinx | palate, palette, pallet | shone, shown |
| key, quay | pause, paws | sighs, size |
| knead, need | peace, piece | slay, sleigh |
| knew, new | peak, peek | soar, sore |
| knight, night | peal, peel | sole, soul |
| knot, not | pedal, peddle | some, sum |
| know, no | peer, pier | son, sun |
| knows, nose | pi, pie | staid, stayed |
| lain, lane | plain, plane | stair, stare |
| laps, lapse | plum, plumb | stake, steak |
| lead, led | pole, poll | stationary, stationery |
| leak, leek | pore, pour | steal, steel |
| lessen, lesson | pray, prey | step, steppe |
| lie, lye | pride, pried | straight, strait |
| links, lynx | prince, prints | suite, sweet |
| lo, low | principal, principle | tail, tale |
| load, lode | profit, prophet | taper, tapir |
| loan, lone | quarts, quartz | taught, taut |
| made, maid | rain, reign, rein | tea, tee |
| mail, male | raise, rays | team, teem |
| main, mane | rap, wrap | tear, tier |
| maize, maze | read, reed | their, there, they're |
| mall, maul | read, red | threw, through |
| manner, manor | real, reel | throne, thrown |
| marshal, martial | right, write | thyme, time |
| meat, meet, mete | ring, wring | to, too, two |
| medal, meddle, metal | road, rode | toe, tow |
| might, mite | roe, row | vail, vale, veil |
| moan, mown | root, route | vain, vane, vein |
| moose, mousse | rose, rows | wade, weighed |
| muscle, mussel | rote, wrote | waist, waste |
| naval, navel | rough, ruff | wait, weight |
| nay, neigh | rung, wrung | walk, wok |
| none, nun | rye, wry | war, wore |
| oh, owe | sac, sack | ware, wear |
| one, won | sail, sale | we, wee |
| or, ore | scene, seen | weak, week |
| overdo, overdue | sea, see | who's, whose |
| paced, paste | seam, seem | wood, would |
| packed, pact | | yoke, yolk |

# Hyphenated Words

A **hyphen** is a punctuation mark that is used to divide words into syllables or to connect them to make compound words. When compound words are first formed, they are written with hyphens. Eventually, however, their spelling changes so that they are written as single words, closed up, without hyphens. See, for example, the list of compound words on pages 15 and 16. Hyphens are still used in writing the compound words listed below.

| | | |
|---|---|---|
| all-out | half-mast | push-up |
| baby-sit | hide-and-seek | quick-tempered |
| brand-new | jack-in-the-box | quick-witted |
| brother-in-law | jack-o'-lantern | right-handed |
| by-product | king-size | run-in |
| cold-blooded | know-it-all | second-guess |
| cross-eyed | life-size | self-conscious |
| custom-built | light-footed | self-made |
| deep-sea | made-to-order | self-service |
| double-cross | made-up | small-time |
| double-decker | middle-aged | thin-skinned |
| drive-in | old-fashioned | third-rate |
| dry-clean | one-half | walkie-talkie |
| father-in-law | one-sided | walk-up |
| go-between | on-line | well-fixed |
| go-getter | out-of-date | well-groomed |
| grown-up | pinch-hit | worn-out |
| half-baked | ping-pong | would-be |

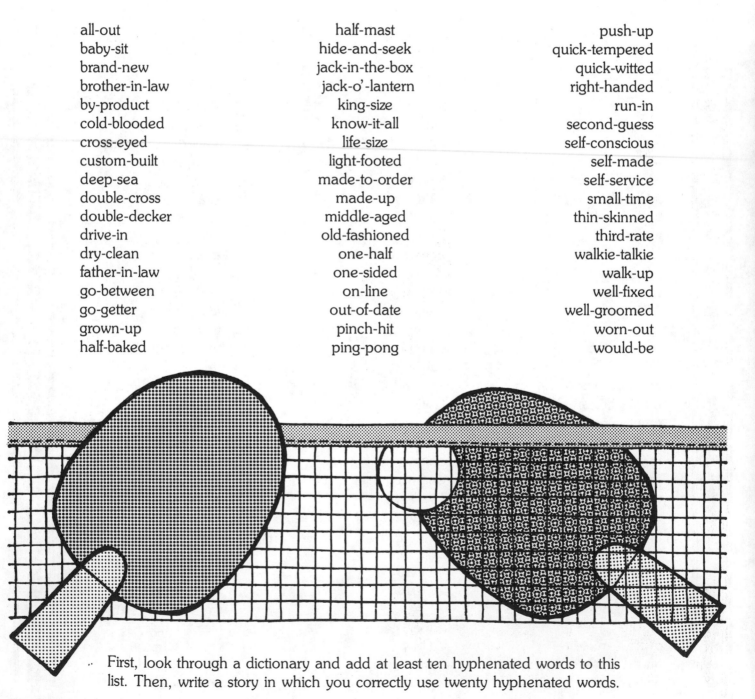

First, look through a dictionary and add at least ten hyphenated words to this list. Then, write a story in which you correctly use twenty hyphenated words.

# Nouns

A **noun** is the name of a person, place, thing, quality, or idea.

| | | |
|---|---|---|
| appetite | igloo | river |
| audience | jacket | signature |
| bachelor | journalism | sociology |
| bobcat | kangaroo | territory |
| committee | knowledge | trestle |
| Congress | Linda | unicycle |
| deputy | literature | Utah |
| disease | macaroni | Venus |
| errand | misery | virus |
| example | nostalgia | weevil |
| fender | nucleus | wrath |
| florist | ocean | xylem |
| gasoline | organization | xylophone |
| ghost | photography | yam |
| hat | pleasure | yogurt |
| heart | quadrangle | zephyr |
| idea | quota | zest |
| | reconstruction | |

# Plurals

A **noun** is the name of a person, place, thing, quality, or idea. A noun that is **singular** names only one person, place, thing, quality, or idea. A noun that is **plural** names more than one.

The plurals of many singular nouns are formed simply by adding the letter *s* to the end of the noun.

| | | | |
|---|---|---|---|
| ant | ants | monster | monsters |
| book | books | pencil | pencils |
| card | cards | pool | pools |
| girl | girls | ring | rings |
| hat | hats | school | schools |

The plurals of most nouns ending in the letters *ch*, *s*, *sh*, *x*, and *z* are formed by adding the letters *es* to the end of the noun.

| | | | |
|---|---|---|---|
| ax | axes | guess | guesses |
| box | boxes | match | matches |
| branch | branches | sandwich | sandwiches |
| bush | bushes | speech | speeches |
| church | churches | tax | taxes |
| fox | foxes | watch | watches |
| gas | gases | wish | wishes |

To form the plural of a noun ending in *y* preceded by a vowel, add the letter *s* to the end of the noun.

| | | | |
|---|---|---|---|
| boy | boys | monkey | monkeys |
| chimney | chimneys | tray | trays |
| donkey | donkeys | trolley | trolleys |
| journey | journeys | turkey | turkeys |
| key | keys | volley | volleys |

To form the plural of a noun ending in *y* preceded by a consonant, change the *y* to *i* and add the letters *es*.

| | | | |
|---|---|---|---|
| berry | berries | lily | lilies |
| body | bodies | penny | pennies |
| bunny | bunnies | sky | skies |
| city | cities | story | stories |
| daisy | daisies | tragedy | tragedies |

To form the plural of a noun ending in *f* preceded by a vowel, simply add the letter *s* to the end of the noun.

| | | | |
|---|---|---|---|
| belief | beliefs | reef | reefs |
| chef | chefs | roof | roofs |

# Plurals
## (continued)

To form the plural of a noun ending in *f* preceded by a consonant, change the *f* to *v* and add the letters *es*.

| | | | |
|---|---|---|---|
| calf | calves | self | selves |
| elf | elves | shelf | shelves |
| half | halves | wharf | wharves |
| | wolf | wolves | |

To form the plural of a noun ending in *o* preceded by a vowel, simply add the letter *s* to the end of the noun.

| | | | |
|---|---|---|---|
| bamboo | bamboos | radio | radios |
| cameo | cameos | ratio | ratios |
| folio | folios | rodeo | rodeos |
| portfolio | portfolios | studio | studios |

To form the plural of a noun ending in *o* preceded by a consonant, add the letters *es* to the end of the noun.

| | | | |
|---|---|---|---|
| cargo | cargoes | mosquito | mosquitoes |
| echo | echoes | potato | potatoes |
| embargo | embargoes | tomato | tomatoes |
| hero | heroes | veto | vetoes |

Some nouns ending in *o* preceded by a consonant are an exception to this rule. The plurals of these nouns are formed simply by adding the letter *s*.

| | | | |
|---|---|---|---|
| alto | altos | piano | pianos |
| Eskimo | Eskimos | soprano | sopranos |

For some nouns, the singular and plural forms are exactly the same.

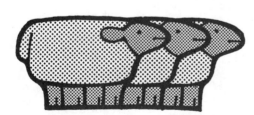

corps
deer
fowl
moose
salmon
sheep

For some nouns, the plurals cannot be formed by following the rules. These nouns are irregular, and their plurals must be memorized.

| | | | |
|---|---|---|---|
| child | children | man | men |
| foot | feet | mouse | mice |
| goose | geese | ox | oxen |
| | woman | women | |

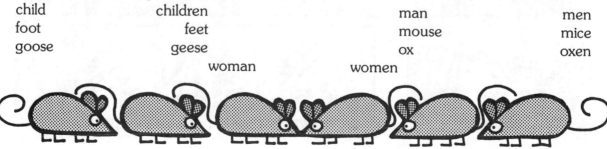

# Plurals of English Words Derived From Latin

In Latin, nouns have gender. They can be masculine, feminine, or neuter. In general, singular masculine nouns end in the letters *us*. The plural form of these nouns is made by changing this word ending from *us* to *i*. Singular feminine nouns end in the letter *a*. The plural form of these nouns is made by changing this ending from *a* to *ae*. Singular neuter nouns end in the letters *um*. The plural form of these nouns is made by changing the ending from *um* to either *a* or *i*.

In some instances, words that have come into English from Latin have retained their Latin plural form exclusively. In other instances, an English plural has been added to the Latin one so that the word actually has two acceptable plural forms.

| Singular Form | Plural Forms | |
| --- | --- | --- |
| | **Latin** | **English** |
| alga | algae | algas |
| alumna | alumnae | |
| alumnus | alumni | |
| aquarium | aquaria | aquariums |
| bacterium | bacteria | |
| cactus | cacti | cactuses |
| candelabrum | candelabra | candelabrums |
| curriculum | curricula | curriculums |
| datum | data | |
| gladiolus | gladioli | gladioluses |
| hiatus | hiati | hiatuses |
| hippopotamus | hippopotami | hippopotamuses |
| larva | larvae | |
| nebula | nebulae | nebulas |
| octopus | octopi | octopuses |
| paramecium | paramecia | parameciums |
| radius | radii | radiuses |
| stratum | strata | |
| syllabus | syllabi | syllabuses |
| vertebra | vertebrae | vertebras |

# Prefixes

A **prefix** is a letter or sequence of letters attached to the beginning of a word, base, or phrase.

| Prefixes | Definitions | Examples |
|---|---|---|
| a- | in, on | abed, ashore |
| ab-, abs- | from, away, off | absent, absolve |
| alti- | high, height | altimeter, altitude |
| ambi- | both | ambidextrous, ambiguous |
| ante- | before | antebellum, antecedent |
| anti- | against, opposite of | antifreeze, antislavery, antiwar |
| aut-, auto- | self, same one | autograph, automobile |
| ben-, bene- | good, well | benediction, benefactor, benefit |
| bi- | two, occurring every two, twice | bicycle, biweekly |
| biblio- | book | bibliography, bibliophile |
| bio- | life, living matter | biography, biology |
| circum- | around | circumnavigate, circumscribe |
| co- | with, together, joint, jointly | coauthor, coexist |
| contra-, contro- | against, contrary, contrasting | contradict, controversy |
| demi- | half | demigod, demitasse |
| dis- | do the opposite of, exclude from, opposite or absence of, not | disable, disappear, disbelief |
| dys- | abnormal, difficult, bad | dyslexia, dystrophy |
| equi- | equal, equally | equidistant, equivalent |
| ex- | from, out of, not, former | export, ex-president, extend |
| extra- | outside, beyond | extracurricular, extraneous, extraordinary |
| fore- | in front of, previous | forecast, forehead |
| geo- | earth | geography, geology |
| hemi- | half | hemisphere, hemistich |
| hydro- | water | hydrofoil, hydroplane |
| hyper- | too much, over | hyperactive, hypersensitive |
| il-, im-, in- | not, without | illegal, impossible |
| inter- | between, among, jointly, together | interlock, international, interstate |
| intra- | within, inside | intramural, intrastate |
| mal- | bad, badly, abnormal, inadequate | maladjusted, malevolent |

# Prefixes
## (continued)

| Prefixes | Definitions | Examples |
|---|---|---|
| micr-, micro- | small, minute, minutely | microcosm, microphone |
| mis- | bad, badly, wrong, wrongly | misbehave, misdeed, misprint |
| mono- | single, one | monologue, monosail |
| multi- | many, multiple, more than two | multicolored, multiplex |
| non- | not | nonsense, nonstop |
| oct-, octa-, octo- | eight | octagon, octave, octet |
| orth-, ortho- | straight, upright, vertical, correct, corrective | orthodontics, orthodox |
| over- | above, more than is necessary, excessive, excessively | overact, overcoat |
| pan- | all | panacea, panorama |
| ped-, pedi- | foot, feet | pedal, pedicure, pedigree |
| per- | throughout, thoroughly | perfection, perform |
| poly- | many, several, much | polygon, polyhedral |
| post- | after, subsequent, later | posthumous, postpone |
| pre- | prior to, before, in front of | prefix, preschool |
| pro- | earlier than, forward, in front of, taking the place of, favoring | pro-American, proceed, proclaim, profess, pronate |
| pseud-, pseudo- | false, spurious | pseudonym, pseudopodium |
| re- | again, anew, back, backward | rebound, recall |
| retro- | backward, back, situated behind | retroactive, retrospect |
| sub- | under, beneath, below, subordinate, secondary, next lower than or inferior to | submarine, subtract |
| super- | over and above; higher in quality, quantity, or degree; more than | superbowl, superior |
| tele- | far | telescope, television |
| trans- | across, beyond, through | transfer, transport |
| tri- | three, once in every three | triangle, triplets |
| ultra- | beyond, extreme, extremely | ultramodern, ultraviolet |
| un- | not, do the opposite of, deprive of | unfinished, unlucky |
| uni- | one, single | unicycle, unilateral |
| vice- | acting for, next in rank to | vice-president, viceroy |

# Prepositions

A **preposition** is a word that can be combined with a noun or pronoun to form a phrase that tells something about some other word in a sentence.

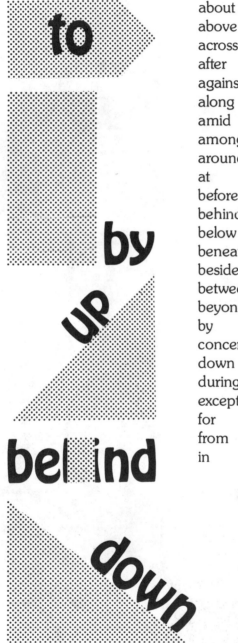

| | |
|---|---|
| about | inside |
| above | into |
| across | of |
| after | off |
| against | on |
| along | onto |
| amid | out |
| among | outside |
| around | over |
| at | past |
| before | round |
| behind | since |
| below | through |
| beneath | throughout |
| beside | to |
| between | toward |
| beyond | under |
| by | underneath |
| concerning | until |
| down | unto |
| during | up |
| except | upon |
| for | with |
| from | within |
| in | without |

# Pronouns

A **pronoun** is a word used in place of a noun. A pronoun may stand for the name of a person, place, thing, quality, or idea.

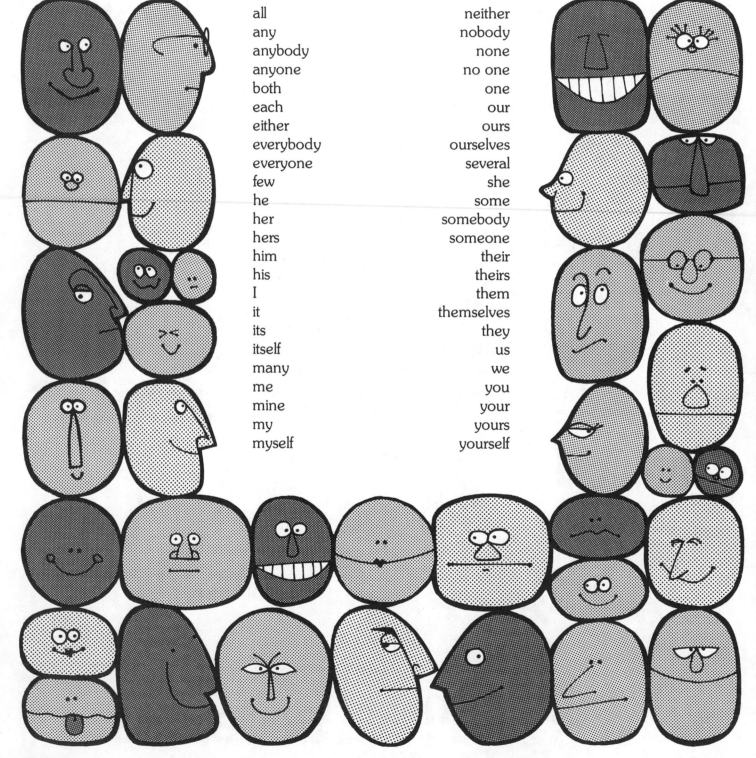

| | |
|---|---|
| all | neither |
| any | nobody |
| anybody | none |
| anyone | no one |
| both | one |
| each | our |
| either | ours |
| everybody | ourselves |
| everyone | several |
| few | she |
| he | some |
| her | somebody |
| hers | someone |
| him | their |
| his | theirs |
| I | them |
| it | themselves |
| its | they |
| itself | us |
| many | we |
| me | you |
| mine | your |
| my | yours |
| myself | yourself |

# Punctuation Rules

## Use a *period* .

- after a sentence that is a statement or command.
- after an abbreviation.
- after an initial.

## Use a *comma* ,

- in a date to separate the day from the year and the year from the rest of the sentence.
- between words or phrases in a series.
- to set off *yes* and *no* at the beginning of a sentence.
- when giving a location or an address to separate the name of a city from the name of a state, the name of a state from the name of a country, and the name of a state or country from the rest of the sentence.
- before a conjunction when it joins two independent clauses.
- after the words *however* and *therefore* when they are used to join clauses in a compound sentence.
- in direct address to separate the name of the person being spoken to from what is being said.
- to separate a quotation from the rest of the sentence unless a question mark or exclamation point is needed.
- after the greeting in a personal letter and after the closing in all letters.

## Use a *question mark* ?

- after a sentence that asks a question.
- after a question in a quotation.

## Use an *exclamation point* !

- after a word, sentence, or quotation that shows strong feeling.

# Punctuation Rules
## (continued)

## Use a *colon* :

- after the greeting in a business letter.
- at the beginning of a list of things in a sentence.
- to separate hours and minutes when writing times.

## Use a *semicolon* ;

- in a compound sentence between principal clauses that are not joined by a conjunction.
- in a compound sentence before a conjunction that joins clauses in which there is internal punctuation.
- before the words *however* and *therefore* when they are used to join clauses in a compound sentence.

## Use an *apostrophe* ,

- to show that one or more letters have been left out of a word.
- with the letter *s* to form the possessive case of most singular nouns.

## Use *quotation marks* " "

- before and after words that are being or have been spoken or written by someone.
- before and after the titles of articles, chapters, short poems, short stories, and songs.

## Use *parentheses* ( )

- to enclose parts of a sentence, such as explanations or comments, that could be omitted without making the sentence incomplete or changing its meaning.

## Use a *hyphen* -

- at the end of a line in a word that is broken and continued on the following line.
- when dividing words into syllables for spelling or pronunciation purposes.

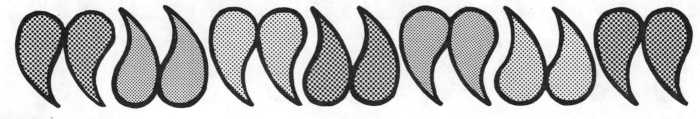

# Roots and Combining Forms

A **root** is the simple element from which a more complex word is derived, often by means of the addition of prefixes, suffixes, and/or other combining forms.

| Roots | Definitions | Examples |
|---|---|---|
| act | do | action |
| -agogue | leader | demagogue |
| agr-, ager | field | agriculture |
| altus, alte | high | altitude |
| alter | other (of two) | alternate |
| annus, anno | year | annual |
| anthrop-, anthropo-, -anthrop | human being, man | misanthrop |
| aqui, aqua- | water | aquatic |
| arch- | chief, principal | anarchy |
| astr-, astro- | star | astronomy |
| aut-, auto- | self, same one | autobiography |
| brevi- | short | abbreviation |
| cand | white, bright, shining | incandescent |
| captus | take, seize, hold | capture |
| caput, capitis | head | cap, capital |
| cent | hundred | century, percent |
| chron-, chrono- | time | chronological |
| citare | put in motion, summon | citation |
| clarus | clear | clarity |
| cogito | turn over in the mind, think | cogitate |
| cogna-, cogni- | know | recognize |
| cosm-, cosmo-, -cosm | order, world | cosmopolitan |
| cred- | believe | incredible |
| culpa | blame, guilt, sin | culprit |
| cycle | circle, ring, wheel | bicycle |
| dem-, demo- | people, populace, population | democracy |
| derm-, derma, -derm | skin | epidermis |
| dict- | say, speak | diction, edict |
| doc-, doct- | instruct, teach | docent, doctor |
| dominus | master of the house, lord, ruler | dominate |

# Roots and Combining Forms
## (continued)

| Roots | Definitions | Examples |
|---|---|---|
| flex | bend | flexible |
| flor, flora | flower | floral, florist |
| flux | flow | influx |
| fort | strong | fortify |
| *fragilis* | frail; easily broken | fragile |
| fus- | pour, melt | fusion |
| -gon | angle | polygon |
| -gram | drawing, writing | telegram |
| *gratus* | pleasing, thankful | gratitude, gratuitous |
| *gregarius* | of or relating to a crowd, flock, or herd | gregarious |
| hem-, hema-, hemo- | blood | hemorrhage |
| hydr-, hydro- | water | hydrofoil |
| *iacto* | to throw, cast, or fling away | eject, interject |
| is-, iso- | equal, homogeneous, uniform | isometric |
| *liber* | to free | liberate |
| *locus* | a single place | location |
| *logos, logi* | *word, words* | *monologue* |
| *magnus* | great, large | magnify, magnitude |
| *manus* | the hand | manufacture |
| *mare* | the sea | marine, maritime |
| mega- | great, large | megaphone |
| *mitto, mittere* | to send or dispatch | missive, remit, transmit |
| *mobilito* | to set in motion | mobilize |
| *navigo* | to sail | navigate |
| ne-, neo- | new | neoclassic |
| *nego, negare* | to say no | negate, negative |
| -nomy | system of laws governing or sum or knowledge regarding | agronomy, autonomy |
| *novus* | fresh, new, young, inexperienced | novel, novice |
| ocul-, oculo- | having to do with the *eye* | binoculars, ocular |
| pan- | all | Pan-American, panorama |

# Roots and Combining Forms
## (continued)

| Roots | Definitions | Examples |
|---|---|---|
| paed-, ped- | child | pediatrics |
| phil-, philo- | loving; having an affinity for | philanthropist |
| phon-, phono- | sound, voice, speech | phonograph |
| phot-, photo- | light | photography, photon |
| porto, portare | to bear, bring, or carry | portable, transport |
| prior, primus | former, first | primacy, primary |
| psych-, psycho- | brain, mind, soul, spirit | psychic, psychoanalysis, psychotherapy |
| pyr-, pyro- | fire, heat | pyrogenic, pyromania |
| rogo, rogare | to ask or question | interrogate |
| rumpere, ruptum | to break or shatter | interrupt, rupture |
| scribere, scriptum | to write | prescribe, script |
| secare, sectum | to cut | dissect, intersection |
| solus, soli | alone, only | solely, solitary |
| somnus | sleep, slumber | insomnia, somnambulate |
| sono, sonare | to sound, resound, or make a noise | resonant, sonata, sonorous, unison |
| struo, struere, structum | to put together, to put in order, to build | construct, destructive, structure |
| techno- | art, craft, skill | technique, technology |
| tempus, temporis | a period of time | contemporary, temporal |
| tenuo, tenuare | to make thin, fine, slender, or slight | attenuated, tenuous |
| termino, terminare | to bound, limit, or make an end to | coterminous, terminate |
| terra | earth, land | terrain, terrarium |
| testor, testare | to bear witness to; to give evidence of | testify |
| therm-, thermo- | heat | thermos, thermometer |
| torquare, tortum | to twist, wind, or wrench | contort, distort, torsion |
| tribuere, tributum | to divide out or allot; to assign, give, or pay to | tributary, tribute |
| turbo, turbare | to agitate, to throw into disorder or confusion | disturb, turbulence |

# Similes

A **simile** is a statement in which one thing is said to be like, or the same as, another thing.

as big as all outdoors
as black as coal
as blind as a bat
as brave as a lion
as brown as a berry
as busy as a bee
as clean as a whistle
as clear as crystal
as cool as a cucumber
as easy as pie
as flat as a pancake
as fresh as a daisy
as good as gold
as happy as a lark
as hard as a rock
as high as a kite
as light as a feather
as mad as a hornet
as meek as a lamb

as neat as a pin
as old as the hills
as pale as a ghost
as pretty as a picture
as proud as a peacock
as quick as a wink
as quiet as a mouse
as red as a beet
as sharp as a tack
as slippery as an eel
as slow as molasses in January
as sly as a fox
as smooth as silk
as stiff as a board
as straight as an arrow
as strong as an ox
as stubborn as a mule
as warm as toast
as white as a sheet

as wise as an owl

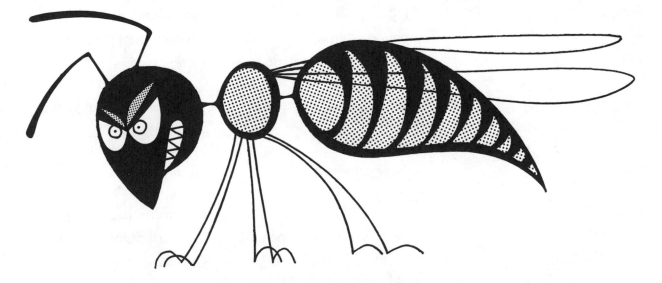

Just for fun, think of or make up some other similes and write them down. Then, select five similes from the ones listed on this page or the ones you have written and draw a picture to illustrate each one.

# Slang

**Slang** is an informal, often colorful, nonstandard vocabulary composed of old words to which new meanings have been assigned or new words that have been made up.

| | |
|---|---|
| **bag** | *noun*, a special talent or interest |
| **blast** | *noun*, a good time, a wild party |
| **blew it** | *verb*, missed an opportunity, failed |
| **bop** | *noun*, a dance popular in the fifties<br>*verb*, to hit or strike |
| **bummer** | *noun*, a bad deal, a wretched experience |
| **cool** | *adj.*, great or fine |
| **cop out** | *noun*, the act of giving up or taking the easy way out |
| **dig** | *verb*, to understand |
| **downer** | *noun*, a depressing experience |
| **drag** | *noun*, a boring thing |
| **dynamite** | *interj.*, fantastic |
| **heavy** | *adj.*, outstanding, deeply meaningful |
| **ice** | *noun*, diamonds |
| **ivories** | *noun*, the keys on a piano, especially the white ones |
| **jive** | *verb*, to tease or intentionally mislead |
| **lifer** | *noun*, a person serving a life sentence in prison |
| **nerd** | *noun*, a dull, boring person |
| **nutty** | *adj.*, crazy, but in an amusing way |
| **pad** | *noun*, one's living quarters |
| **plastic** | *adj.*, false, insincere |
| **rad** | *adj.*, fantastic, super, terrific |
| **slop** | *noun*, food that is both ill prepared and unattractively served |
| **spaced out** | *adj.*, out of touch with reality |
| **turkey** | *noun*, an awkward, inferior person or thing |
| **zap** | *verb*, to destroy |
| **zilch** | *noun*, nothing |
| **zip** | *noun*, zero or nothing |

Write a short story using slang words from this list or from your own vocabulary. Underline each slang word you use. Illustrate your story.

# Suffixes

A **suffix** is a letter or sequence of letters that has a specific definition and may be added to the end of a word, base, or phrase to change its meaning.

| Suffixes | Definitions | Examples |
|---|---|---|
| -able, -ible | capable or worthy of | changeable, collectible |
| -age | action or process; rate of; fee | dosage, postage |
| -ance, -ancy | act, process, or state of being | brilliance, fragrance |
| -ant, -ent | one who performs a specified action | confidant, defendant |
| -dom | office; state or fact of being | dukedom, freedom |
| -ence | act, process, or state of being | absence |
| -er, -or | one who; that which | banker, editor |
| -ful | full of; number or quantity that fills | cupful, roomful, shameful |
| -fy | to make; to invest with the attributes of | simplify, citify |
| -hood | condition, time, or instance of | boyhood, motherhood |
| -ion | act, condition, state, or process of | exploration, operation |
| -ish | characteristic of or relating to | girlish |
| -ism | belief or practice of | intellectualism |
| -ist | one who performs a specified action; one who advocates a particular doctrine or position | communist, florist |
| -ity, -ty, -y | quality, state, or degree of | civility |
| -ive | tending to | supportive |
| -ize | to cause to conform to; to become like; to engage in | theorize, westernize |
| -logue, -log | speech or discourse; student or specialist | monologue, dialogue, ideologue |
| -logy | oral or written expression; doctrine, theory, or study of | biology, criminology |
| -ment | act, process, or state of being; concrete result of an action | entanglement, government |
| -ness | state, condition, quality, or degree of | happiness |
| -ory | having the quality of; being characterized by; a place or thing for | compulsory, laboratory |
| -osis | act, condition or process of | metamorphosis |
| -ous, -ose | full of, having, or possessing the qualities of | anxious, comatose |
| -ship | state of being; the art, office, or skill of | brinksmanship, friendship |
| -some | causing or characterized by | awesome, lonesome |
| -tude | state, condition, quality, or degree of | gratitude |
| -ward | in the direction of | upward |
| -y | characterized by, full of, like, or inclined to | dusty, sleepy |

# Syllables

Here is a list of rules for dividing words into syllables.

1. A syllable is a group of letters sounded together.

2. Each syllable must have at least one vowel sound; a word cannot have more syllables than vowel sounds.

3. Words pronounced as one syllable should not be divided.

   dive                  helped                  through

4. A word containing two consonants between two vowels (**vccv**) is divided between the two consonants.

   vc cv                 vc cv                   vc cv
   cor-rect              pret-ty                 sis-ter

5. In a two-syllable word containing a single consonant between two vowels (**vcv**), the consonant usually begins the second syllable.

   v cv                  v cv
   po-tion               to-day

6. In a word ending in **-le**, the consonant immediately preceding the **-le** usually begins the last syllable.

   can-dle               mar-ble                 ta-ble

7. Compound words usually are divided between their word parts.

   down-stairs           rain-bow                sun-shine

Here is a list of rules for the way syllables are accented.

1. In a two-syllable word containing a double consonant, the first syllable is usually accented.

   hap′ py               rib′ bon

2. In a two-syllable word where the second syllable has two vowels, the second syllable is usually accented.

   con ceive′            de fraud′               pre mier′

3. In words ending in **-ion**, **-tion**, **-sion**, **-ial**, and **-ical**, the syllable preceding these endings is usually accented.

   dis cus′ sion         ex ten′ sion            of fi′ cial

4. In a word containing a prefix, the accent usually falls on or within the root word.

   com pose′             in doors′               re ply′

5. In a compound word, the accent usually falls on or within the first word.

   black′ board          court′ house            farm′ hand

but-ter-scotch ma-ple pep-per-mint

lic-o-rice lime choc-o-late tof-fee

# Synonyms

| | | |
|---|---|---|
| abrupt-sudden | false-untrue | obvious-apparent |
| adjust-fix | fast-quick | odor-smell |
| aid-assist | fear-fright | often-frequently |
| alone-solitary | fierce-ferocious | opinion-view |
| anger-rage | forgive-excuse | oppose-resist |
| answer-reply | genuine-real | pain-ache |
| arouse-awaken | gleam-shine | peculiar-odd |
| beg-plead | govern-rule | petty-trivial |
| blank-empty | grief-sorrow | piece-part |
| brave-fearless | happen-occur | promise-pledge |
| buy-purchase | hardy-strong | quiver-shake |
| calm-serene | honest-sincere | reasonable-fair |
| caution-warn | hurry-rush | recall-remember |
| choice-option | identical-alike | refuse-decline |
| clear-plain | ill-sick | reimburse-repay |
| close-near | imitate-copy | sensible-wise |
| coarse-rough | inquire-ask | separate-disconnect |
| coy-shy | late-tardy | severe-harsh |
| danger-peril | leave-depart | shiver-shake |
| decline-refuse | liberty-freedom | silly-foolish |
| decrease-lessen | limp-slack | small-tiny |
| dense-thick | marvelous-wonderful | task-job |
| desire-want | meek-mild | teach-instruct |
| detach-separate | mend-repair | tease-taunt |
| disappear-vanish | merit-worth | tight-snug |
| divulge-disclose | misty-foggy | timid-shy |
| dubious-doubtful | mix-blend | tranquil-peaceful |
| easy-simple | modern-recent | useless-worthless |
| elect-choose | moist-damp | value-worth |
| empty-vacant | necessary-essential | verdict-judgment |
| enemy-rival | need-require | whole-entire |
| enormous-gigantic | nimble-spry | worthy-honorable |
| extraordinary-unusual | normal-ordinary | zone-area |

# Tricky Words

**accede**, *verb:* to agree
**exceed**, *verb:* to surpass

**accept**, *verb:* to receive
**except**, *verb:* to leave out

**adapt**, *verb:* to change or adjust
**adept**, *adv.:* expert, proficient, skillful
**adopt**, *verb:* to accept; to receive as one's own

**affect**, *verb:* to influence
**effect**, *verb:* to bring about
**effect**, *noun:* the result

**aisle**, *noun:* a passageway between sections of seats
**isle**, *noun:* a small island

**all ready**, *adj.:* completely prepared
**already**, *adv.:* before now, previously

**allude**, *verb:* to make brief or vague reference
**elude**, *verb:* to dodge or slip away from
**illude**, *verb:* to trick or deceive in the manner of a magician

**allusion**, *noun:* a reference
**illusion**, *noun:* something that deceives, misleads, or plays tricks upon

**all ways**, *adv.:* in every possible way
**always**, *adv.:* at all times; forever

**annual**, *adj.:* occurring yearly
**biannual**, *adj.:* occurring twice a year
**biennial**, *adj.:* occurring once every two years

**ascent**, *noun:* the act of climbing or going up
**assent**, *noun:* agreement or approval

**assay**, *verb:* to analyze or test
**essay**, *verb:* to attempt

**avenge**, *verb:* to punish in just payment for wrong done
**revenge**, *noun:* a personal attempt to get even

**berth**, *noun:* a resting place
**birth**, *noun:* the beginning of life

**beside**, *prep.:* at the side of; next to
**besides**, *prep.:* in addition to; moreover

**capital**, *noun:* a city that is the seat of government
**capitol**, *noun:* the building in which a legislative body deliberates

**complement**, *noun:* a completing part
**compliment**, *noun:* an expression of admiration

**confidant**, *noun:* a person in whom one confides
**confident**, *adj.:* certain

**conscience**, *noun:* sense of right
**conscientious**, *adj.:* governed by conscience; meticulous, careful
**conscious**, *adj.:* aware of an inward state and/or an outward fact

**consul**, *noun:* a government representative
**council**, *noun:* an assembly of persons convened for deliberation
**counsel**, *noun:* advice

# Tricky Words
## (continued)

**continual**, *adj.:* recurring in steady and rapid succession
**continuous**, *adj.:* uninterrupted

**decent**, *adj.:* conforming to standards of propriety, good taste, or morality
**descent**, *noun:* the act of going from a higher to a lower level
**dissent**, *noun:* difference of opinion; disagreement

**deduct**, *verb:* to take away an amount or quantity from a total
**subtract**, *verb:* to take one number from another

**deprecate**, *verb:* to express disapproval or regret
**depreciate**, *verb:* to lessen in value

**directions**, *noun:* guidance or step-by-step instructions for reaching a goal, place, or destination
**instructions**, *noun:* an outline of procedures for the accomplishment of a task

**discreet**, *adj.:* wise, prudent, judicious
**discrete**, *adj.:* disconnected, separate

**elicit**, *verb:* to draw forth or bring out; to evoke
**illicit**, *adj.:* not permitted; unlawful

**eliminate**, *verb:* to get rid of
**illuminate**, *verb:* to supply with light

**emigrate**, *verb:* to leave one's own country for another
**immigrate**, *verb:* to come into a country of which one is not a native for permanent residence

**former**, *adj.:* the first of two
**latter**, *adj.:* the second of two; the end, last, or final

**imply**, *verb:* to express indirectly; to hint at or suggest
**infer**, *verb:* to draw a conclusion or conclusions based on facts or premises

**incredible**, *adj.:* unbelievable
**incredulous**, *adj.:* skeptical, disbelieving

**ingenious**, *adj.:* skillful in contriving; inventive
**ingenuous**, *adj.:* artless, naïve, innocent

**lay**, *verb:* to place
**lie**, *verb:* to recline

**mania**, *noun:* a craze
**phobia**, *noun:* a fear

**persecute**, *verb:* to oppress or harass
**prosecute**, *verb:* to initiate criminal action against

**precede**, *verb:* to be, come, or go ahead or in front of
**proceed**, *verb:* to continue after a pause; to go on in an orderly way

**principal**, *adj.:* most important
**principal**, *noun:* a chief or head man or woman
**principle**, *noun:* a rule or code of conduct

**rout**, *noun:* an overwhelming defeat
**route**, *noun:* a line or direction of travel

**stationary**, *adj.:* immovable
**stationery**, *noun:* letter paper and/or other materials for writing

**turbid**, *adj.:* foul, muddy
**turgid**, *adj.:* swollen

# incredulous

# Verbs

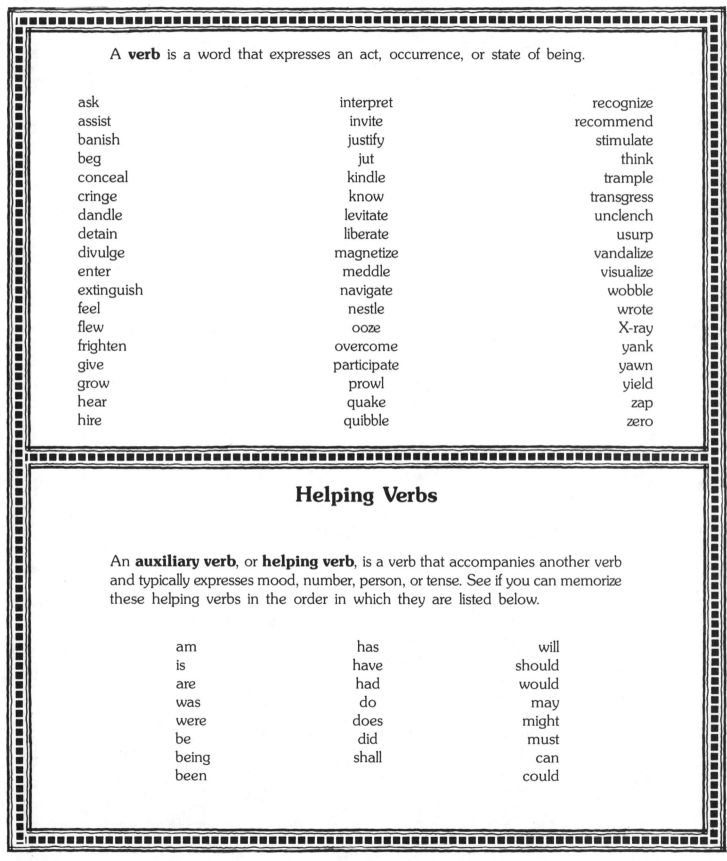

A **verb** is a word that expresses an act, occurrence, or state of being.

| | | |
|---|---|---|
| ask | interpret | recognize |
| assist | invite | recommend |
| banish | justify | stimulate |
| beg | jut | think |
| conceal | kindle | trample |
| cringe | know | transgress |
| dandle | levitate | unclench |
| detain | liberate | usurp |
| divulge | magnetize | vandalize |
| enter | meddle | visualize |
| extinguish | navigate | wobble |
| feel | nestle | wrote |
| flew | ooze | X-ray |
| frighten | overcome | yank |
| give | participate | yawn |
| grow | prowl | yield |
| hear | quake | zap |
| hire | quibble | zero |

# Helping Verbs

An **auxiliary verb**, or **helping verb**, is a verb that accompanies another verb and typically expresses mood, number, person, or tense. See if you can memorize these helping verbs in the order in which they are listed below.

| | | |
|---|---|---|
| am | has | will |
| is | have | should |
| are | had | would |
| was | do | may |
| were | does | might |
| be | did | must |
| being | shall | can |
| been | | could |

# Words for Sensations

## Sound

| | | | | |
|---|---|---|---|---|
| bang | growl | shriek | | |
| boom | gurgle | sizzle | | |
| brouhaha | hiss | slam | | |
| bubble | howl | smack | | |
| buzz | hum | snap | | |
| cackle | jingle | sniff | | |
| chatter | moan | splash | | |
| chime | murmur | sputter | | |
| clang | mutter | squeak | | |
| clatter | plink | squeal | | |
| click | plop | swish | | |
| clop | pop | thud | | |
| crackle | purr | thump | | |
| crash | rattle | tick | | |
| croak | ring | tinkle | | |
| crunch | roar | twang | | |
| din | rumble | wail | | |
| drone | rustle | wheeze | | |
| fizz | scream | whimper | | |
| flap | screech | whine | | |
| flutter | shout | whisper | | |
| grind | | yell | | |

## Touch

| | |
|---|---|
| brittle | oily |
| bumpy | prickly |
| coarse | ribbed |
| cold | rough |
| cool | rubbery |
| crumbly | sandy |
| damp | satiny |
| dirty | scaly |
| fluffy | scratchy |
| furry | sharp |
| fuzzy | silky |
| greasy | slippery |
| gritty | smooth |
| gummy | soft |
| hairy | spiny |
| hard | squishy |
| heavy | sticky |
| hot | stringy |
| knobbed | velvety |
| light | warm |
| lumpy | woolly |
| moist | wrinkled |

## Sight

| | |
|---|---|
| bright | gloomy |
| clear | glow |
| cloudy | muddy |
| dark | murky |
| dim | opaque |
| dull | pale |
| dusk | radiant |
| faded | scintillate |
| gleam | shimmer |
| glimmer | shine |
| glint | shiny |
| glisten | sparkle |
| glitter | twinkle |

## Smell

| | |
|---|---|
| acrid | pungent |
| aroma | rancid |
| bouquet | rank |
| foul | reek |
| fragrance | scent |
| fragrant | smoky |
| moldy | stench |
| musty | stink |
| odor | stuffy |
| odoriferous | sulfurous |
| perfume | |

## Taste

| |
|---|
| acid |
| ambrosial |
| bitter |
| delicious |
| peppery |
| piquant |
| salty |
| savory |
| sour |
| spicy |
| sweet |
| tangy |
| tart |
| vinegary |
| zesty |

# Word of the Week

Here is a list of new words to add to your vocabulary. If you learn one word each week, you'll have the entire list mastered in a year!

**adorn** (ə - dôrn′) *verb*—to add beauty to; decorate: *I will **adorn** my hat with ribbons.*

**apathy** (ap′ - ə - thē) *noun*—lack of feeling or interest; indifference: *He was filled with **apathy** after losing his job.*

**bawl** (bôl) *verb*—to shout or cry loudly: *I heard her **bawl** when she cut her finger.*

**bountiful** (boun′ - tə - fəl) *adj.*—more than enough; plentiful; abundant: *The farmer was proud of his **bountiful** crop.*

**chasm** (kaz′ - əm) *noun*—deep opening or crack in the earth; gap; gorge: *We could not cross the wide **chasm**.*

**condone** (kən - dōn′) *verb*—to forgive or overlook: *I cannot **condone** your bad manners.*

**diligent** (dil′ - ə - jənt) *adj.*—steady and careful; hardworking and industrious: *She is a **diligent** student.*

**dwindle** (dwin′ - dəl) *verb*—to become smaller or less; to shrink: *Lack of rain caused the water supply to **dwindle**.*

**eccentric** (ek - sen′ - trik) *adj.*—different; odd; peculiar: *Everyone laughed at the **eccentric** woman who dyed her hair green.*

**explicit** (ek - splis′ - ət) *adj.*—clearly expressed; distinctly stated; definite: *We found the house easily because of his **explicit** directions.*

**flit** (flit) *verb*—to move lightly and quickly from one place to another; dart: *We saw the hummingbird **flit** among the flowers.*

**frivolous** (friv′ - ə - ləs) *adj.*—not serious; silly: ***Frivolous** behavior is out of place in a church or courtroom.*

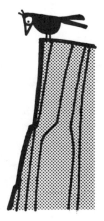

# Word of the Week
## (continued)

**girder** (gur′ - dər) *noun*—a large, horizontal beam of concrete, steel, or wood used as a main support: *The construction worker lowered the **girder** in place to support the floor.*

**gnarled** (närld) *adj.*—having a rough, twisted or knotted look: *There is a **gnarled** oak tree in the park. His leathery hands had been **gnarled** by time and hard work.*

**heifer** (hef′ - ər) *noun*—a young cow that has not had a calf: *The **heifer** was grazing in the pasture.*

**humiliate** (hyōō - mil′ - ē - āt) *verb*—make feel ashamed: *I will not **humiliate** you in front of your friends.*

**impudent** (im′ - pyə - dənt) *adj.*—not well mannered; shamelessly bold; very rude: *The **impudent** student argued with the professor.*

**isolate** (ī′ - sə - lāt) *verb*—separate from others; place or set apart: *It is wise to **isolate** patients with contagious diseases.*

**jovial** (jō′ - vē - əl) *adj.*—full of fun; jolly: *The child was in a **jovial** mood on her birthday.*

**jubilant** (jōō′ - bə - lənt) *adj.*—expressing or showing joy: *The team members were **jubilant**.*

**katydid** (kā′ - tē - did) *noun*—a large, green grasshopper: *The **katydid** hopped on our grass.*

**knoll** (nōl) *noun*—a small, rounded hill; mound: *We had a picnic on the grassy **knoll**.*

**loiter** (loi′ - tər) *verb*—stand around; linger idly: *Do not **loiter** in the halls.*

**luminous** (lōō′ - mə - nəs) *adj.*—shining by its own light; full of light; bright: *The sun and stars are **luminous**.*

**melancholy** (mel′ - ən - kol - ē) *adj.*—sad or gloomy; low in spirits: *She was in a **melancholy** mood.*

# Word of the Week
## (continued)

**mumble** (mum′ - bəl) *verb*—speak softly and unclearly: *If you **mumble**, I cannot under-stand you.*

**nimble** (nim′ - bəl) *adj.*—light and quick in movement; active and surefooted; agile: *The ballerina was graceful and **nimble**.*

**noble** (nō′ - bəl) *adj.*—being of high birth, rank, or title; showing greatness of mind or character; possessing superior qualities, magnificent: *Although his beginning was humble, his actions were **noble**.*

**ominous** (om′ - ə - nəs) *adj.*—unfavorable; threatening; telling of bad luck or trouble to come: *The **ominous** clouds warned us that a storm was approaching.*

**optional** (op′ - shə - nəl) *adj.*—not required; left to one's choice: *The chemistry class was **optional** for juniors.*

**pulsate** (pul′ - sāt) *verb*—beat; throb; move rhythmically: *The doctor could see the artery **pulsate** with each beat of his patient's weakened heart.*

**punctual** (pungk′ - choo - əl) *adj.*—on time; prompt: *He makes a habit of being **punctual** no matter where he goes.*

**quench** (kwench) *verb*—put an end to by satisfying: *On a hot, dry day, you can **quench** your thirst by drinking lemonade.*

**querulous** (kwer′ - əl - əs) *adj.*—complaining; fretful: *The sick boy was very **querulous**.*

**relic** (rel′ - ik) *noun*—a thing left from the past: *The vase was a **relic** from grandmother's day.*

**rustic** (rus′ - tik) *adj.*—belonging to the country rather than the city; rural; simple, plain, unsophisticated: *They live in a **rustic** farmhouse.*

**scant** (skant) *adj.*—inadequate in size or amount; barely enough: *It was hard for us to give our patients adequate treatment because we had a **scant** supply of medicine.*

**stifle** (stī′ - fəl) *verb*—to hold back; suppress; stop: *Vainly I tried to **stifle** my yawn.*

# Word of the Week
## (continued)

**tapir** (tā′ - pər) *noun*—a large piglike mammal with a long nose: *The **tapir** lives in tropical America and southern Asia.*

**tedious** (tē′ - dē - əs) *adj.*—long and tiring: *Her job on the assembly line was very **tedious**.*

**uncanny** (un - kan′ - ē) *adj.*—strange and mysterious: *He had an **uncanny** ability to predict the future.*

**urban** (ər′ - bən) *adj.*—having to do with cities or city life: *They missed their **urban** life-style when they moved to the farm.*

**valiant** (val′ - yənt) *adj.*—brave; courageous: *The fire fighter put up a **valiant** battle against the flames.*

**verge** (vərj) *noun*—the point at which something begins; brink; border: *She was on the **verge** of falling asleep when the phone rang.*

**wilt** (wilt) *verb*—droop or fade; become limp: *The delicate flower will **wilt** in this hot sun.*

**witty** (wit′ - ē) *adj.*—amusing in a clever way: *The comedian told a **witty** joke.*

**xylem** (zī′ - ləm) *noun*—fleshy or woody part of plants: *The **xylem** carries water and minerals absorbed by the roots up through the plant.*

**xylophone** (zī′ - lə - fōn) *noun*—a musical instrument made of metal or wooden bars of varying lengths, which are sounded by striking: *She played the **xylophone** in the school band.*

**yearn** (yərn) *verb*—feel a deep desire or longing: *I **yearn** to go on a long vacation.*

**yowl** (youl) *noun*—long, loud wailing sound: *The **yowl** of the wolf could be heard throughout the forest.*

**zeal** (zēl) *noun*—eagerness; enthusiasm: *She worked with **zeal** on her science fair project.*

**zephyr** (zef′ - ər) *noun*—soft, gentle wind; mild breeze: *A **zephyr** blew across the plains.*

# Consonant Blends – Initial

## bl

| | |
|---|---|
| black | blimp |
| blade | blind |
| blame | blink |
| blanch | bloat |
| blank | block |
| blanket | blond |
| blare | blood |
| blast | bloom |
| blaze | blouse |
| bleach | blow |
| bleak | blown |
| bleat | blue |
| bleed | bluff |
| blend | blur |
| bless | blush |

## br

| | |
|---|---|
| brace | brick |
| brag | bride |
| braid | bright |
| brain | brim |
| brake | bring |
| bran | brink |
| branch | broad |
| brand | broke |
| brass | brook |
| brave | broom |
| bread | broth |
| break | brother |
| breed | brown |
| breeze | browse |
| bribe | brush |

## ch

| | |
|---|---|
| chain | cheese |
| chair | chest |
| chalk | chew |
| champ | chick |
| chance | chief |
| change | chill |
| chant | chimp |
| chap | chin |
| charm | china |
| chart | chip |
| chase | chirp |
| chat | choke |
| cheap | choose |
| cheat | chop |
| check | chum |
| cheek | chunk |
| cheer | churn |

## cl

| | |
|---|---|
| clack | clever |
| clad | click |
| claim | climb |
| clammy | clinch |
| clamp | cling |
| clash | cloak |
| clasp | clock |
| class | clog |
| claw | close |
| clay | clot |
| clean | cloth |
| clear | clove |
| cleat | clown |
| clench | clump |
| clerk | clutch |

# Consonant Blends — Initial
## (continued)

### cr

| | |
|---|---|
| crab | crept |
| crack | crest |
| craft | crew |
| cramp | crib |
| crane | crime |
| crash | crisp |
| crate | crook |
| crater | crop |
| crawl | cross |
| craze | crow |
| creak | crowd |
| cream | crown |
| crease | cruel |
| credit | cruise |
| creep | crust |

### dr

| | |
|---|---|
| drab | dried |
| draft | drift |
| drag | drill |
| dragon | drink |
| drain | drip |
| drake | drive |
| drama | drizzle |
| drank | drone |
| drape | droop |
| draw | drop |
| drawer | drove |
| dread | drug |
| dream | drum |
| drench | drunk |
| dress | dry |

### fl

| | |
|---|---|
| flab | flex |
| flag | flick |
| flake | flier |
| flame | flinch |
| flank | fling |
| flap | flip |
| flare | float |
| flash | flock |
| flat | floor |
| flavor | flop |
| flaw | flour |
| flea | flow |
| fleck | flower |
| fled | flown |
| flesh | fly |

### fr

| | |
|---|---|
| frail | fritter |
| frame | fro |
| fray | frock |
| freak | frog |
| freckle | frolic |
| free | from |
| freeze | frond |
| fresh | front |
| fret | frontier |
| friction | frost |
| friend | frown |
| frill | froze |
| fringe | fruit |
| frisk | fry |

### gl

| | |
|---|---|
| glacier | glint |
| glad | glitter |
| glamour | gloat |
| glance | glob |
| gland | globe |
| glare | gloom |
| glass | glory |
| glaze | gloss |
| gleam | glossary |
| glean | glove |
| glee | glow |
| glib | glue |
| glide | glum |
| glimmer | glut |
| glimpse | |

### gr

| | |
|---|---|
| grab | greet |
| grace | grid |
| grade | grief |
| grain | grill |
| grand | grim |
| grant | grin |
| grape | grind |
| graph | grip |
| grass | grit |
| grate | groan |
| grave | groom |
| gray | ground |
| graze | group |
| grease | grow |
| great | growl |
| greed | gruff |
| green | grunt |

# Consonant Blends – Initial
## (continued)

### pl

| | |
|---|---|
| place | pleat |
| plague | pledge |
| plaid | plenty |
| plain | plod |
| plan | plot |
| plane | plow |
| planet | plug |
| plank | plum |
| plant | plumb |
| plaster | plump |
| plate | plunge |
| play | plural |
| plaza | plus |
| plead | ply |
| please | |

### pr

| | |
|---|---|
| praise | prime |
| pram | prince |
| prance | print |
| prank | prior |
| preach | private |
| premium | prize |
| prep | probe |
| press | prod |
| pretend | profit |
| pretty | prone |
| pretzel | proof |
| prey | prop |
| price | prose |
| pride | proud |
| prim | pry |

### sh

| | |
|---|---|
| shack | shell |
| shade | shift |
| shake | shine |
| shall | ship |
| shame | shirt |
| shape | shop |
| share | shore |
| shark | short |
| shave | shot |
| shawl | should |
| she | shout |
| shed | shove |
| sheep | show |
| sheet | shut |
| shelf | shy |

### sl

| | |
|---|---|
| slab | slid |
| slack | slim |
| slam | slink |
| slander | slip |
| slang | sliver |
| slant | slob |
| slap | slosh |
| slash | slot |
| slat | slow |
| slate | slug |
| slave | slum |
| sled | slur |
| sleek | slush |
| sleep | sly |
| slick | |

### sm

| | |
|---|---|
| smack | smock |
| small | smog |
| smart | smoke |
| smash | smolder |
| smear | smooch |
| smell | smother |
| smile | smudge |
| smirk | smuggle |
| smite | |

### th

| | |
|---|---|
| that | thing |
| thaw | think |
| the | third |
| their | thirty |
| them | this |
| then | those |
| there | though |
| these | thought |
| they | thud |
| thick | thumb |
| thin | thump |

### st

| | |
|---|---|
| stab | stitch |
| stack | stock |
| staff | stole |
| stair | stomp |
| stake | stone |
| stale | stop |
| stamp | store |
| stand | street |
| stare | stress |
| stash | strict |
| stem | struck |
| step | stuff |
| stick | stump |
| still | stun |
| sting | stunt |

### wh

| | |
|---|---|
| whale | which |
| wharf | while |
| what | whine |
| wheat | whip |
| wheel | whirl |
| when | white |
| where | why |

# Consonant Blends—Final

## -ck

| | |
|---|---|
| back | hock |
| black | lack |
| block | lick |
| brick | lock |
| buck | luck |
| clack | mock |
| click | nick |
| clock | pack |
| crack | pick |
| crock | pluck |
| deck | quick |
| duck | rack |
| flack | sack |
| fleck | sock |
| flock | tack |

## -ct

| | |
|---|---|
| abstract | elect |
| act | enact |
| affect | exact |
| collect | expect |
| conduct | fact |
| conflict | indict |
| connect | inflict |
| convict | inject |
| correct | insect |
| deduct | neglect |
| depict | object |
| detect | select |
| direct | suspect |
| effect | tact |
| eject | tract |

## -ft

| |
|---|
| aft |
| cleft |
| craft |
| draft |
| drift |
| gift |
| graft |
| left |
| lift |
| loft |
| raft |
| rift |
| shaft |
| shift |
| swift |

## -ld

| |
|---|
| bald |
| bold |
| build |
| child |
| cold |
| field |
| guild |
| hold |
| mild |
| mold |
| scald |
| shield |
| told |
| wild |
| yield |

## -mp

| | |
|---|---|
| blimp | primp |
| bump | pump |
| camp | ramp |
| champ | romp |
| chimp | scamp |
| chomp | shrimp |
| cramp | skimp |
| damp | slump |
| dump | stamp |
| grump | stomp |
| jump | stump |
| lamp | thump |
| limp | tramp |
| lump | trump |
| plump | vamp |

## -nd

| | |
|---|---|
| and | found |
| band | friend |
| behind | gland |
| bend | grind |
| beyond | ground |
| blend | hand |
| blond | hind |
| command | land |
| contend | mound |
| defend | remind |
| demand | round |
| depend | send |
| end | strand |
| expand | trend |
| extend | wind |

# Consonant Blends — Final
## (continued)

### -ng

| | |
|---|---|
| bang | sang |
| bring | sing |
| clang | slang |
| cling | sling |
| fang | slung |
| fling | spring |
| gang | sprung |
| hang | sting |
| hung | string |
| king | strong |
| long | stung |
| lung | sung |
| pang | swing |
| rang | wing |
| ring | zing |

### -nk

| | |
|---|---|
| bank | pink |
| blank | plank |
| blink | prank |
| brink | rank |
| bunk | rink |
| clink | sank |
| crank | sink |
| drank | skunk |
| drink | slink |
| flank | spank |
| frank | spunk |
| junk | stink |
| link | sunk |
| mink | tank |
| monk | think |

### -nt

agent
aunt
bent
cent
chant
client
count
current
decent
dent
distant
event
front
glint
grant
haunt
hint
hunt
implant
infant
instant
joint
lent
moment
print
sent
splint
tent
vacant
went

### -pt

adapt
adept
adopt
attempt
concept
corrupt
disrupt
erupt
except
interrupt
kept
prompt
receipt
slept
wept

### -sk

ask
bask
brisk
cask
desk
disk
dusk
flask
frisk
husk
mask
musk
risk
task
tusk

### -st

| | |
|---|---|
| adjust | honest |
| artist | host |
| best | invest |
| boast | just |
| cast | last |
| coast | least |
| contest | must |
| crest | nest |
| dentist | past |
| dust | roast |
| enlist | suggest |
| feast | toast |
| fist | vest |
| frost | yeast |
| gust | zest |

# Long Words
## Five Syllables

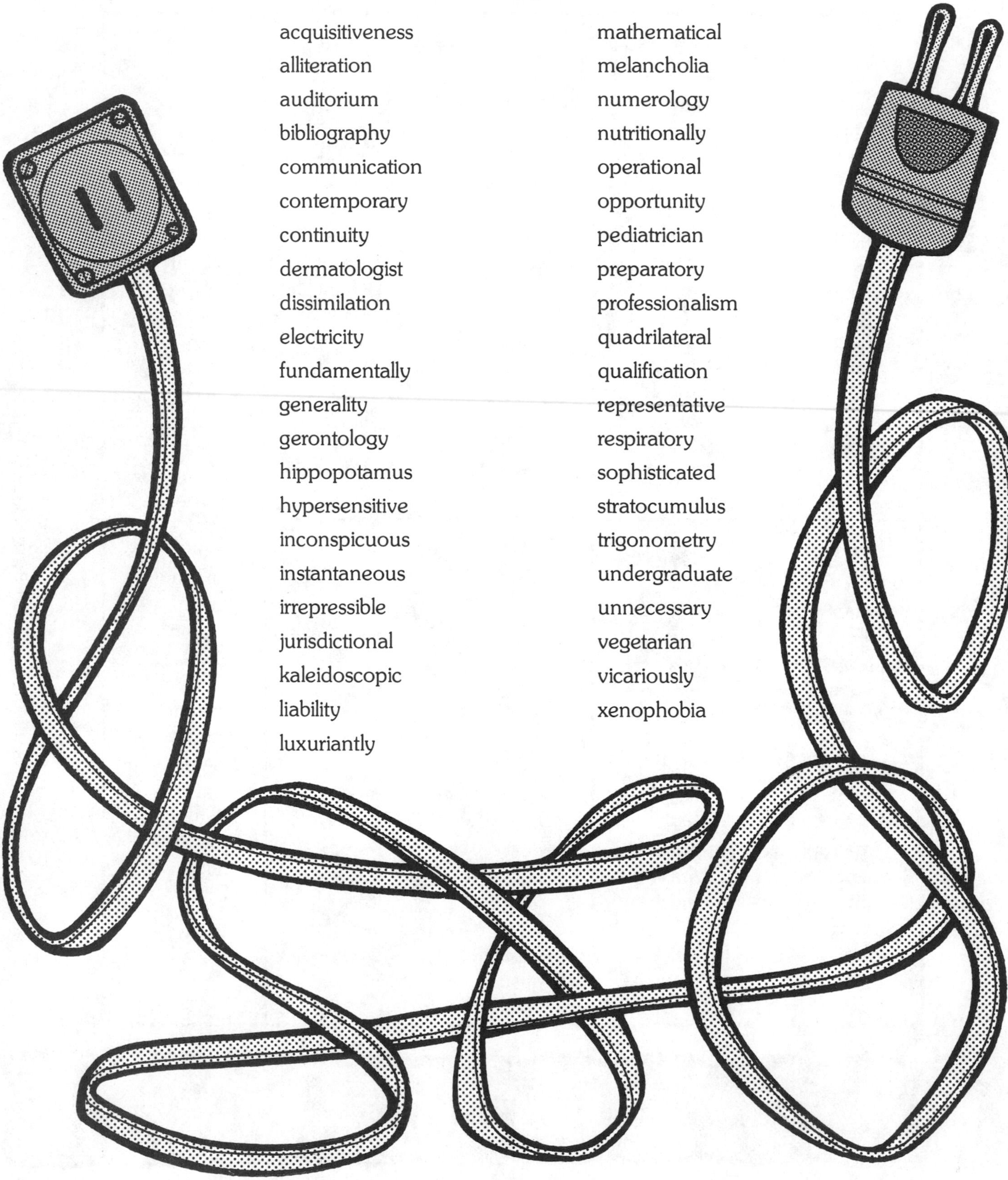

acquisitiveness
alliteration
auditorium
bibliography
communication
contemporary
continuity
dermatologist
dissimilation
electricity
fundamentally
generality
gerontology
hippopotamus
hypersensitive
inconspicuous
instantaneous
irrepressible
jurisdictional
kaleidoscopic
liability
luxuriantly

mathematical
melancholia
numerology
nutritionally
operational
opportunity
pediatrician
preparatory
professionalism
quadrilateral
qualification
representative
respiratory
sophisticated
stratocumulus
trigonometry
undergraduate
unnecessary
vegetarian
vicariously
xenophobia

# Longer Words
## Six Syllables

autobiography

beneficiary

bioenergetics

compartmentalizing

compatibility

congregationalism

conversationalist

convertability

disciplinarian

disproportionally

ecclesiasticism

encyclopedia

equivocatory

eventuality

exemplification

externalization

extraprofessional

gyrostabilizer

hallucinatory

inconsequentially

intercommunicate

jurisdictionally

metaphysically

microscopically

mythologically

neuropsychiatry

nonparticipating

onomatopoeia

originality

paleontology

parenthetically

prestidigitation

pronunciamento

reorganization

representational

respectability

sentimentality

sesquicentennial

subordinationism

susceptibility

territorialism

totalitarian

transubstantiation

ultramicroscopic

unintelligible

unsophisticated

unsuitability

vegetarianism

vulnerability

# Longest Words
## Seven Syllables or More

axiomatically
differentiability
electrotherapeutics
hydrometeorology
incorrigibility
indefensibility
insusceptibility
micropaleontology
microphotometrically
neurophysiology
nonrepresentationalism
onomasiology
psychobiological
septuagenarian
territoriality
thermoelectromotive
unapologetically
unceremoniously
unreliability
utilitarianism

1. Use a dictionary to discover the meanings of at least five of the words on this list.

2. Use a dictionary to help you add ten words to this list.

3. Use a dictionary to find and list words with nine or ten syllables.

# Rhyming Words

| -ab | -ack | -ag | -ake | -all | -am |
|---|---|---|---|---|---|
| cab | back | bag | bake | all | am |
| fab | black | flag | brake | ball | bam |
| gab | crack | gag | cake | call | dam |
| grab | flack | hag | drake | fall | ham |
| jab | lack | jag | fake | gall | jam |
| lab | pack | lag | flake | hall | lamb |
| nab | quack | nag | lake | mall | Pam |
| slab | rack | rag | make | pall | ram |
| stab | sack | sag | quake | small | Sam |
| tab | slack | shag | rake | stall | tam |
|  | smack | snag | sake | tall | yam |
|  | stack | tag | shake | wall |  |
|  |  |  | snake |  |  |
|  |  |  | stake |  |  |
|  |  |  | take |  |  |
|  |  |  | wake |  |  |

| -an | -ank | -ap | -at | -ay |
|---|---|---|---|---|
| an | bank | cap | at | bay |
| ban | blank | clap | bat | clay |
| bran | crank | flap | brat | day |
| can | drank | gap | cat | fray |
| clan | flank | lap | chat | gay |
| Dan | frank | map | fat | gray |
| fan | hank | nap | flat | hay |
| Jan | plank | rap | gnat | jay |
| man | rank | sap | hat | lay |
| Nan | sank | slap | mat | may |
| pan | spank | tap | Nat | pay |
| plan | tank | trap | pat | play |
| ran | thank | wrap | rat | pray |
| scan | yank | yap | rat | ray |
| tan |  | zap | sat | say |
| than |  |  | scat | stay |
| van |  |  | slat | sway |
|  |  |  | spat | tray |
|  |  |  | that | way |
|  |  |  | vat |  |

# Rhyming Words
## (continued)

| -eak | -ear | -eat | -ed | -end | -et | -ick | -ig |
|---|---|---|---|---|---|---|---|
| beak | clear | beat | bed | bend | bet | brick | big |
| cheek | dear | cheat | bled | blend | get | chick | dig |
| leak | drear | cleat | bred | end | jet | flick | fig |
| meek | ear | eat | dead | fend | let | kick | gig |
| peak | fear | feat | fed | lend | met | lick | jig |
| peek | gear | heat | fled | mend | net | nick | pig |
| reek | hear | meat | led | send | pet | pick | rig |
| seek | leer | meet | red | spend | set | sick | twig |
| sleek | rear | neat | said | tend | vet | slick | wig |
| weak | sear | pleat | shed | trend | wet | stick | |
| week | shear | seat | shred | vend | yet | tick | |
| | sneer | sheet | sled | | | trick | |
| | spear | treat | sped | | | wick | |
| | tear | wheat | wed | | | | |
| | year | | | | | | |

| -est | -ill | -in | -ing | -ink | -ip | -it | -ob |
|---|---|---|---|---|---|---|---|
| best | bill | bin | bring | blink | dip | bit | bob |
| chest | chill | din | cling | clink | drip | fit | cob |
| jest | dill | fin | ding | drink | flip | flit | gob |
| nest | drill | gin | fling | link | hip | hit | job |
| pest | fill | kin | king | mink | lip | kit | knob |
| rest | gill | pin | ring | pink | nip | knit | mob |
| test | hill | sin | sing | rink | rip | lit | rob |
| vest | ill | skin | sling | sink | sip | mitt | slob |
| west | kill | spin | spring | stink | slip | nit | snob |
| wrest | mill | thin | sting | think | snip | pit | sob |
| zest | nil | tin | swing | wink | strip | sit | throb |
| | pill | win | thing | | tip | slit | |
| | quill | | wing | | trip | wit | |
| | skill | | wring | | whip | writ | |
| | spill | | | | zip | | |
| | still | | | | | | |
| | will | | | | | | |

# Rhyming Words
## (continued)

| -ock | -od | -og | -oom | -op | -ot | -y |
|------|-----|-----|------|-----|-----|-----|
| block | clod | cog | bloom | bop | cot | by |
| clock | cod | dog | boom | cop | dot | cry |
| dock | God | flog | broom | crop | got | die |
| flock | mod | fog | doom | drop | hot | eye |
| hock | nod | frog | fume | fop | jot | fly |
| knock | plod | hog | gloom | hop | lot | fry |
| lock | pod | jog | groom | lop | not | high |
| mock | prod | log | loom | mop | pot | I |
| rock | rod | smog | room | plop | rot | lie |
| sock | shod | tog | tomb | pop | shot | my |
| | sod | | zoom | plop | slot | pie |
| | Todd | | | slop | sot | rye |
| | | | | sop | spot | sigh |
| | | | | stop | tot | sty |
| | | | | top | | tle |
| | | | | | | try |
| | | | | | | why |

| -ud | -ug | -un | -unk | -ut |
|-----|-----|-----|------|-----|
| bud | bug | bun | bunk | but |
| cud | dug | done | clunk | cut |
| dud | hug | fun | drunk | gut |
| flood | jug | gun | dunk | hut |
| Jud | lug | none | hunk | jut |
| mud | mug | one | junk | nut |
| thud | pug | pun | punk | putt |
| | rug | run | stunk | rut |
| | slug | son | sunk | shut |
| | tug | sun | trunk | Tut |
| | | ton | | |
| | | won | | |

Name _____

# Create a Language List

Think of a language-related topic that interests you. On the lines below, create a list that reflects this topic. Illustrate your list and give it a title.

_____

_____

_____

_____

_____

_____

_____

_____

_____

_____

# Social Studies

# Chief Justices of the U.S. Supreme Court

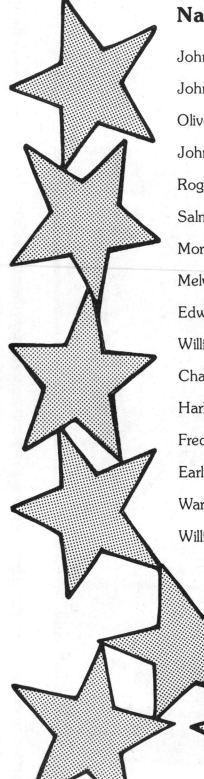

| Name | Term of Office |
| --- | --- |
| John Jay | 1789–1795 |
| John Rutledge | 1795 |
| Oliver Ellsworth | 1796–1800 |
| John Marshall | 1801–1835 |
| Roger Taney | 1836–1864 |
| Salmon Chase | 1864–1873 |
| Morrison Waite | 1874–1888 |
| Melville Fuller | 1888–1910 |
| Edward White | 1910–1921 |
| William Taft | 1921–1930 |
| Charles Hughes | 1930–1941 |
| Harlan Stone | 1941–1946 |
| Frederick Vinson | 1946–1953 |
| Earl Warren | 1953–1969 |
| Warren Burger | 1969–1986 |
| William Rehnquist | 1986– |

# Explorers

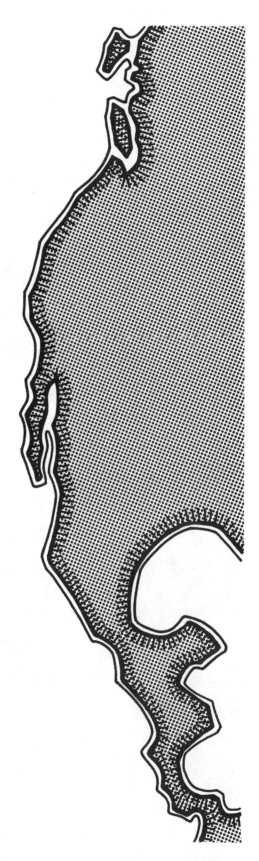

Edwin E. Aldrin, Jr.

Neil A. Armstrong

Lucas Vásquez de Ayllon

William Baffin

Vasco Núñez de Balboa

Robert A. Bartlett

Charles William Beebe

Vitus Bering

Daniel Boone

James Bowie

James Bridger

James Bruce

Robert O'Hara Burke

Sir Richard Francis Burton

Richard E. Byrd

John Cabot

Pedro Álvares Cabral

Juan Rodríquez Cabrillo

René Auguste Caillié

Kit Carson

Jacques Cartier

Samuel de Champlain

Hugh Clapperton

William Clark

Christopher Columbus

James Cook

Francisco Vásquez de Coronado

Hernando Cortes

William Dampier

Hernando de Soto

# Explorers
## (continued)

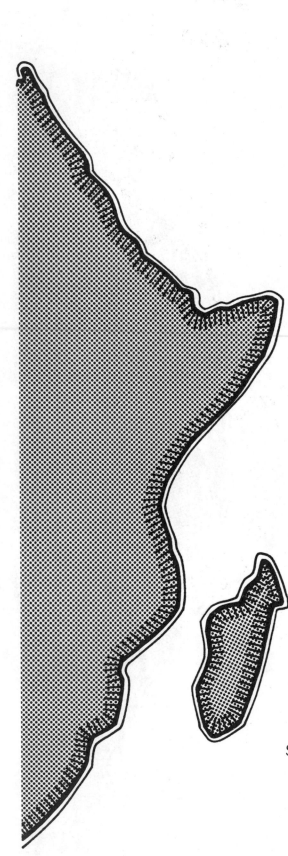
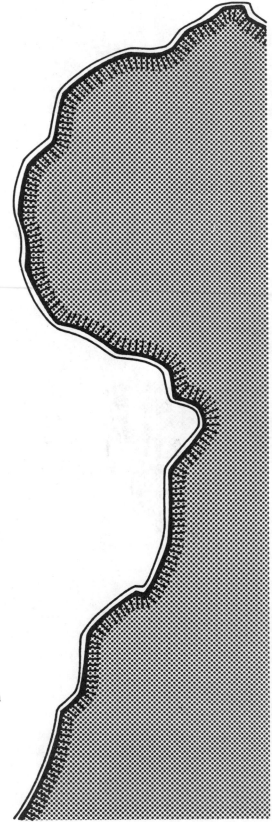

Bartholomeu Dias

Sir Francis Drake

Sieur Duluth

Leif Ericson

Edward John Eyre

Sir John Franklin

John C. Frémont

Sir Martin Frobisher

Yuri A. Gagarin

Vasco da Gama

Louis Hennepin

Sir Edmund Hillary

Henry Hudson

Louis Jolliet

Sieur de La Salle

Alexei A. Leonov

Meriwether Lewis

David Livingstone

James A. Lovell, Jr.

Ferdinand Magellan

Jacques Marquette

Tenzing Norgay

Mungo Park

Robert E. Peary

Zebulon Pike

Francisco Pizarro

Sir Walter Raleigh

Robert Falcon Scott

Sir Ernest Henry Shackleton

# Explorers
## (continued)

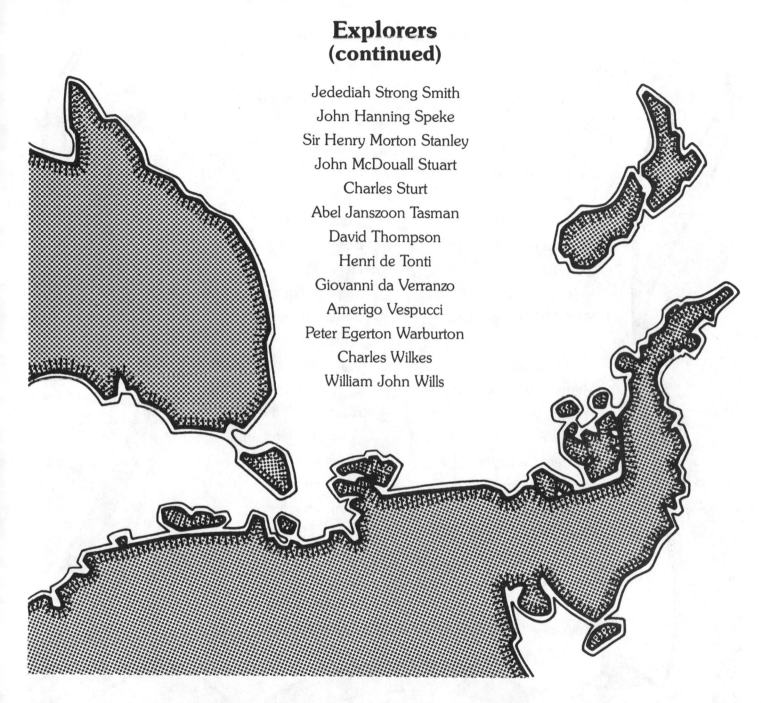

Jedediah Strong Smith

John Hanning Speke

Sir Henry Morton Stanley

John McDouall Stuart

Charles Sturt

Abel Janszoon Tasman

David Thompson

Henri de Tonti

Giovanni da Verranzo

Amerigo Vespucci

Peter Egerton Warburton

Charles Wilkes

William John Wills

1. Divide a sheet of paper into eight columns. Label the columns with these headings: **Africa**, **Australia and the Pacific Ocean**, **Europe**, **North America**, **the Polar Regions**, **South America**, **Space**, and **Undersea**. Then, write the names of explorers from this list under these headings according to the areas they explored.

2. Do some research to discover the nationalities of at least twenty of these explorers.

3. Select two explorers from this list. Read about their accomplishments and compare their lives. In what ways were they similar? In what ways were they different?

# Famous Americans

Maude Adams

Jane Addams

Marian Anderson

Susan B. Anthony

Virginia Apgar

John Jacob Astor

John James Audubon

Clara Barton

Alexander Graham Bell

Mary McLeod Bethune

Elizabeth Blackwell

Daniel Boone

Margaret Wise Brown

Pearl S. Buck

Luther Burbank

Andrew Carnegie

Hattie Carnegie

Emma Perry Carr

George Washington Carver

Mary Cassatt

Willa Cather

Henry Clay

Katharine Cornell

Hilda Doolittle (H.D.)

Amelia Earhart

Thomas Alva Edison

Medgar W. Evers

Edna Ferber

Geraldine Ferraro

Dorothy Canfield Fisher

Henry Ford

Stephen Foster

Benjamin Franklin

Robert Fulton

William Lloyd Garrison

Theodor Geisel

Elizabeth Meriwether Gilmer

John H. Glenn, Jr.

Ulysses S. Grant

Alex Haley

Sonja Henie

Patrick Henry

Billie Holiday

Elias Howe

Mahalia Jackson

Helen Keller

# Famous Americans
## (continued)

Francis Scott Key

Martin Luther King, Jr.

Dorothea Lange

Emma Lazarus

Robert E. Lee

Henry Wadsworth Longfellow

Amy Lowell

Clare Boothe Luce

Douglas MacArthur

Carson McCullers

Hattie McDaniel

Horace Mann

James Wilson Marshall

John Marshall

Thurgood Marshall

Margaret Mead

Samuel F. B. Morse

Anna Mary Robertson Moses

Sandra Day O'Connor

Georgia O'Keefe

Dorothy Rothschild Parker

Linus Pauling

Emily Price Post

Joseph Pulitzer

Paul Revere

Sally Ride

John Roosevelt (Jackie) Robinson

John D. Rockefeller

Anna Eleanor Roosevelt

Elihu Root

Nellie Tayloe Ross

Helena Rubinstein

Jonas Edward Salk

Beverly Sills

B. F. Skinner

Cornelia Otis Skinner

Harriet Beecher Stowe

Maria Tallchief

Henry David Thoreau

Harriet Tubman

Booker T. Washington

Daniel Webster

Noah Webster

Marcus Whitman

Walt Whitman

Eli Whitney

Laura Ingalls Wilder

Thornton Niven Wilder

Roger Williams

Charles E. Yeager

Brigham Young

Mildred (Babe) Didrikson Zaharias

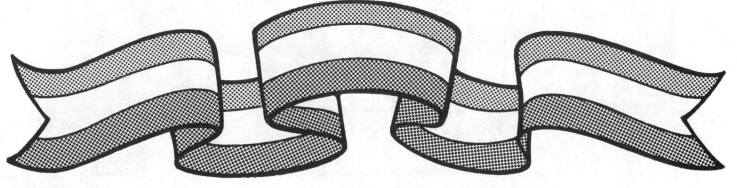

# Firsts for American Women

| | |
|---|---|
| **Jane Addams** | first American woman to win the Nobel peace prize |
| **Marian Anderson** | first black to sing with the Metropolitan opera |
| **Clara Barton** | founder of the American Red Cross |
| **Elizabeth Blackwell** | first woman doctor of medicine in modern times |
| **Pearl S. Buck** | first American woman to win the Nobel prize for literature |
| **Shirley Chisholm** | first black woman to serve in the U.S. Congress |
| **Isadora Duncan** | first American woman interpretive dancer |
| **Amelia Earhart** | American aviatrix who became the first woman to cross the Atlantic Ocean in an airplane |
| **Rebecca Latimer Felton** | became by appointment the first woman to serve in the U.S. Senate |
| **Patricia Harris** | first black woman to serve as a U.S. ambassador |
| **Clare Boothe Luce** | first woman to represent the United States in a major diplomatic post |
| **Susanna Madora** | first woman elected mayor |
| **Maria Mitchell** | first woman astronomer and discoverer of a comet |
| **Sandra Day O'Connor** | first woman justice of the U.S. Supreme Court |
| **Frances Perkins** | first woman appointed to serve in a presidential cabinet |
| **Jeanette Rankin** | first woman elected to the U.S. Congress |
| **Nellie Tayloe Ross** | first woman governor in the United States |
| **Elizabeth Cochrane Seaman** (*Pseudonym:* **Nellie Bly**) | American journalist who set a record by traveling around the world in 72 days, 6 hours, and 11 minutes |
| **Victoria Clafin Woodhull** | first woman to run for president of the United States |

# Leaders of the Revolutionary War

John Adams

Samuel Adams

Ethan Allen

Benedict Arnold

John Barry

George Rogers Clark

George Clinton

Silas Deane

Henry Dearborn

Benjamin Franklin

Horatio Gates

Nathanael Greene

Nathan Hale

John Hancock

Patrick Henry

Esek Hopkins

John Jay

Thomas Jefferson

John Paul Jones

Henry Knox

Charles Lee

Henry Lee

Richard Henry Lee

Robert R. Livingston

Francis Marion

George Mason

Robert Morris

William Moultrie

James Otis

Thomas Paine

Israel Putnam

Rufus Putnam

Paul Revere

Arthur St. Clair

Haym Salomon

Philip J. Schuyler

John Stark

Artemas Ward

Seth Warner

Joseph Warren

George Washington

Anthony Wayne

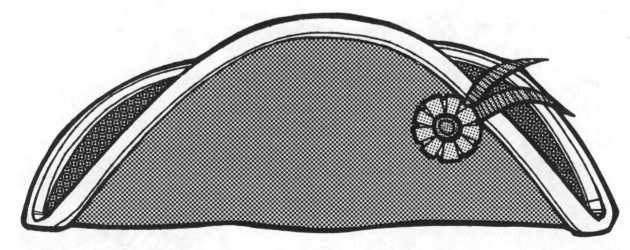

Do the research necessary to classify the people on this list as either military leaders or civilian leaders.

# Presidents of the United States

| Name | Term | Party |
|------|------|-------|
| 1. George Washington | 1789-1797 | Federalist |
| 2. John Adams | 1797-1801 | Federalist |
| 3. Thomas Jefferson | 1801-1809 | Democratic-Republican |
| 4. James Madison | 1809-1817 | Democratic-Republican |
| 5. James Monroe | 1817-1825 | Democratic-Republican |
| 6. John Quincy Adams | 1825-1829 | Democratic-Republican |
| 7. Andrew Jackson | 1829-1837 | Democrat |
| 8. Martin Van Buren | 1837-1841 | Democrat |
| 9. William H. Harrison | 1841 | Whig |
| 10. John Tyler | 1841-1845 | Whig |
| 11. James K. Polk | 1845-1849 | Democrat |
| 12. Zachary Taylor | 1849-1850 | Whig |
| 13. Millard Fillmore | 1850-1853 | Whig |
| 14. Franklin Pierce | 1853-1857 | Democrat |
| 15. James Buchanan | 1857-1861 | Democrat |
| 16. Abraham Lincoln | 1861-1865 | Republican |
| 17. Andrew Johnson | 1865-1869 | Democrat |
| 18. Ulysses S. Grant | 1869-1877 | Republican |
| 19. Rutherford B. Hayes | 1877-1881 | Republican |
| 20. James A. Garfield | 1881 | Republican |
| 21. Chester A. Arthur | 1881-1885 | Republican |
| 22. Grover Cleveland | 1885-1889 | Democrat |
| 23. Benjamin Harrison | 1889-1893 | Republican |
| 24. Grover Cleveland | 1893-1897 | Democrat |
| 25. William McKinley | 1897-1901 | Republican |

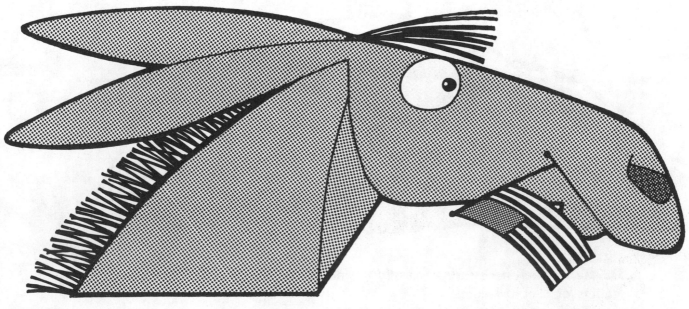

# Presidents of the United States
## (continued)

| Name | Term | Party |
|---|---|---|
| 26. Theodore Roosevelt | 1901–1909 | Republican |
| 27. William Howard Taft | 1909–1913 | Republican |
| 28. Woodrow Wilson | 1913–1921 | Democrat |
| 29. Warren G. Harding | 1921–1923 | Republican |
| 30. Calvin Coolidge | 1923–1929 | Republican |
| 31. Herbert C. Hoover | 1929–1933 | Republican |
| 32. Franklin D. Roosevelt | 1933–1945 | Democrat |
| 33. Harry S. Truman | 1945–1953 | Democrat |
| 34. Dwight D. Eisenhower | 1953–1961 | Republican |
| 35. John F. Kennedy | 1961–1963 | Democrat |
| 36. Lyndon B. Johnson | 1963–1969 | Democrat |
| 37. Richard M. Nixon | 1969–1974 | Republican |
| 38. Gerald R. Ford | 1974–1977 | Republican |
| 39. James Earl ("Jimmy") Carter | 1977–1981 | Democrat |
| 40. Ronald W. Reagan | 1981– | Republican |

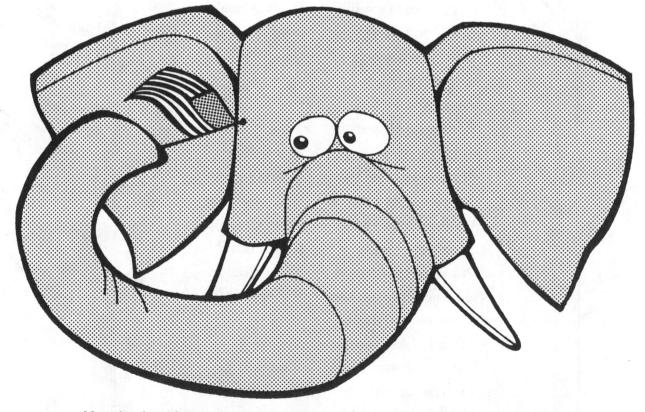

Use the list of presidents to make up a trivia game of presidential firsts. For example, by doing some research, determine who was the first president to (1) be married while in office, (2) resign from office, (3) use a telephone, or (4) be telecast in color.

# Signers of the Declaration of Independence

Fifty-six members of the Continental Congress signed the Declaration of Independence, the historic document in which the American colonies declared their freedom from British rule.

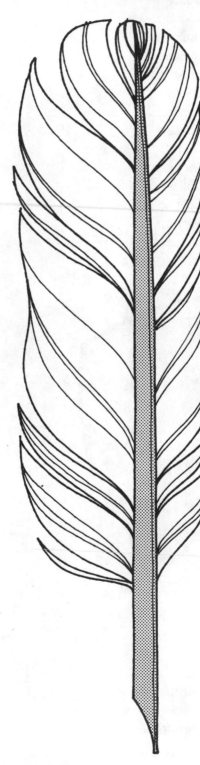
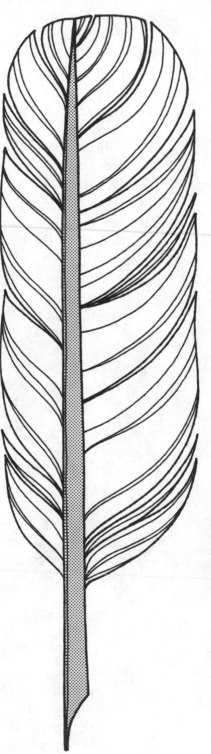

| | |
|---|---|
| **John Adams** | Massachusetts |
| **Samuel Adams** | Massachusetts |
| **Josiah Bartlett** | New Hampshire |
| **Carter Braxton** | Virginia |
| **Charles Carroll** | Maryland |
| **Samuel Chase** | Maryland |
| **Abraham Clark** | New Jersey |
| **George Clymer** | Pennsylvania |
| **William Ellery** | Rhode Island |
| **William Floyd** | New York |
| **Benjamin Franklin** | Pennsylvania |
| **Elbridge Gerry** | Massachusetts |
| **Button Gwinnett** | Georgia |
| **Lyman Hall** | Georgia |
| **John Hancock** | Massachusetts |
| **Benjamin Harrison** | Virginia |
| **John Hart** | New Jersey |
| **Joseph Hewes** | North Carolina |
| **Thomas Heyward, Jr.** | South Carolina |
| **William Hooper** | North Carolina |
| **Stephen Hopkins** | Rhode Island |
| **Francis Hopkinson** | New Jersey |
| **Samuel Huntington** | Connecticut |
| **Thomas Jefferson** | Virginia |
| **Francis Lightfoot Lee** | Virginia |
| **Richard Henry Lee** | Virginia |
| **Francis Lewis** | New York |
| **Philip Livingston** | New York |

# Signers of the Declaration of Independence
## (continued)

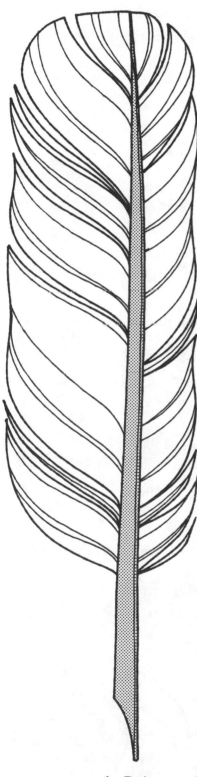
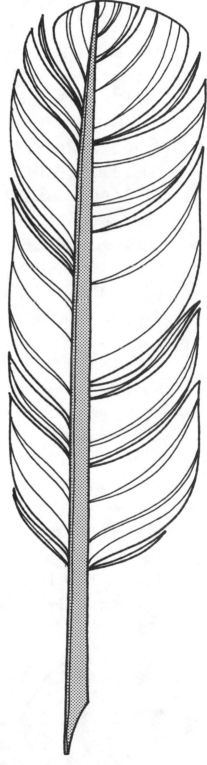

| | |
|---|---|
| **Thomas Lynch, Jr.** | South Carolina |
| **Thomas McKean** | Delaware |
| **Arthur Middleton** | South Carolina |
| **Lewis Morris** | New York |
| **Robert Morris** | Pennsylvania |
| **John Morton** | Pennsylvania |
| **Thomas Nelson, Jr.** | Virginia |
| **William Paca** | Maryland |
| **Robert T. Paine** | Massachusetts |
| **John Penn** | North Carolina |
| **George Read** | Delaware |
| **Caesar Rodney** | Delaware |
| **George Ross** | Pennsylvania |
| **Benjamin Rush** | Pennsylvania |
| **Edward Rutledge** | South Carolina |
| **Roger Sherman** | Connecticut |
| **James Smith** | Pennsylvania |
| **Richard Stockton** | New Jersey |
| **Thomas Stone** | Maryland |
| **George Taylor** | Pennsylvania |
| **Matthew Thornton** | New Hampshire |
| **George Walton** | Georgia |
| **William Whipple** | New Hampshire |
| **William Williams** | Connecticut |
| **James Wilson** | Pennsylvania |
| **John Witherspoon** | New Jersey |
| **Oliver Wolcott** | Connecticut |
| **George Wythe** | Virginia |

1. Pick one of the signers on this list and do research to learn more about him.
2. Make a chart or bar graph showing how many signers were from each colony.

# World-Famous Leaders

Konrad Adenauer (1876-1967)

Alexander the Great (356-323 B.C.)

Attila the Hun (*ca.* 406-453)

Menahem Begin (1913-        )

David Ben-Gurion (1886-1973)

Otto von Bismarck (1815-1898)

Simón Bolívar (1783-1830)

Ralph Bunche (1904-1971)

Gaius Julius Caesar (100-44 B.C.)

Fidel Castro (1927-        )

Charlemagne (742-814)

Chiang Kai-shek (1887-1975)

Winston Churchill (1874-1965)

Cleopatra (69-30 B.C.)

Crazy Horse (1849-1877)

Oliver Cromwell (1599-1658)

Cyrus the Great (*ca.* 600-529 B.C.)

Moshe Dayan (1915-1981)

Charles de Gaulle (1890-1970)

Porfirio Díaz (1830-1915)

Dwight D. Eisenhower (1890-1969)

Elizabeth I (1523-1603)

Elizabeth II (1926-        )

Valery Giscard d'Estaing (1926-        )

Farouk I (1920-1965)

Frederick the Great (1712-1786)

Genghis Khan (1162-1227)

Indira Nehru Gandhi (1917-1984)

Mahatma Gandhi (1869-1948)

Geronimo (1829-1909)

Henry VIII (1491-1547)

Hirohito (1901-        )

Adolf Hitler (1889-1945)

Ho Chi Minh (1890-1969)

Chief Joseph (*ca.* 1840-1904)

Benito Pablo Juarez (1806-1872)

Nikita Khrushchev (1894-1971)

Thomas E. Lawrence (1888-1935)

Nikolai Lenin (1870-1924)

Louis XIV (1638-1715)

Douglas MacArthur (1880-1964)

Mao Tse-tung (1893-1976)

Golda Meir (1898-1978)

Benito Mussolini (1883-1945)

Napoleon I (1769-1821)

George S. Patton (1885-1945)

Erwin Rommel (1891-1944)

Franklin D. Roosevelt (1882-1945)

Anwar el-Sadat (1918-1981)

Santa Anna (*ca.* 1795-1876)

Joseph Stalin (1879-1953)

Tecumseh (*ca.* 1768-1813)

Tutankhamen (fl. *ca.* 1358 B.C.)

# Canadian Provinces and Territories

| Provinces and Territories | Capitals |
| --- | --- |
| Alberta | Edmonton |
| British Columbia | Victoria |
| Manitoba | Winnipeg |
| New Brunswick | Fredericton |
| Newfoundland | Saint John's |
| Northwest Territories | Yellowknife |
| Nova Scotia | Halifax |
| Ontario | Toronto |
| Prince Edward Island | Charlottetown |
| Quebec | Quebec |
| Saskatchewan | Regina |
| Yukon Territory | Whitehorse |

# Continents of the World

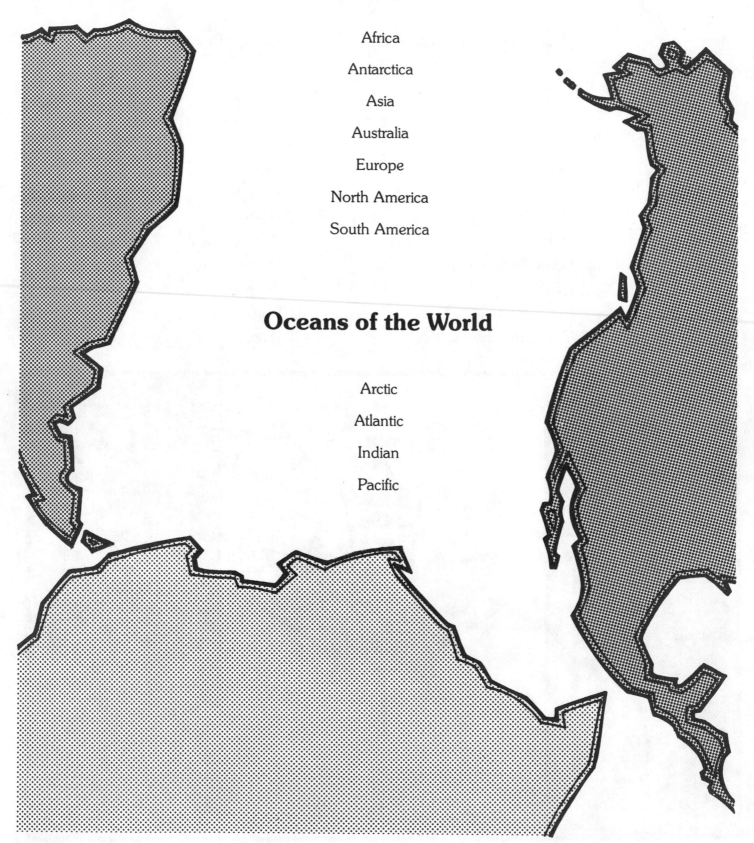

Africa

Antarctica

Asia

Australia

Europe

North America

South America

# Oceans of the World

Arctic

Atlantic

Indian

Pacific

# Deserts of the World

A **desert** is a region that experiences little rainfall, grows sparse vegetation, and is incapable of supporting a population of any size without an artificial water supply.

## Africa
Arabian (Eastern)
Kalahari
Libyan
Namib
Nubian
Sahara

## Asia
Gobi
Kara Kum
Kavir (Dasht-i-Kavir)
Kyzyl Kum
Lut (Dasht-i-Lut)
Nafud (An Nafud)
Negev
Rub al-Khali (Empty Quarter)
Syrian
Taklamakan
Thar (Great Indian)

## Australia
Gibson
Great Sandy
Great Victoria
Simpson

## North America
Black Rock
Colorado Desert
Death Valley
Mojave
Painted Desert
Sonoran

## South America
Atacama
Sechura

1. Locate each one of these deserts on a regional or world map.

2. Do research to discover the differences among tropical deserts, polar deserts, and middle latitude deserts.

3. Select a desert from this list. Do research to find out what kinds of plant and animal life are found there.

# Islands of North America

| | |
|---|---|
| Alcatraz | Manitoulin Islands |
| Aleutian Islands | Martha's Vineyard |
| Anticosti | Mount Desert Island |
| Bermuda | Nantucket |
| Cape Breton Island | Newfoundland |
| Dry Tortugas | Padre Island |
| Ellis Island | Pribilof Islands |
| Florida Keys | Prince Edward Island |
| Governors Island | Queen Charlotte Islands |
| Isle Royale National Park | Sable Island |
| Liberty Island | Saint Pierre and Miquelon |
| Long Island | Southampton Island |
| Mackinac Island | Staten Island |
| Magdalen Islands | Thousand Islands |
| Manhattan Island | Vancouver Island |

This is a partial listing and includes only some of the islands of North America. Many islands, such as Santa Catalina off the coast of California and both Camano and Whidbey in Puget Sound, have been omitted. Look up the names of some of the omitted islands in your area and add them to this list.

# Longest Rivers

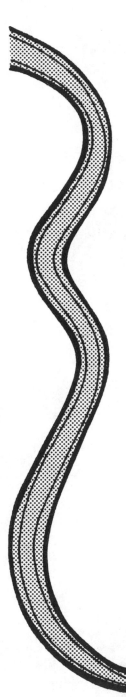

| Name | Location | Length in Miles |
|---|---|---|
| Nile | Africa | 4,145 |
| Amazon | South America | 4,000 |
| Yangtze | Asia | 3,915 |
| Huang Ho | Asia | 2,903 |
| Congo | Africa | 2,900 |
| Amur | Asia | 2,744 |
| Lena | Asia | 2,734 |
| Irtysh | Asia | 2,640 |
| Mackenzie | North America | 2,635 |
| Mekong | Asia | 2,600 |
| Niger | Africa | 2,590 |
| Yenisey | Asia | 2,543 |
| Paraná | South America | 2,485 |
| Mississippi | North America | 2,348 |
| Missouri | North America | 2,315 |
| Murray-Darling | Australia | 2,310 |
| St. Lawrence | North America | 2,280 |
| Ob | Asia | 2,268 |
| Volga | Europe | 2,194 |
| Purús | South America | 2,100 |
| Madeira | South America | 2,013 |
| São Francisco | South America | 1,988 |
| Yukon | North America | 1,979 |
| Rio Grande | North America | 1,885 |
| Brahmaputra | Asia | 1,800 |
| Indus | Asia | 1,800 |
| Danube | Europe | 1,777 |
| Japurá | South America | 1,750 |
| Euphrates | Asia | 1,700 |
| Zambezi | Africa | 1,700 |
| Tocantins | South America | 1,677 |

# Missions of California
## (in the order of their founding)

| Name | Year Founded | Location |
| --- | --- | --- |
| 1. San Diego de Alcalá | 1769 | San Diego |
| 2. San Carlos Borromeo del Carmelo | 1770 | Monterey |
| 3. San Antonio de Padua | 1771 | near King City |
| 4. San Gabriel Arcángel | 1771 | San Gabriel |
| 5. San Luis Obispo de Tolosa | 1772 | San Luis Obispo |
| 6. San Francisco de Asís | 1776 | San Francisco |
| 7. San Juan Capistrano | 1776 | San Juan Capistrano |
| 8. Santa Clara de Asís | 1777 | Santa Clara |
| 9. San Buenaventura | 1782 | Ventura |
| 10. Santa Barbara Virgen y Mártir | 1786 | Santa Barbara |
| 11. La Purísima Concepción | 1787 | near Lompoc |
| 12. Santa Cruz | 1791 | Santa Cruz |
| 13. Nuestra Senora de la Soledad | 1791 | Soledad |
| 14. San José de Guadalupe | 1797 | near San Jose |
| 15. San Juan Bautista | 1797 | San Juan Bautista |
| 16. San Miguel Arcángel | 1797 | San Miguel |
| 17. San Fernando Rey de España | 1797 | San Fernando |
| 18. San Luis Rey de Francia | 1798 | Oceanside |
| 19. Santa Inés Virgen y Mártir | 1804 | Solvang |
| 20. San Rafael Arcángel | 1817 | San Rafael |
| 21. San Francisco Solano | 1823 | Sonoma |

# Mountains of the World

## Africa
Atlas Mountains
Kilimanjaro
Mount Kenya

## Asia
Altai Mountains
Annapurna
Ararat
Himalaya
Hindu Kush
Khyber Pass
Krakatoa
Lebanon Mountains
Mount Apo
Mount Carmel
Mount Everest
Mount Fuji
Mount Godwin Austen
Mount Kanchenjunga
Mount Makalu
Mount of Olives
Stanovoy Mountains
Tien Shan
Ural Mountains
Yablonovyy Mountains

## Australia and New Zealand
Mount Cook
Mount Kosciusko
Owen-Stanley Mountains

## Canada
Canadian Shield
Coast Range
Mount Logan
Rocky Mountains
Saint Elias Mountains
Selkirk Mountains

## Europe
Alps
Apennines
Ardennes Mountains
Ben Nevis
Black Forest
Carpathian Mountains
Caucasus Mountains
Jungfrau
Matterhorn
Mont Blanc
Montserrat
Mount Elbrus
Mount Etna
Olympus
Parnassus
Pyrenees
Stromboli
Vesuvius

## Mexico
Ixtacihuatl
Orizaba
Parícutin
Popocatepetl
Sierra Madre

# Mountains of the World
## (continued)

### South America

Aconcagua
Andes Mountains
Chimborazo

Pichincha

Cotopaxi
El Misti
Ojos del Salado

### United States

Adirondack Mountains
Allegheny Mountains
Appalachian Mountains
Blue Ridge Mountains
Cascade Range
Catskill Mountains
Cumberland Mountains
Diamond Head
Great Smoky Mountains
Green Mountains
Kilauea
Lassen Peak
Mauna Kea
Mauna Loa
Mesabi Range
Mount Hood
Mount McKinley

Mount Mitchell
Mount Rainier
Mount Rushmore
Mount St. Helens
Mount Shasta
Mount Washington
Mount Whitney
Olympic Mountains
Ozark Mountains
Pikes Peak
Rocky Mountains
Sierra Madre
Sierra Nevada
Stone Mountains
Teton Range
Wasatch Range
White Mountains

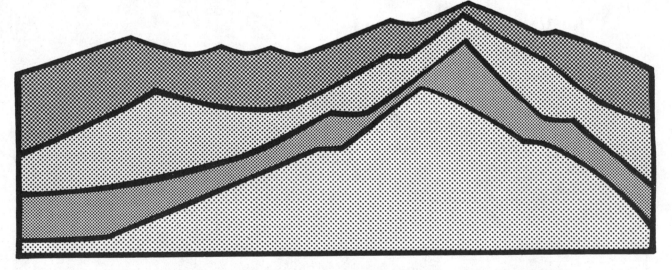

1. Select ten mountains from this list and use a bar graph to compare their heights.

2. Pretend that you are climbing one of the mountains on this list. Write a story telling about your preparations for the climb, your reasons for attempting to scale this peak, the things you see and feel as you ascend, and/or your adventures and misadventures along the way.

# Nations of the World

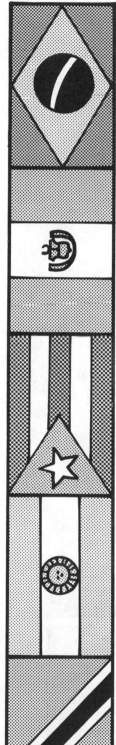

## North America

| Nation | Capital |
| --- | --- |
| United States | Washington, D.C. |
| Bahamas | Nassau |
| Barbados | Bridgetown |
| Belize | Belmopan |
| Canada | Ottawa |
| Costa Rica | San Jose |
| Cuba | Havana |
| Dominica | Roseau |
| Dominican Republic | Santo Domingo |
| El Salvador | San Salvador |
| Grenada | Saint George's |
| Guatemala | Guatemala City |
| Haiti | Port-au-Prince |
| Honduras | Tegucigalpa |
| Jamaica | Kingston |
| Mexico | Mexico City |
| Nicaragua | Managua |
| Panama | Panama |
| Saint Lucia | Castries |
| Saint Vincent and the Grenadines | Kingstown |
| Trinidad and Tobago | Port-of-Spain |

## South America

| Nation | Capital |
| --- | --- |
| Argentina | Buenos Aires |
| Bolivia | Sucre (legal), La Paz (de facto) |
| Brazil | Brasilia |
| Chile | Santiago |
| Colombia | Bogota |
| Ecuador | Quito |
| Guyana | Georgetown |
| Paraguay | Asunción |
| Peru | Lima |
| Suriname | Paramaribo |
| Uruguay | Montevideo |
| Venezuela | Caracas |

# Nations of the World
## (continued)

## Africa

| Nation | Capital | Nation | Capital |
|---|---|---|---|
| Algeria | Algiers | Madagascar | Antananarivo |
| Angola | Luanda | Malawi | Lilongwe |
| Benin | Porto-Novo | Mali | Bamako |
| Botswana | Gaborone | Mauritania | Nouakchott |
| Burundi | Bujumbura | Mauritius | Port Louis |
| Cameroon | Yaounde | Morocco | Rabat |
| Central African Republic | Bangui | Mozambique | Maputo |
| Chad | N'Djamena | Niger | Niamey |
| Comoros | Moroni | Nigeria | Lagos |
| Congo | Brazzaville | Rwanda | Kigali |
| Djibouti | Djibouti | Senegal | Dakar |
| Egypt | Cairo | Sierra Leone | Freetown |
| Equatorial Guinea | Malabo | Somalia | Mogadishu |
| Ethiopia | Addis Ababa | South Africa | Cape Town |
| Gabon | Libreville | Sudan | Khartoum |
| Gambia | Banjul | Swaziland | Mbabane |
| Ghana | Accra | Tanzania | Dar-es-Salaam |
| Guinea | Conakry | Togo | Lomé |
| Guinea-Bissau | Bissau | Tunisia | Tunis |
| Ivory Coast | Abidjan | Uganda | Kampala |
| Kenya | Nairobi | Upper Volta | Ouagadougou |
| Lesotho | Maseru | Zaire | Kinshasa |
| Liberia | Monrovia | Zambia | Lusaka |
| Libya | Tripoli | Zimbabwe | Harare |

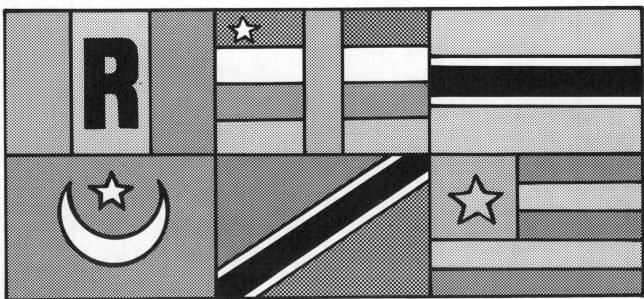

# Nations of the World
## (continued)

## Asia

| Nation | Capital | Nation | Capital |
|---|---|---|---|
| Afghanistan | Kabul | Maldives | Male |
| Bahrain | Manama | Mongolia | Ulaanbaatar |
| Bangladesh | Dacca | Nauru | Yaren |
| Bhutan | Thimphu | Nepal | Kathmandu |
| Burma | Rangoon | Oman | Muscat |
| Cambodia (Kampuchea) | Phnom Penh | Pakistan | Islamabad |
| China | Peking | Papua New Guinea | Port Moresby |
| China (Taiwan) | Taipei | Philippines | Quezon City |
| Cyprus | Nicosia | Qatar | Doha |
| India | New Delhi | Saudi Arabia | Riyadh |
| Indonesia | Jakarta | Singapore | Singapore |
| Iran | Teheran | Solomon Islands | Honiara |
| Iraq | Baghdad | Sri Lanka | Colombo |
| Israel | Jerusalem | Syria | Damascus |
| Japan | Tokyo | Thailand | Bangkok |
| Jordan | Amman | Turkey | Ankara |
| Kiribati | Tarawa | Union of Soviet Socialist | |
| North Korea | Pyongyang | Republics | Moscow |
| South Korea | Seoul | United Arab Emirates | Abu Dhabi |
| Kuwait | Kuwait | Vietnam | Hanoi |
| Laos | Vientiane | Western Samoa | Apia |
| Lebanon | Beirut | North Yemen | Sanaa |
| Malaysia | Kuala Lumpur | South Yemen | Aden |

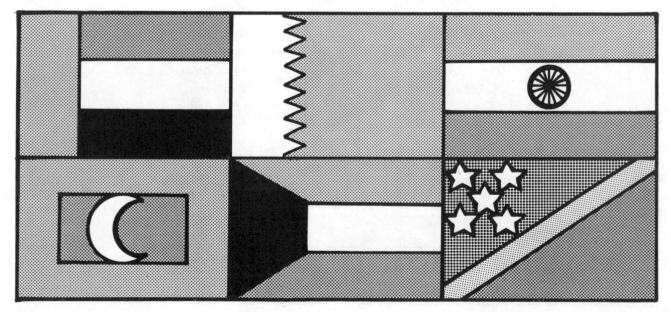

# Nations of the World
## (continued)

## Europe

| Nation | Capital | Nation | Capital |
|--------|---------|--------|---------|
| Albania | Tirana | Luxembourg | Luxembourg |
| Andorra | Andorra la Vella | Malta | Valletta |
| Austria | Vienna | Monaco | Monaco-Ville |
| Belgium | Brussels | Netherlands | Amsterdam |
| Bulgaria | Sofia | Norway | Oslo |
| Czechoslovakia | Prague | Poland | Warsaw |
| Denmark | Copenhagen | Portugal | Lisbon |
| Finland | Helsinki | Romania | Bucharest |
| France | Paris | San Marino | San Marino |
| East Germany | East Berlin | Spain | Madrid |
| West Germany | Bonn | Sweden | Stockholm |
| Greece | Athens | Switzerland | Bern |
| Hungary | Budapest | United Kingdom of Great | |
| Iceland | Reykjavik | Britain and Northern | |
| Ireland | Dublin | Ireland | London |
| Italy | Rome | Vatican City | (in Rome, Italy) |
| Liechtenstein | Vaduz | Yugoslavia | Belgrade |

## Other

| Nation | Capital |
|--------|---------|
| Antigua and Barbuda | St. John's |
| Australia | Canberra |
| Cape Verde | Mindelo |
| Fiji | Suva |
| New Zealand | Wellington |
| Seychelles | Victoria |

# Places of Interest to Visit

| | |
|---|---|
| airport | mission |
| animal shelter | movie |
| aquarium | national park |
| art gallery | natural history museum |
| art museum | packing plant |
| bakery | park |
| bank | pet shop |
| beach | photography studio |
| botanical gardens | planetarium |
| bus station | post office |
| circus | printing company |
| college | radio station |
| computer store | repair shop |
| concert | restaurant |
| construction site | science museum |
| courthouse | sports event |
| dairy | supermarket |
| factory | telephone company |
| farm | television station |
| government building | theater |
| grocery store | theme park |
| historical site | train station |
| hospital | university |
| hotel | veterinarian's office |
| library | zoo |

# States, Their Capitals, and Their Abbreviations

| State Name | Capital | Standard Abbreviation | Two-Letter Abbreviation |
|---|---|---|---|
| Alabama | Montgomery | Ala. | AL |
| Alaska | Juneau | Alaska | AK |
| Arizona | Phoenix | Ariz. | AZ |
| Arkansas | Little Rock | Ark. | AR |
| California | Sacramento | Calif. | CA |
| Colorado | Denver | Colo. | CO |
| Connecticut | Hartford | Conn. | CT |
| Delaware | Dover | Del. | DE |
| Florida | Tallahassee | Fla. | FL |
| Georgia | Atlanta | Ga. | GA |
| Hawaii | Honolulu | Hawaii | HI |
| Idaho | Boise | Idaho | ID |
| Illinois | Springfield | Ill. | IL |
| Indiana | Indianapolis | Ind. | IN |
| Iowa | Des Moines | Iowa | IA |
| Kansas | Topeka | Kans. | KS |
| Kentucky | Frankfort | Ky. | KY |
| Louisiana | Baton Rouge | La. | LA |
| Maine | Augusta | Maine | ME |
| Maryland | Annapolis | Md. | MD |
| Massachusetts | Boston | Mass. | MA |
| Michigan | Lansing | Mich. | MI |
| Minnesota | Saint Paul | Minn. | MN |
| Mississippi | Jackson | Miss. | MS |
| Missouri | Jefferson City | Mo. | MO |
| Montana | Helena | Mont. | MT |
| Nebraska | Lincoln | Nebr. | NE |
| Nevada | Carson City | Nev. | NV |
| New Hampshire | Concord | N.H. | NH |
| New Jersey | Trenton | N.J. | NJ |
| New Mexico | Santa Fe | N.Mex. | NM |
| New York | Albany | N.Y. | NY |
| North Carolina | Raleigh | N.C. | NC |
| North Dakota | Bismarck | N.Dak. | ND |
| Ohio | Columbus | Ohio | OH |
| Oklahoma | Oklahoma City | Okla. | OK |
| Oregon | Salem | Oreg. | OR |
| Pennsylvania | Harrisburg | Pa. | PA |
| Rhode Island | Providence | R.I. | RI |
| South Carolina | Columbia | S.C. | SC |
| South Dakota | Pierre | S.Dak. | SD |
| Tennessee | Nashville | Tenn. | TN |
| Texas | Austin | Tex. | TX |
| Utah | Salt Lake City | Utah | UT |
| Vermont | Montpelier | Vt. | VT |
| Virginia | Richmond | Va. | VA |
| Washington | Olympia | Wash. | WA |
| West Virginia | Charleston | W.Va. | WV |
| Wisconsin | Madison | Wis. | WI |
| Wyoming | Cheyenne | Wyo. | WY |

# Thirteen Original Colonies
## (in order of their adoption of the Constitution)

| Colony | Date of Adoption |
|--------|------------------|
| 1. Delaware | December 7, 1787 |
| 2. Pennsylvania | December 12, 1787 |
| 3. New Jersey | December 18, 1787 |
| 4. Georgia | January 2, 1788 |
| 5. Connecticut | January 9, 1788 |
| 6. Massachusetts | February 6, 1788 |
| 7. Maryland | April 28, 1788 |
| 8. South Carolina | May 23, 1788 |
| 9. New Hampshire | June 21, 1788 |
| 10. Virginia | June 25, 1788 |
| 11. New York | July 26, 1788 |
| 12. North Carolina | November 21, 1789 |
| 13. Rhode Island | May 29, 1790 |

# Volcanic Eruptions

A **volcano** is an opening in the earth's surface through which rock fragments, hot gases, and lava erupt, or burst forth. Volcanoes occur when melted rock from within the earth blasts through the surface.

| Date | Name | Place |
|---|---|---|
| 1400 B.C. | Thera | Santorini, Greece |
| August 24, A.D. 79 | Mount Vesuvius | Pompeii, Italy |
| First century A.D. | Stromboli | Lipari Islands, Italy |
| 1169 | Mount Etna | Sicily, Italy |
| April 1815 | Mount Tambora | Sumbawa, Indonesia |
| 1832 | Mauna Loa | Hawaii, United States |
| 1877 | Cotopaxi | near Quito, Equador |
| August 26, 1883 | Krakatoa | Sunda Strait, Indonesia |
| May 8, 1902 | Mount Pelee | Martinique, West Indies |
| June 6, 1912 | Mount Katmai | Alaska, United States |
| 1919 | Mount Kelud | Java, Indonesia |
| February 20, 1943 | Parícutin | Michoacan, Mexico |
| January 18, 1951 | Mount Lamington | Papua, New Guinea |
| 1951 | Hibokhibok | Northern Mindanao, Philippines |
| March 1963 | Mount Agung | Bali, Indonesia |
| November 1963 | Surtsey | Surtsey, Iceland |
| September 28, 1965 | Mount Taal | Luzon, Philippines |
| April 28, 1966 | Mount Kelud | Java, Indonesia |
| July 29, 1968 | Mount Arenal | Costa Rica |
| February 20, 1979 | Mount Sinila | Java, Indonesia |
| September 12, 1979 | Mount Etna | Sicily, Italy |
| May 18, 1980 | Mount St. Helens | Washington, United States |
| March 28, 1982 | El Chichon | Pichucalco, Mexico |
| April 9, 1982 | Galunggung | Java, Indonesia |

# Careers

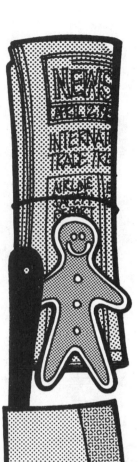

| | |
|---|---|
| actor | comptroller |
| administrator | computer analyst |
| archaeologist | computer programmer |
| architect | construction worker |
| artist | dancer |
| assembler | dentist |
| astronaut | designer |
| attorney | developer |
| author | director |
| bailiff | editor |
| baker | electrician |
| barber | engineer |
| beautician | entertainer |
| biologist | farmer |
| bookkeeper | fire fighter |
| broadcaster | florist |
| builder | gardener |
| bus driver | geographer |
| butcher | geologist |
| buyer | illustrator |
| carpenter | insurance agent |
| cartographer | interior decorator |
| cashier | interpreter |
| chauffeur | inventor |
| chef | janitor |
| chemist | jeweler |
| choreographer | journalist |
| cinematographer | judge |
| composer | keypunch operator |

# Careers
## (continued)

| | |
|---|---|
| librarian | psychologist |
| linguist | publisher |
| locksmith | rancher |
| mail carrier | realtor |
| mechanic | receptionist |
| meteorologist | reporter |
| musician | salesperson |
| nurse | scuba diver |
| optometrist | seamstress |
| painter | secretary |
| pharmacist | social worker |
| photographer | teacher |
| physical therapist | therapist |
| physician | travel agent |
| pilot | truck driver |
| plumber | typesetter |
| poet | typist |
| police officer | undertaker |
| probation officer | veterinarian |
| professor | welder |

FOR SAL
ROLLING HIL
REALTY

From this list, select a career that interests you. Find out more about the educational requirements, the working conditions, the salary, the advantages, the disadvantages, and the employment outlook for people who choose to pursue this career.

# Coins of the United States

| Coin | Portrait |
|------|----------|
| Cent | Abraham Lincoln |
| Nickel | Thomas Jefferson |
| Dime | Franklin D. Roosevelt |
| Quarter | George Washington |
| Half Dollar | John F. Kennedy |
| Dollar | Dwight D. Eisenhower |

# Currency of the United States

| Denomination | Portrait | Design on Back |
|--------------|----------|----------------|
| $1 | George Washington | Great Seal of the United States |
| $2 | Thomas Jefferson | Declaration of Independence |
| $5 | Abraham Lincoln | Lincoln Memorial |
| $10 | Alexander Hamilton | U.S. Treasury Building |
| $20 | Andrew Jackson | The White House |
| $50 | Ulysses S. Grant | U.S. Capitol |
| $100 | Benjamin Franklin | Independence Hall |
| $500 | William McKinley | large $500 sign |
| $1,000 | Grover Cleveland | large $1,000 sign |
| $5,000 | James Madison | large $5,000 sign |
| $10,000 | Salmon P. Chase | large $10,000 sign |
| $100,000 | Woodrow Wilson | large $100,000 sign |

# Colonial Terms

| | |
|---|---|
| batten | meeting house |
| bayberry | minuet |
| blacksmith | musket |
| breeches | New England Primer |
| candles | pewter |
| cards | pillory |
| colonists | plague |
| common house | plantation |
| dame schools | powder horn |
| dasher | Puritans |
| doublet | ruff |
| fiddler | rushlight |
| flax | Quakers |
| flint | quilting bee |
| gristmill | sconce |
| hatchet | smock |
| heddles | snuffer |
| hornbook | spinning wheel |
| house-raising | tallow |
| indigo | tankard |
| lantern | tinder |
| loom | town crier |
| lye | venison |
| mansion | |

# Communication

**Communication** is a process by which information is exchanged between individuals or groups by means of a mutually understood system of symbols, signs, or actions. Below are listed some means of communication.

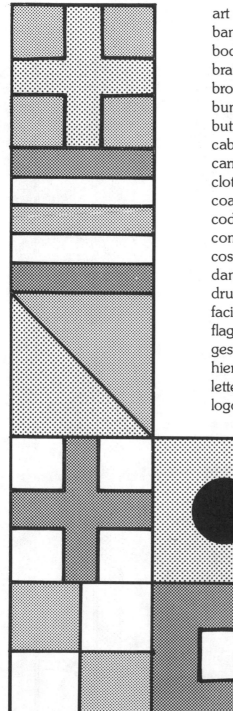

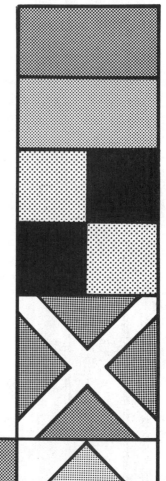

art
banners
body language
braille
brochures
bumper stickers
buttons
cable
carrier pigeon
clothing
coat of arms
code
computer
costumes
dance
drums
facial expressions
flags
gestures
hieroglyphics
letters
logos

magazines
mail
masks
Morse code
music
newspapers
pennants
pictographs
postcards
posters
radio
satellite
semaphore
sign language
signs
sky writing
smoke signals
symbols
telegrams
telegraph
telephone
television

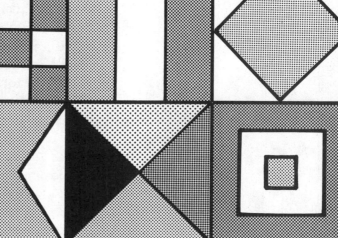

# Constitution of the United States

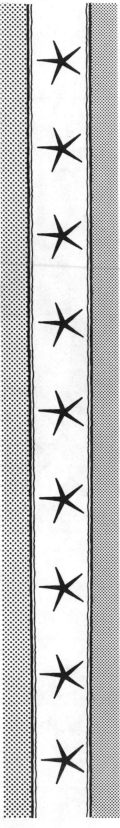

## Original Constitution

Preamble

Article
1. The Legislature
2. The Executive Departments
3. The Judicial Departments
4. Relations Among States
5. Amending the Constitution
6. Role of the National Government
7. Ratification

## Bill of Rights

Amendment
1. Religious and Political Freedoms
2. Right to Bear Arms
3. Quartering Troops
4. Search and Seizure
5. Rights of Accused Persons
6. Right to a Speedy, Public Trial
7. Trial by Jury in Civil Cases
8. Limits of Fines and Punishments
9. Rights of the People
10. Powers of the States and People

## Additional Amendments

11. Lawsuits Against States
12. Election of Executives
13. Abolition of Slavery
14. Civil Rights
15. Right to Vote
16. Income Tax
17. Direct Election of Senators
18. Prohibition
19. Women's Suffrage
20. "Lame Duck" Session
21. Repeal of Prohibition
22. Limit on Presidential Terms
23. Voting in District of Columbia
24. Abolition of Poll Taxes
25. Presidential Succession
26. Voting Age Lowered to Eighteen

# Geographical Jargon

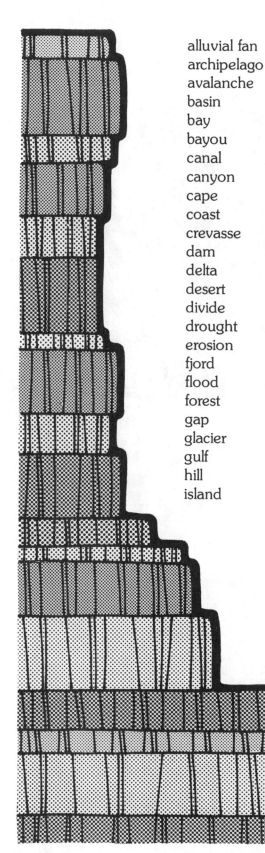

| | |
|---|---|
| alluvial fan | isthmus |
| archipelago | lagoon |
| avalanche | lake |
| basin | levee |
| bay | mesa |
| bayou | mountain |
| canal | mouth |
| canyon | ocean |
| cape | pampa |
| coast | peninsula |
| crevasse | plain |
| dam | plateau |
| delta | reef |
| desert | reservoir |
| divide | river |
| drought | sea |
| erosion | silt |
| fjord | sound |
| flood | strait |
| forest | swamp |
| gap | tributary |
| glacier | valley |
| gulf | veldt |
| hill | waterfall |
| island | wetlands |

# Government Addresses

Central Intelligence Agency (CIA)
Washington, D.C.    20505

Council on Environmental Quality
722 Jackson Place, N.W.
Washington, D.C.    20006

Department of Defense
The Pentagon
Washington, D.C.    20301

Department of the Interior
18th and C Streets, N.W.
Washington, D.C.    20240

Department of Justice
Constitution Avenue and 10th Street, N.W.
Washington, D.C.    20530

Department of the Treasury
15th Street and Pennsylvania Avenue, N.W.
Washington, D.C.    20220

Environmental Protection Agency (EPA)
401 M Street, S.W.
Washington, D.C.    20460

Federal Reserve System
20th Street and Constitution Avenue, N.W.
Washington, D.C.    20551

Office of the Vice-President
Executive Office Building
Washington, D.C    20501

The White House
1600 Pennsylvania Avenue, N.W.
Washington, D.C.    20500

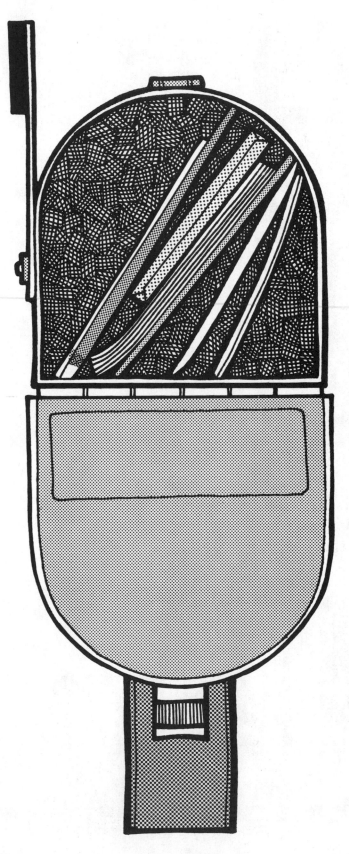

# Languages of the World

A **language** is the words, their pronunciations, and the methods for combining them used and understood by a considerable community. Linguistic experts estimate that more than six hundred languages are spoken in the world today. This number does not include languages, such as Ionian, Latin, Moabite, and Phoenician, which are no longer spoken and are said to be **dead languages**. Below is a list of the twenty-nine languages of the world which have more than thirty million speakers each.

Amoy-Swatow Chinese
Arabic
Bengali
Bhojpuri
Cantonese
Eastern Hindi
English
French
German
Gujarati
Hindu with Urdu
Italian
Japanese
Javanese
Korean
Mandarin Chinese
Marathi
Panjabi
Polish
Portuguese
Russian
Spanish
Tamil
Telugu
Thai with Lao
Turkish
Ukrainian
Vietnamese
Wu [Shanghai] Chinese

# Law Terms

accessory
accomplice
affidavit
alias
alibi
appeal
arraignment
arson
assault and battery
autopsy
bail
bill of attainder
bona fide
bribery
brief
burglary
complaint
confession
conspiracy
contempt
crime
curfew
deposition
Doe, John
embezzlement
equity
evidence
extortion
felony
forgery
fraud
habeas corpus

hearing
homicide
incompetence
indictment
injunction
inquest
judgment
jury
larceny
libel
malice
manslaughter
minor
misdemeanor
murder
oath
perjury
robbery
slander
smuggling
subpoena
suit
summons
testimony
treason
trial
vagrancy
vandalism
witness
writ
writ of assistance
writ of mandamus

# Money of the World

A **monetary unit** is the standard unit of value of a currency. For example, the monetary unit in the United States is the dollar. All of the money used in this country is either a fraction or a multiple of one dollar. Below are listed some examples of the monetary units used in different countries around the world.

| | |
|---|---|
| afghani | leu |
| baht | lev |
| balboa | lira |
| birr | mark |
| bolívar | markka |
| cedi | naira |
| colón | ouguiya |
| córdoba | peseta |
| cruzeiro | peso |
| dinar | pound |
| dirham | quetzal |
| dollar | rand |
| drachma | rial |
| escudo | ringgit |
| forint | riyal |
| franc | ruble |
| gourde | rupee |
| guaraní | rupiah |
| guilder | shekel |
| kina | shilling |
| kip | sol |
| koruna | sucre |
| krona | syli |
| krone | taka |
| kwacha | tughrik |
| kwanza | won |
| kyat | yen |
| lek | yuan |
| lempira | zaire |
| leone | zloty |

1. Do some research to match each one of these monetary units with the country or countries in which it is used.

2. Make a chart showing the values of at least ten of these monetary units as measured in U.S. dollars.

# Renaissance Terms and Topics

The word **Renaissance** means "rebirth." This word is used to name the period of European history which began during the fourteenth century and lasted about three hundred years.

Battle of Agincourt
Black Death
Giovanni Boccaccio
Anne Boleyn
Botticelli
Cervantes
château
chiaroscuro
Christendom
Manuel Chrysoloras
classics
Dante
Donatello
*Don Quixote de la Mancha*
Elizabeth I
exploration
Guy Fawkes
Florence, Italy
frescoes
Great Schism
El Greco
Gunpowder Plot

Johann Gutenberg
Henry VIII
Huguenots
humanism
Hundred Years' War
Joan of Arc
Leonardo da Vinci
Machiavelli
Martin Luther
Medici
Michelangelo
*Mona Lisa*
Petrarch
*Pietà*
Sir Walter Raleigh
Raphael
Reformation
Richelieu
Luca della Robbia
Savonarola
William Shakespeare
Titian

# Social Studies Topics

advertising
American Indians
architecture
art
California missions
Canada (or any other country)
careers
castles
Civil War
colonial life
communication
Congress
Constitution
crime
Dark Ages
Declaration of Independence
early civilization
economics
Egypt
elections
Eskimos
Europe
explorers
famous men in history
famous women in history
Federal Bureau of Investigation (FBI)
Florida (or any other state)

French Revolution
geography
Hellenic Age
human rights
League of Nations
Lewis and Clark expedition
maps and map making
Middle East
national parks
Olympics
pioneers
pony express
presidents
Renaissance
Revolutionary War
stock market
Stone Age
Supreme Court
transportation
underground railroad
United Nations
voyages and discoveries
War of 1812
westward movement
White House
world neighbors
world of the future

# State Tourism Agencies

**Alabama**
Alabama Bureau of Tourism and
Travel
532 S. Perry Street
Montgomery, AL 36104-4614

**Alaska**
Alaska Division of Tourism
Pouch E
Juneau, AK 99811

**Arizona**
Arizona Office of Tourism
1480 E. Bethany Home Road
Phoenix, AZ 85014

**Arkansas**
Arkansas Department of Parks and
Tourism
1 Capitol Mall
Little Rock, AR 72201

**California**
California Office of Tourism
1121 L Street, Suite 103
Sacramento, CA 95814

**Colorado**
Colorado Tourism Board
5500 S. Syracuse Street, Suite 267
Englewood, CO 80111

**Connecticut**
Tourism Division
Connecticut Department of Economic
Development
210 Washington Street
Hartford, CT 06106

**Delaware**
State Travel Service
Delaware Development Office
99 Kings Highway, P. O. Box 1401
Dover, DE 19903

**District of Columbia**
Washington Convention and Visitors
Association
1575 Eye Street, N.W., Suite 250
Washington, DC 20005

**Florida**
Florida Division of Commerce
107 W. Gaines Street
Tallahassee, FL 32301

**Georgia**
Tourist Division
Georgia Department of Industry and
Trade
230 Peachtree Street, N.W.
P. O. Box 1776
Atlanta, GA 30301

**Hawaii**
Hawaii Visitors Bureau
2270 Kalakaua Avenue, Suite 801
Honolulu, HI 96815

**Idaho**
Idaho Travel Council
State Capitol Building, Room 108
Boise, ID 83720

**Illinois**
Illinois Office of Tourism
100 W. Randolf Street, Suite 3-400
Chicago, IL 60601

**Indiana**
Tourism Development Division
Indiana Department of Commerce
1 N. Capitol, Suite 700
Indianapolis, IN 46204-2288

**Iowa**
Department of Economic
Development
200 E. Grand Avenue
Des Moines, IA 50309

**Kansas**
Travel and Tourism Division
Kansas Department of Economic
Development
400 W. 8th Street, 5th floor
Topeka, KS 66603-3957

**Kentucky**
Department of Travel Development
Capitol Plaza Tower, 22nd floor
Frankfort, KY 40601

**Louisiana**
Louisiana Office of Tourism
P. O. Box 94291
Baton Rouge, LA 70804-9291

**Maine**
State Development Office
Executive Department
189 State Street
State House Station 59
Augusta, ME 04333

**Maryland**
Maryland Office of Tourist
Development
Department of Economic and
Community Development
45 Calvert Street
Annapolis, MD 21401

**Massachusetts**
Spirit of Massachusetts
Department of Commerce
100 Cambridge Street
Boston, MA 02202

**Michigan**
Michigan Travel Bureau
P. O. Box 30226
Lansing, MI 48909

**Minnesota**
Minnesota Office of Tourism
35 Jackson Street
Farm Credit Building, Room 250
St. Paul, MN 55101

**Mississippi**
Division of Tourism
Mississippi Department of Economic
Development
1301 Walter Sillars Building
P. O. Box 22825
Jackson, MS 39201

**Missouri**
Missouri Division of Tourism
P. O. Box 1055
Jefferson City, MO 65102

**Montana**
Montana Travel Promotion
1424 9th Avenue
Helena, MT 59620-0411

**Nebraska**
Nebraska Travel and Tourism
Department of Economic
Development
P. O. Box 94666
301 Centennial Mall South
Lincoln, NE 68509

**Nevada**
Nevada Commission on Tourism
Capitol Complex, Suite 207
Carson City, NV 89710

**New Hampshire**
State of New Hampshire
Office of Vacation Travel
105 Loudon Road
P. O. Box 856
Concord, NH 03301

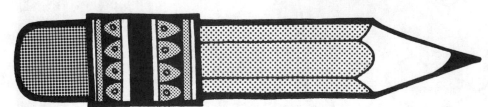

# State Tourism Agencies
## (continued)

**New Jersey**
New Jersey Department of Commerce
and Economic Development
Division of Travel and Tourism
CN 826
Trenton, NJ 08625

**New Mexico**
New Mexico Economic Development
and Tourism Department
1100 St. Francis Drive
Santa Fe, NM 87503

**New York**
Department of Commerce
Tourism Division
1 Commerce Plaza
Albany, NY 12245

New York City
New York Tourism Bureau
P. O. Box 992
Latham, NY 12110

**North Carolina**
North Carolina Department of
Commerce
Division of Travel and Tourism
430 N. Salisbury Street
Raleigh, NC 27611

**North Dakota**
North Dakota Tourism Promotion
Liberty Memorial Building
Capital Grounds
Bismarck, ND 58505

**Ohio**
Office of Travel and Tourism
P. O. Box 1001
Columbus, OH 43266-0101

**Oklahoma**
Oklahoma Tourism and Recreation
Division of Marketing Services
500 Will Rogers Building
Oklahoma City, OK 73105

**Oregon**
Tourism Division
Oregon Economic Development
Department
595 Cottage Street, N.E.
Salem, OR 97310

**Pennsylvania**
Bureau of Travel Development
416 Forum Building
Harrisburg, PA 17120

**Rhode Island**
Tourism and Promotion Department
Department of Economic
Development
7 Jackson Walkway
Providence, RI 02903

**South Carolina**
Department of Parks, Recreation, and
Tourism
1205 Pendleton Street
Edgar A. Brown Building
Columbia, SC 29201

**South Dakota**
South Dakota Tourism
711 Wells Avenue
Pierre, SD 57501

**Tennessee**
Tennessee Tourist Development
320 6th Avenue, N.
Nashville, TN 37219

**Texas**
Texas Tourist Development Agency
Capitol Station
P. O. Box 12208
Austin, TX 78711

**Utah**
Utah Travel Council
Council Hall/Capitol Hill
Salt Lake City, UT 84114

**Vermont**
Vermont Travel Division
Agency of Development and
Community Affairs
134 State Street
Montpelier, VT 05602

**Virginia**
Virginia Division of Tourism
101 N. 9th Street, Suite 500
Richmond, VA 23219

**Washington**
Travel Development Division
Department of Commerce and
Economic Development
101 General Administration Building
Olympia, WA 98504

**West Virginia**
Department of Commerce
Tourism Division
State Capitol, Building 6, Room B564
1900 Washington Street, E.
Charleston, WV 25305

**Wisconsin**
Division of Tourism
123 W. Washington Avenue
P. O. Box 7970
Madison, WI 53707

**Wyoming**
Wyoming Travel Commission
Frank Norris Jr. Travel Center
Cheyenne, WY 82002-0660

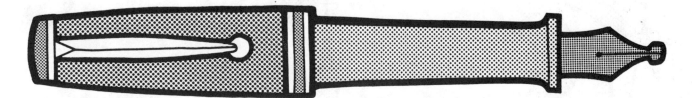

1. Write to the tourism agency for the state in which you live requesting information. When it comes, have fun reading and learning more about your state.

2. Write and request information from the tourism agency for a state you would like to visit.

# Things That Travel on Land

| | |
|---|---|
| ambulance | pedicab |
| automobile | perambulator |
| bicycle | roller skates |
| bus | scooter |
| camel | skateboard |
| carriage | snowmobile |
| cart | stagecoach |
| chariot | streetcar |
| coach | subway |
| dogsled | taxicab |
| donkey | tractor |
| elevator | train |
| escalator | tram |
| helicopter | travois |
| horse | tricycle |
| jinrikisha | trolley |
| monorail | truck |
| moped | unicycle |
| motorcycle | wagon |

# Things That Travel on Water

| | | |
|---|---|---|
| argosy | felucca | prau |
| barge | ferryboat | punt |
| bark | float | raft |
| barkentine | frigate | rowboat |
| bireme | galleon | sailboat |
| brig | galliot | sampan |
| brigantine | gig | schooner |
| caïque | gondola | scow |
| canoe | houseboat | shallop |
| caravel | hovercraft | sharpie |
| carrack | hydrofoil | skiff |
| catamaran | hydroplane | sloop |
| clipper | junk | smack |
| coracle | kayak | steamship |
| corvette | ketch | submarine |
| cruiser | launch | surfboat |
| cutter | lifeboat | tugboat |
| destroyer | lugger | wherry |
| dhow | motorboat | xebec |
| dinghy | outrigger | yacht |
| dugout | pontoon | yawl |

Make a **Water Transportation** booklet in which you describe and draw pictures of at least twenty of these vessels.

# Wars

| Name | Dates | Who Fought? |
|------|-------|-------------|
| Greco-Persian War | 499-478 B.C. | Greek states versus Persia |
| Peloponnesian War | 431-404 B.C. | Sparta versus Athens |
| Punic Wars | 264-146 B.C. | Rome versus Carthage |
| Norman Conquest | A.D. 1066 | Normandy versus England |
| Crusades | 1096-1291 | Christianity versus Islam |
| Hundred Years' War | 1338-1453 | England versus France |
| French and Indian War | 1755-1763 | England versus France |
| Seven Years' War | 1756-1763 | Prussia versus Austria, France, and Russia |
| Revolutionary War | 1775-1783 | American Colonies versus England |
| Napoleonic Wars | 1796-1815 | France versus Austria, England, Prussia, and Russia |
| War of 1812 | 1812-1815 | United States versus England |
| Mexican War | 1846-1848 | United States versus Mexico |
| Crimean War | 1854-1856 | England, France, Sardinia, and Turkey versus Russia |
| U.S. Civil War | 1861-1865 | Union (North) versus Confederacy (South) |
| Franco-Prussian War | 1870-1871 | France versus Prussia |
| Spanish-American War | 1898 | United States versus Spain |
| Boer War | 1899-1902 | England versus the Transvaal Republic and the Orange Free State |
| Russo-Japanese War | 1904-1905 | Russia versus Japan |
| World War I | 1914-1918 | Allies (Belgium, England, France, Russia, and Serbia) versus Central Powers (Austria-Hungary and Germany) |
| World War II | 1941-1945 | Allies (England, France, United States, and the USSR) versus Axis Powers (Germany, Italy, and Japan) |
| Indochinese War | 1946-1954 | Communists versus the French |
| Korean War | 1950-1952 | South Korea and United Nations forces versus invading forces from Communist-supported North Korea |
| Vietnam War | 1959-1973 | Communist-led soldiers from North Vietnam versus the South Vietnamese government supported by the United States |

Do research to learn the names and some of the provisions of the treaties that were signed at the ends of these wars.

# Bonus Ideas for Social Studies

1. Choose a topic from one of the social studies lists, and do research on this topic. Then, use your topic as the basis for a pictorial scroll. On a long strip of butcher or shelf paper, draw a series of pictures and write a brief caption for each one. Attach each end of the paper strip to a dowel. Cut a screen-sized opening in one side of a cardboard box. Mount the dowels so that the scroll can be rolled past this opening and the pictures can be viewed through it.

2. Select a topic from one of the social studies lists and research it thoroughly. Wrap a medium-sized cube-shaped box in colored butcher, construction, or shelf paper. Paste interesting information and pictures about your topic on all sides of the box. Display your fact cube for classmates to enjoy.

3. Pick a topic from one of the social studies lists and research it thoroughly. Use cardboard, clay, papier-mâché, Popsicle sticks, soap, sugar cubes, or other appropriate media to construct a model related to this topic.

4. Select a famous woman from the list on page 68. Do research to learn more about her life and contributions. Then, design a postage stamp in her honor.

5. Using the state names and capitals on page 88, create a matching game to play with a friend.

6. Select an address of a government agency or building listed on page 98. Write a letter requesting booklets, pamphlets, and any free information they may distribute. Be sure to include your name and return address.

Name _____

# Create a Social Studies List

Think of a social studies topic that interests you. On the lines below, create a list that reflects this topic. Illustrate your list and give it a title.

_____

_____

_____

_____

_____

_____

_____

_____

_____

# Science

# Animal Groups

a **bevy** of larks or quail

a **brood** of birds

a **cast** of hawks

a **cete** of badgers

a **clowder** of cats

a **clutch** of chicks

a **colony** of ants, beavers, or rabbits

a **covert** of coots

a **covey** of partridges or quail

a **drift** of hogs

a **drove** of pigs or sheep

a **fall** of woodcocks

a **flight** of birds

a **flock** of chickens or goats

a **gaggle** of geese

a **gam** of whales

a **gang** of buffalo or elk

a **herd** of cattle, elephants, or horses

a **hive** of bees

a **muster** of peacocks

a **nide** of pheasants

a **pack** of dogs or wolves

a **pod** of seals or whales

a **pride** of lions

a **rafter** of turkeys

a **school** of fish

a **shoal** of fish or whales

a **skulk** of foxes

a **sloth** of bears

a **sord** of mallards

a **swarm** of bees

a **troop** of kangaroos or monkeys

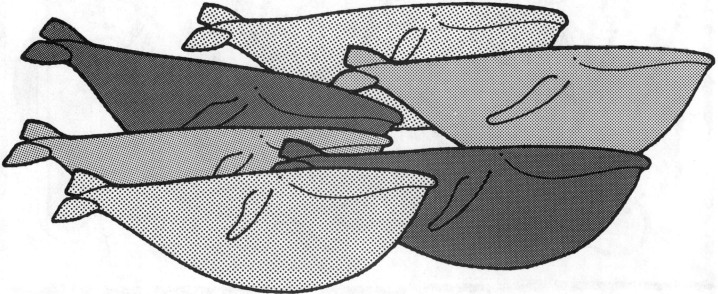

# Animal Offspring

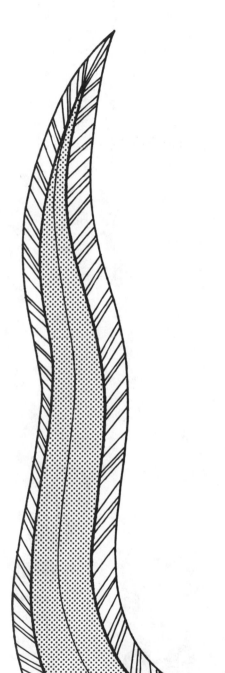

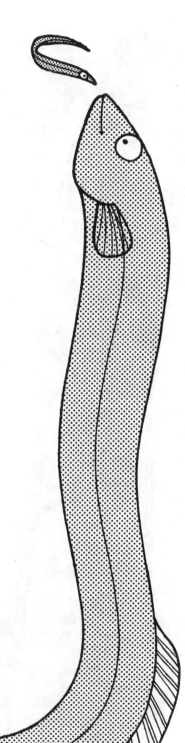

| Animal | Young |
|---|---|
| antelope | kid |
| bear | cub |
| beaver | kit, pup |
| bobcat | kit |
| cat | kitten |
| cattle | calf |
| chicken | chick |
| deer | fawn |
| dog | pup |
| donkey | foal, colt |
| duck | duckling |
| eagle | eaglet |
| eel | leptocephalus |
| elephant | calf |
| fish | fry |
| fox | cub, kit, whelp |
| giraffe | calf |
| goat | kid |
| goose | gosling |

# Animal Offspring
## (continued)

| Animal | Young |
|---|---|
| hawk | eyas |
| hog | piglet, shoat |
| horse | foal, colt (male), filly (female) |
| kangaroo | joey |
| lion | cub |
| ostrich | chick |
| otter | whelp |
| oyster | spat |
| rabbit | kit, kitten |
| rhinoceros | calf |
| seal | pup, whelp |
| sheep | lamb, lambkin, teg |
| swan | cygnet |
| tiger | cub |
| turkey | poult |
| whale | calf |
| wolf | cub, whelp |
| zebra | colt |

# Birds

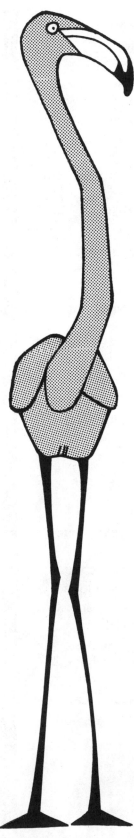

adjutant
albatross
anhinga
auk
avocet
bird of paradise
bittern
bluebird
bobolink
bobwhite
booby
bowerbird
brant
cahow
cardinal
cassowary
cedar waxwing
chat
chickadee
chicken
cockatoo
cock of the rock
coly
condor
coot
cormorant
courser
crow
cuckoo
curlew
dipper
dodo
dove
duck
eagle
egret
emu
falcon
flamingo
flicker
flycatcher
frogmouth

goldfinch
goose
goshawk
grebe
grosbeak
guinea fowl
gull
hawk
heron
honey guide
hornbill
hummingbird
ibis
jackdaw
jay
kea
kestrel
killdeer
kingfisher
kiwi
kookaburra
loon
lorikeet
lovebird
lyrebird
macaw
magpie
marabou
meadlowlark
mockingbird
myna
nightingale
nightjar
nuthatch
oriole
osprey
ostrich
ovenbird
owl
oyster catcher
parakeet
parrot
partridge

peafowl
pelican
penguin
petrel
pheasant
pigeon
puffin
quail
quetzal
rail
raven
rhea
roadrunner
robin
secretary bird
skua
skylark
sparrow
spoonbill
starling
stork
sunbird
swallow
swan
swift
tailorbird
tanager
tern
thrush
tinamou
toucan
touraco
towhee
trogon
turkey
vulture
warbler
weaverbird
whippoorwill
whydah
woodpecker
wren

# Classification of Animals

Scientists classify all members of the animal kingdom using a system of seven categories: **phylum**, **subphylum**, **class**, **order**, **family**, **genus**, and **species**. The phyla are the largest groups into which the animal kingdom is divided. For example, man belongs to the phylum **Chordata**, the subphylum **Vertebrata**, the class **Mammalia**, the subclass **Eutheria**, the order **Primates**, the family **Hominidae**, the genus **Homo**, and the species **sapiens**. Below are listed some of the categories used by scientists to classify animals.

| | |
|---|---|
| Protozoa | Simple, one-celled animals, including amebas, euglenas, malarial parasites, and paramecia. |
| Porifera | Sponges, the simplest of the many-celled animals. |
| Coelenterata | Corals, hydra, jellyfishes, and sea anemones. |
| Annelida | Segmented worms, including clamworms, earthworms, and leeches. |
| Arthropoda | Joint-footed animals. |
|   Crustacea | Crustaceans, including crabs, lobsters, crayfishes, and sowbugs. |
|   Chilopoda | Centipedes. |
|   Diplopoda | Millipedes and thousand-legged worms. |
|   Arachnoidea | Spiders, scorpions, mites, and ticks. |
|   Insecta | Probably the largest group of animals. Includes bees and wasps, beetles, butterflies and moths, crickets and grasshoppers, flies, termites, and others. |
| Mollusca | Mollusks. |
|   Gastropoda | Abalones, slugs, and snails. |
|   Pelecypoda | Clams, mussels, oysters, and scallops. |
|   Cephalopoda | Squids, cuttlefishes, and octopuses. |
| Echinodermata | Includes sand dollars, sea cucumbers, sea urchins, and starfishes. |
| Chordata | Chordates; bilaterally symmetrical animals with a notochord. |
|   Vertebrata | Vertebrates; animals with a definite head, a well-developed brain, a bony support structure, and a backbone, or spine. |
|     Cyclostomata | Cyclostomes, including lampreys and hagfishes. |
|     Chondrichthyses | Cartilaginous fishes, including rays, sharks, and skates. |
|     Osteichthys | Bony fishes, including garpike, herring, mackerel, and sturgeon. |
|     Amphibia | Amphibians, including frogs, newts, salamanders, and toads. |
|     Reptilia | Reptiles, including alligators, crocodiles, lizards, snakes, and turtles. |
|     Aves | Birds, the only animals that have feathers. |
|     Mammalia | Mammals, the only animals that have true hair. |
|       Eutheria | Placental mammals. |
|         Primates | Lemurs, tarsiers, monkeys, apes, and man. |

# Dog Breeds

The American Kennel Club (AKC) is the main organization of dog breeders in the United States. It recognizes more than one hundred breeds in six groups. The following list includes some examples from each category.

## Sporting Group

American Water Spaniel
Cocker Spaniel
Curly-Coated Retriever
English Setter
Golden Retriever
Irish Setter
Labrador Retriever
Pointer
Sussex Spaniel
Vizsla

## Hound Group

Afghan Hound
Basenji
Basset Hound
Beagle
Bloodhound
Borzoi
Dachshund
Greyhound
Irish Wolfhound
Whippet

## Toy Group

Chihuahua
English Toy Spaniel
Italian Greyhound
Japanese Chin
Maltese
Miniature Pinscher
Papillon
Pekingese
Shih Tzu
Yorkshire Terrier

## Working Group

Akita
Alaskan Malamute
Bearded Collie
Boxer
Bullmastiff
Collie
Doberman Pinscher
German Shepherd
Great Dane
Samoyed

## Terrier Group

Airedale Terrier
Australian Terrier
Bull Terrier
Cairn Terrier
Fox Terrier
Irish Terrier
Scottish Terrier
Skye Terrier
Welsh Terrier
West Highland White Terrier

## Nonsporting Group

Bichon Frise
Boston Terrier
Bulldog
Chow Chow
Dalmation
French Bulldog
Keeshond
Lhasa Apso
Poodle
Schipperke

1. Select ten dog breeds from this list. Do research to discover the place and probable date of origin for each breed.
2. Select one dog group listed above and do research to add more breed names to that list.

# Fishes

| | | | |
|---|---|---|---|
| alewife | dolphin | marlin | sawfish |
| amber jack | drum | menhaden | sculpin |
| anableps | eel | minnow | scup |
| anchovy | electric fish | molly | sea bat |
| anemone | flatfish | mosquito fish | sea horse |
| angelfish | flounder | mudskipper | shad |
| archerfish | flying fish | mullet | shark |
| barracuda | garfish | oarfish | skate |
| bass | goldfish | paddlefish | smelt |
| blackfish | grayling | perch | snapper |
| blindfish | grouper | pickerel | sole |
| bluefish | grunion | pike | spot |
| bocaccio | grunt | pilot fish | sprat |
| bonefish | guppy | pipefish | stickleback |
| bonito | gurnard | piranha | stingray |
| bowfin | haddock | pollack | sturgeon |
| buffalo fish | hagfish | pompano | sunfish |
| bullhead | hake | porcupine fish | swordfish |
| butterfish | halibut | porgy | tarpon |
| candlefish | herring | puffer | tilefish |
| carp | jewfish | pupfish | toadfish |
| catfish | kingfish | ray | torpedo |
| chub | lamprey | redfish | trout |
| cod | lanternfish | remora | tuna |
| coelacanth | leaf fish | roach | turbot |
| cutlass fish | lionfish | rosefish | wahoo |
| darter | lumpfish | sailfish | weakfish |
| discus | lungfish | salmon | whitefish |
| doctorfish | mackerel | sardine | wolf fish |
| dogfish | | | |

1. Classify these fishes as either freshwater fishes or saltwater fishes.
2. Create an entirely new fish by combining the head of one of the fishes on this list with the body of another and the tail of a third. Draw a picture of your new fish, and write a paragraph or two in which you describe how big your fish is, where it lives, what it eats, what distinguishing coloration and markings it has, and any unusual habits of which you may be aware. Don't forget to give your fish a name.

# Habitats

Because different kinds of animals have different needs, they thrive in different kinds of places. An animal's **habitat** is the type of place where that animal naturally lives and grows.

| | |
|---|---|
| coniferous woodlands | rivers |
| deciduous woodlands | rocky shores |
| deserts | sandy shores |
| fields and meadows | seas and oceans |
| lakes | shrubland and chaparral |
| mountains | streams |
| polar regions | swamps, marshes, and wetlands |
| ponds | tropical rain forests |
| prairies and grasslands | tundra |

Give three or more examples of animals that live in each of the habitats listed above. Then, draw a picture or make a shoe box diorama of one of these habitats and some of the animals that are indigenous to it.

# Horses

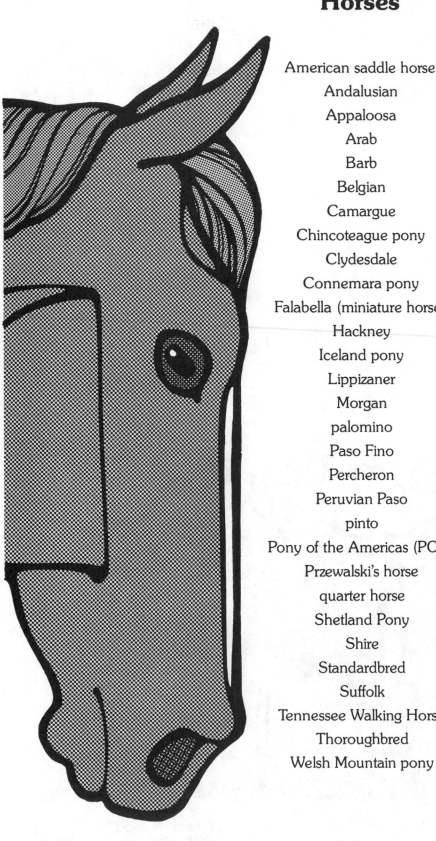
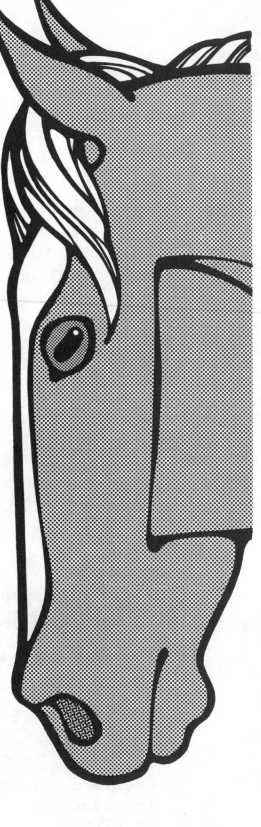

American saddle horse
Andalusian
Appaloosa
Arab
Barb
Belgian
Camargue
Chincoteague pony
Clydesdale
Connemara pony
Falabella (miniature horse)
Hackney
Iceland pony
Lippizaner
Morgan
palomino
Paso Fino
Percheron
Peruvian Paso
pinto
Pony of the Americas (POA)
Przewalski's horse
quarter horse
Shetland Pony
Shire
Standardbred
Suffolk
Tennessee Walking Horse
Thoroughbred
Welsh Mountain pony

# Mammals

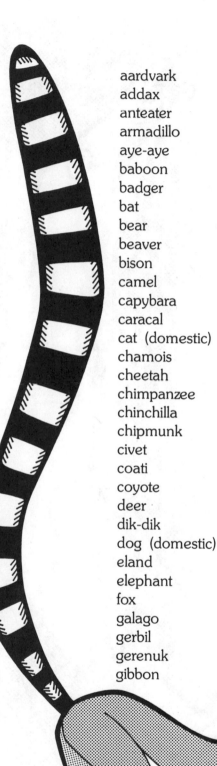

| | | |
|---|---|---|
| aardvark | giraffe | ocelot |
| addax | gnu | okapi |
| anteater | gopher | opossum |
| armadillo | gorilla | orangutan |
| aye-aye | hamster | otter |
| baboon | hartebeest | panda |
| badger | hedgehog | pangolin |
| bat | hippopotamus | peccary |
| bear | horse | platypus |
| beaver | hyena | porcupine |
| bison | hyrax | prairie dog |
| camel | ibex | rabbit |
| capybara | jackal | raccoon |
| caracal | jaguar | rhinoceros |
| cat (domestic) | kangaroo | seal |
| chamois | kinkajou | shrew |
| cheetah | klipspringer | skunk |
| chimpanzee | koala | sloth |
| chinchilla | lemming | squirrel |
| chipmunk | lemur | tapir |
| civet | leopard | thylacine |
| coati | lion | tiger |
| coyote | llama | walrus |
| deer | lynx | warthog |
| dik-dik | manatee | weasel |
| dog (domestic) | markhor | whale |
| eland | marmoset | wolf |
| elephant | mink | wolverine |
| fox | mole | wombat |
| galago | mongoose | woodchuck |
| gerbil | moose | yak |
| gerenuk | mouse | zebra |
| gibbon | musk-ox | zebu |

# Prehistoric Animals

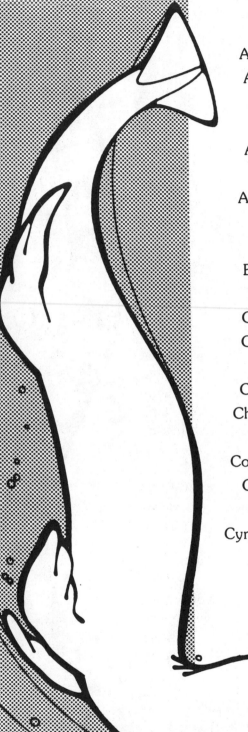

| | |
|---|---|
| Acanthopholis | Dicraeosaurus |
| Albertosaurus | Dicynodon |
| Allosaurus | Dimetrodon |
| Anatosaurus | Dimorphodon |
| Ankylosaurus | Diplodocus |
| Apatosaurus | Edaphosaurus |
| Archaeopteryx | Edmontosaurus |
| Archelon | Euoplocephalus |
| Avimimus | Euparkeria |
| Brachiosaurus | Geosaurus |
| Brontosaurus | Gorgosaurus |
| Camarasaurus | Halticosaurus |
| Camptosaurus | Hesperornis |
| Ceratosaurus | Heterodontosaurus |
| Chasmosaurus | Homeosaurus |
| Chialingosaurus | Hypsilophodon |
| Coelophysis | Icthyosaurus |
| Compsognathus | Iguanodon |
| Corythosaurus | Kentrosaurus |
| Cryptocleidus | Kronosaurus |
| Cymbospondylus | Kritosaurus |
| Cynognathus | Lambeosaurus |
| Dapedius | Megalosaurus |
| Deinonychus | Mesosaurus |
| Diadectes | Monoclonius |

# Prehistoric Animals
## (continued)

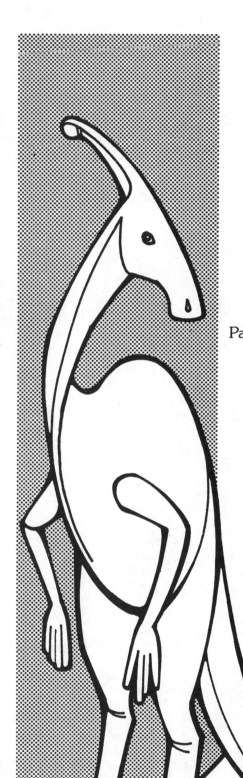

| | |
|---|---|
| Moschops | Psittacosaurus |
| Mystriosaurus | Pteranodon |
| Nemegtosaurus | Pterodactylus |
| Nodosaurus | Quetzalcoatlus |
| Nothosaurus | Rhamphorhynchus |
| Nyctosaurus | Scelidosaurus |
| Omosaurus | Spinosaurus |
| Ophiacodon | Stegosaurus |
| Ornitholestes | Struthiosaurus |
| Ornithomimus | Styracosaurus |
| Pachycephalosaurus | Teratosaurus |
| Pachyophis | Thecodontosaurus |
| Paleoscincus | Theriosuchus |
| Parasaurolophus | Titanosaurus |
| Pentaceratops | Torosaurus |
| Phobosuchus | Trachodon |
| Pinacosaurus | Triceratops |
| Placodus | Trilophosaurus |
| Plateosaurus | Tylosaurus |
| Polacanthus | Tyrannosaurus |
| Polyodontosaurus | Velociraptor |
| Proganochelys | Yaverlandia |
| Protoceratops | Zephyrosaurus |
| Protorosaurus | |

# Prehistoric Dig

The activities on this page are for use with the list of Prehistoric Animals on pages 122 and 123.

1. Make a time line showing which ones of these animals lived during the following geologic periods and systems:

   | | |
   |---|---|
   | Carboniferous | 310-280 million years ago |
   | Permian | 280-230 million years ago |
   | Triassic | 230-190 million years ago |
   | Jurassic | 190-135 million years ago |
   | Cretaceous | 135-63 million years ago |
   | Tertiary | 63-1 million years ago |
   | Quaternary | 1 million years ago |

2. Do research to discover the diet of at least ten of these prehistoric animals. From what you learn, classify each one as either **herbivorous**, or plant-eating; **carnivorous**, or meat-eating; or **omnivorous**, both plant- and meat-eating.

3. Using a globe or map of the world, show where the fossil remains of at least ten of these prehistoric animals were found.

4. Represent the lengths of at least ten of these prehistoric animals on a bar graph.

5. Make a chart on which you compare the dimensions and/or weight of ten prehistoric animals with the dimensions and/or weight of familiar present-day animals or objects.

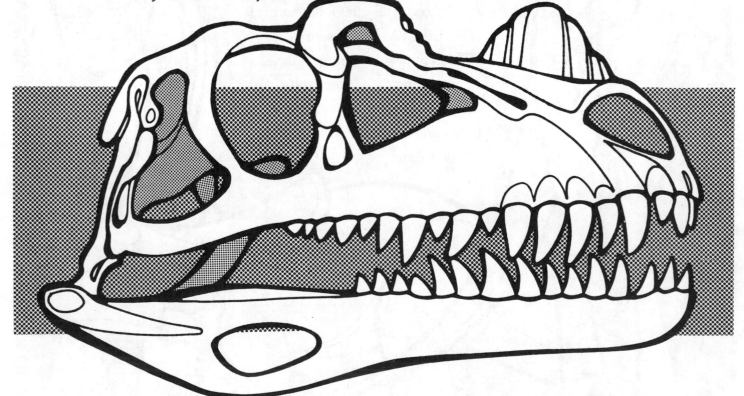

# Reptiles

## Snakes

anaconda
ball python
boa constrictor
boomslang
bull snake
bushmaster
carpet snake
copperhead
coral snake
corn snake
cottonmouth
death adder
diamondback rattlesnake
emerald tree boa
fer-de-lance
gaboon viper
garter snake
hognose snake
horned viper
Indian cobra
indigo snake
king cobra
king snake

krait
mamba
mangrove snake
massasauga
milk snake
puff adder
rainbow boa
rat snake
reticulated python
rhinoceros viper
ring-necked snake
rock python
rosy boa
rubber boa
sea snake
sidewinder
spitting cobra
tiger snake
vine snake
wart snake
water snake
whip snake
worm snake

## Lizards

agama
alligator lizard
anole
blue-tongued skink
chuckwalla
collared lizard
flying lizard
frilled lizard
gila monster
glass snake
goanna
green iguana
horned toad
Komodo dragon
marine iguana
moloch
Nile monitor
plumed basilisk
sand skink
slowworm
sungazer
three-horned chameleon
tokay gecko

## Turtles

Adalbra giant tortoise
big-headed turtle
box turtle
cooter
desert tortoise
diamondback terrapin
Galápagos giant tortoise
gopher tortoise
hawksbill turtle

hinged-back tortoise
leatherback turtle
leopard tortoise
loggerhead turtle
map turtle
marginated tortoise
matamata
painted turtle
pancake tortoise

red-eared turtle
side-necked turtle
slider turtle
snapping turtle
soft-shelled turtle
spotted turtle
star tortoise
stinkpot
wood turtle

## Alligators and Crocodiles

American alligator
black caiman
Chinese alligator
dwarf crocodile

estuarine crocodile
gavial
Nile crocodile
spectacled caiman

# Bones in the Human Body

The entire human skeleton consists of two hundred distinct bones. These bones are distributed as follows:

| | | |
|---|---|---|
| Skull | | 22 |
| Cranium | 8 | |
| Face | 14 | |
| Spine | | 26 |
| Hyoid bone, sternum, ribs | | 26 |
| Upper extremities | | 64 |
| Lower extremities | | 62 |

calcaneus

carpus

cervical vertebrae

clavicle

coccyx

dorsal vertebrae

femur

fibula

humerus

ilium

ischium

lumbar vertebrae

mandible

maxilla

metacarpus

metatarsus

olecranon

patella

peluis

phalanges

pubis

radius

ribs

sacrum

scapula

sternum

tarsus

tibia

ulna

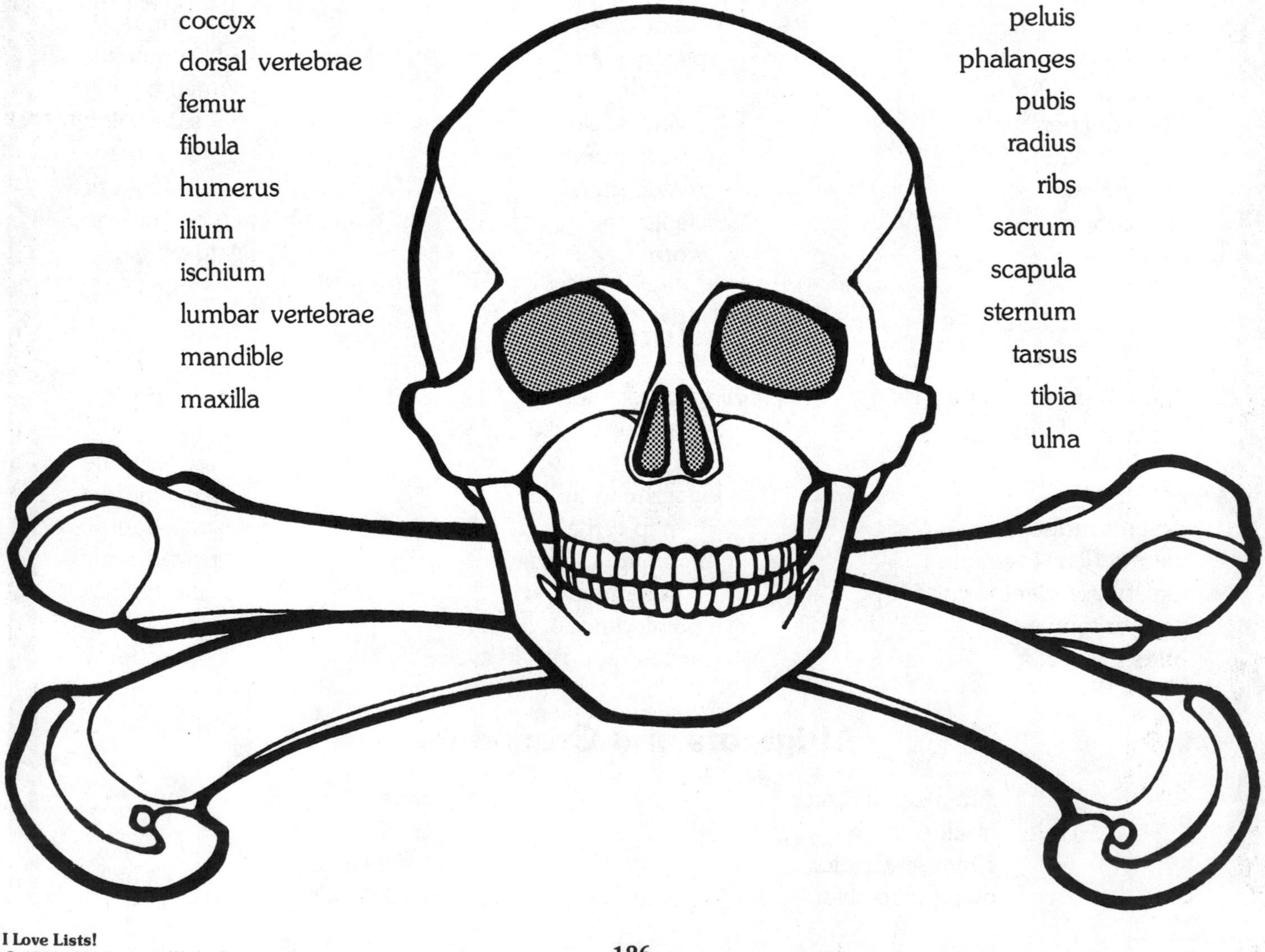

# Itises

Words ending in **-itis** usually name an inflammation. In the list below, the description following each *-itis* tells what part of the human body is inflamed.

| | |
|---|---|
| **appendicitis** | appendix |
| **arthritis** | joint |
| **bronchitis** | bronchi, or tubes branching off at the lower part of the trachea |
| **bursitis** | bursa, a fluid-filled sac in a joint |
| **colitis** | colon, or large intestine |
| **conjunctivitis** | conjunctiva, or transparent membrane lining the front of the eyeball |
| **cystitis** | bladder |
| **dermatitis** | skin |
| **diverticulitis** | diverticula, or abnormal pouches or soft-walled cavities that form along the walls of the intestines |
| **encephalitis** | brain |
| **enteritis** | intestines |
| **gastritis** | stomach |
| **gastroenteritis** | mucous membranes of the intestines and stomach |
| **gingivitis** | gums |
| **hepatitis** | liver |
| **laryngitis** | larynx |
| **mastoiditus** | mastoid cells |
| **myringitis** | the tympanic membrane, or eardrum |

# Itises
## (continued)

| | |
|---|---|
| **nephritis** | kidney |
| **neuritis** | nerve |
| **omphalitis** | navel |
| **ophthalmitis** | eye |
| **osteochondritis** | bone and cartilage |
| **osteomyelitis** | bone and marrow |
| **pancarditis** | structures of the heart |
| **pancreatitis** | pancreas |
| **pericarditis** | pericardium, or tissue covering the heart |
| **periodontitis** | periodontal membrane, or connective tissue covering the cement layer of a tooth |
| **peritonitis** | peritoneum, or membrane that lines the abdominal organs |
| **pharyngitis** | pharynx, or tube that connects the mouth and nasal passages and becomes continuous with the esophagus |
| **phlebitis** | vein |
| **pneumonitis** | lung tissue |
| **rhinitis** | mucous membrane of the nose |
| **sinusitis** | sinus |
| **stomatitis** | soft tissues of the mouth |
| **tendinitis** | tendon |
| **tonsillitis** | tonsils |
| **tracheitis** | trachea |

# Phobias

A **phobia** (fō′ - bē - ə) is an intense abnormal or unreasonable fear of a particular class or type of people, places, things, or situations. Below is a list of words that name phobias. Beside each word is a brief description of the thing feared by a person suffering from this phobia.

| | | | |
|---|---|---|---|
| **acrophobia** | heights | **hypnophobia** | sleep |
| **agoraphobia** | open spaces | **lalophobia** | speech or speaking |
| **ailurophobia** | cats | **mysophobia** | uncleanliness or contamination |
| **amaxophobia** | being or riding in vehicles | **necrophobia** | death or dead bodies |
| **androphobia** | men | **nyctophobia** | night, darkness |
| **apeirophobia** | that which is unlimited or indeterminate | **ophidiophobia** | reptiles, especially snakes |
| **astrophobia** | stars | **pedophobia** | infants or children |
| **autophobia** | being alone with oneself | **phagophobia** | eating |
| **bathophobia** | depths | **phonophobia** | sounds or noise |
| **chionophobia** | snow | **psychrophobia** | cold |
| **claustrophobia** | narrow or closed spaces | **pyrophobia** | flames or fire |
| **cynophobia** | dogs | **thalassophobia** | ocean or sea |
| **demophobia** | people, crowds | **thanatophobia** | death |
| **entomophobia** | insects | **toxicophobia** | drugs or poison |
| **erythrophobia** | the color red | **triskaidekaphobia** | the number 13 |
| **gamophobia** | marriage | **xenophobia** | foreigners or strangers, or anything that is foreign or strange |
| **gynophobia** | women | **zoophobia** | animals |
| **hemophobia** | blood | | |
| **hydrophobia** | water | | |

# Pioneers in Medicine

| Name | Achievements |
| --- | --- |
| **Christiaan N. Barnard** | in 1967, performed the first successful human heart transplant. |
| **Albert C. T. Billroth** | made important contributions in the areas of histology and pathology, and advanced military surgery by citing bacteria as the cause of infection in wounds. |
| **Elizabeth Blackwell** | in 1849, became the first woman doctor of medicine in modern times. |
| **Gerhard Domagk** | in 1934, discovered and performed experimental work with "prontosil," forerunner of sulfanilamide, the first sulfa drug. |
| **Charles Richard Drew** | in 1940, developed a safe and efficient way to store blood plasma in blood banks. |
| **John Franklin Enders** | in 1954, developed a vaccine for measles and later made important discoveries concerning the poliomyelitis virus. |
| **Sir Alexander Fleming** | in 1928, discovered and later developed penicillin. |
| **Sigmund Freud** | developed psychoanalysis as one way of treating mental illness. |
| **Joseph Goldberger** | between 1913 and 1925, discovered the nature of and cure for pellagra. |
| **Stephen Hales** | invented many mechanical devices, including artificial ventilators and, in 1727, inaugurated the science of plant physiology. |
| **William Harvey** | discovered circulation of the blood, a theory which he first expounded in lectures delivered between 1628 and 1651. |
| **Hippocrates** | lived between *ca.* 460 and *ca.* 377 B.C.; called the "father of medicine"; is said to have devised for his students the code of medical ethics which today is administered as an oath to persons seeking to enter medical practice. |

# Pioneers in Medicine
## (continued)

| Name | Achievements |
|---|---|
| **Carl Gustav Jung** | developed analytic psychology as a way of treating mental illness. |
| **Anton von Leeuwenhoek** | made simple microscopes which enabled him to become the first to give an accurate description of red blood corpuscles and to describe bacteria in 1676. |
| **Sir Joseph Lister** | influenced by the discoveries of Pasteur, used carbolic acid to prevent septic infection and, thus, became the founder of antiseptic surgery. |
| **Crawford Williamson Long** | in 1842, became the first to use ether as an anesthetic during surgery. |
| **George Richards Minot** | an authority on blood diseases; in 1934, won the Nobel prize in medicine for research on liver treatment of anemias. |
| **Florence Nightingale** | in 1860, founded an institution for training nurses and, thus, established nursing as a profession. |
| **Louis Pasteur** | was the first to prove that fermentation is caused by minute organisms and to use heating (pasteurization) as a means of killing the organisms and preventing spoilage; also was the first to prove that bacteria cause disease; developed a vaccine for rabies. |
| **Walter Reed** | helped to prove that yellow fever is transmitted by a mosquito, which made it possible to eradicate this disease by eliminating its carriers. |
| **Albert Sabin** | in 1955, developed an oral poliomyelitis vaccine. |
| **Jonas Salk** | in 1953, developed the first successful vaccine for poliomyelitis. |
| **Mary Edwards Walker** | pioneer woman physician who served as a nurse with the Union army during the Civil War and received the Congressional Medal of Honor. |

# Specialty Fields in Medicine

| | |
|---|---|
| **allergy and immunology** | concerned with altered and/or abnormally severe body reactivity to substances or situations |
| **anesthesiology** | study and practice of using drugs or other means to induce a controlled loss of sensation with or without a loss of consciousness |
| **dermatology** | medical and surgical treatment of skin disorders |
| **emergency medicine** | immediate recognition and treatment of acute illnesses and injuries |
| **endocrinology** | diagnosis and treatment of disorders of the endocrine glands, which regulate the complex metabolic process by which the body's cells are nourished, repaired, and/or replaced |
| **family or general practice** | supervision of the total health care of individual adults and/or of family groups |
| **gastroenterology** | diseases and pathology of the stomach and intestines |
| **gynecology** | diseases and disorders of the female reproductive organs |
| **hematology** | diseases and disorders of the blood and blood-forming organs |
| **internal medicine** | complete nonsurgical care of adults |
| **neurology** | diseases and disorders of the nervous system |
| **nuclear medicine** | use of radioactive substances to diagnose and treat disease |
| **obstetrics** | care of women during pregnancy and childbirth |
| **ophthalmology** | diagnosis and treatment of eye and vision disorders using surgery and other corrective techniques |
| **otolaryngology** | medical and surgical treatment of ear, nose, and throat disorders |
| **pathology** | analysis of the causes and effects of disease by examination of visible changes in cells, fluids, tissues, and life processes |
| **pediatrics** | medical care of children from birth through adolescence |
| **preventive medicine** | prevention of disease and disability with an emphasis on analyzing present health services and planning ways to meet future health care needs |
| **psychiatry** | diagnosis and treatment of persons with mental, emotional, or behavioral disorders |
| **radiology** | use of X-rays, ultrasound, nuclear medicine, computer axial tomography (CAT), and magnetic resonance imaging (MRI) for the diagnosis and treatment of disease |
| **surgery** | correction of diseased or injured parts of the body by means of operative treatment |
| **urology** | diagnosis and treatment of abnormalities and diseases of the urinary tract of men, women, and children and of disorders affecting the male reproductive system |

# Astronauts

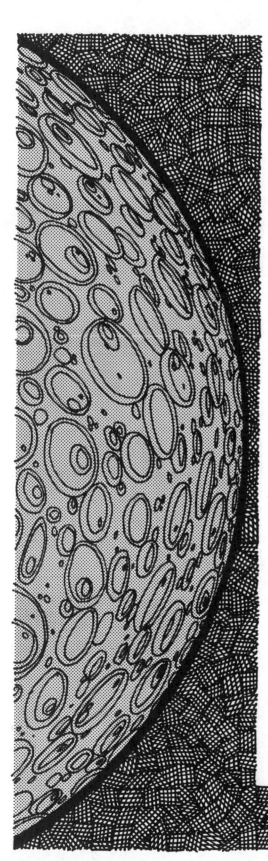
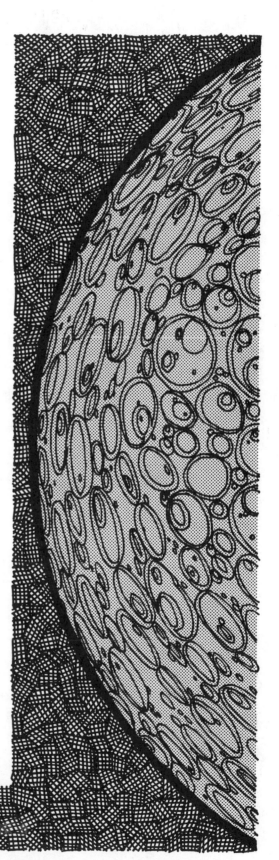

Edwin E. Aldrin, Jr.

Joseph Allen

William A. Anders

Neil A. Armstrong

Alan L. Bean

Karol Bobko

Frank Borman

Vance Brand

M. Scott Carpenter

Gerald P. Carr

Eugene A. Cernan

Roger B. Chaffee

Michael Collins

Charles Conrad, Jr.

L. Gordon Cooper, Jr.

Robert L. Crippen

R. Walter Cunningham

Charles M. Duke, Jr.

Donn F. Eisele

Joe Engle

Ronald E. Evans

John Fabian

C. Gordon Fullerton

Owen K. Garriott

Edward G. Gibson

John H. Glenn, Jr.

Richard F. Gordon, Jr.

Virgil I. Grissom

Fred W. Haise, Jr.

Henry Hartsfield, Jr.

# Astronauts
## (continued)

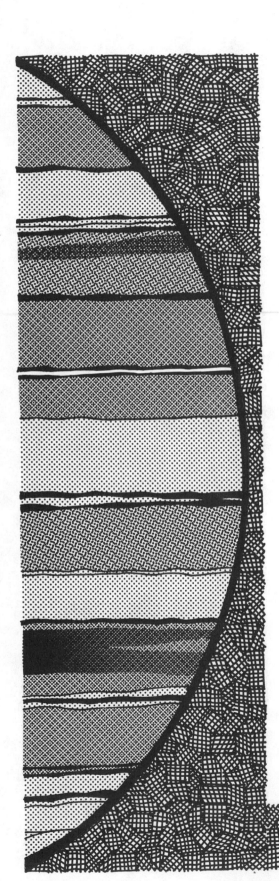

Frederick Hauck

James B. Irwin

Joseph P. Kerwin

William Lenoir

Jack R. Lousma

James A. Lovell, Jr.

James A. McDivitt

Thomas K. Mattingly, II

Edgar D. Mitchell

Story Musgrave

Robert Overmyer

Donald Peterson

William Pogue

Sally K. Ride

Stuart A. Roosa

Walter M. Schirra

Harrison H. Schmitt

Russell L. Schweickart

David R. Scott

Alan B. Shepard, Jr.

Donald K. Slayton

Thomas P. Stafford

John L. Swigart, Jr.

Norman Thagard

Richard Truly

Paul J. Weitz

Edward H. White, II

Alfred M. Worden

John W. Young

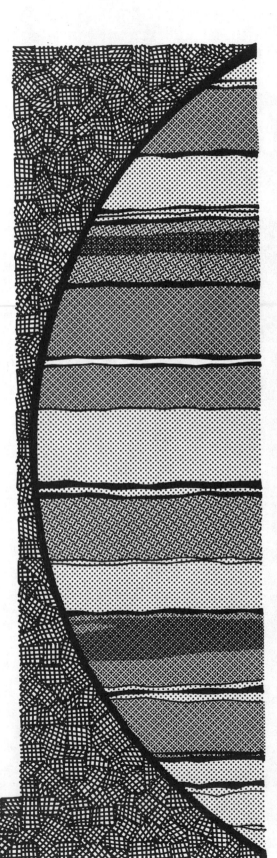

# Comets

A **comet** is a heavenly body that looks like a fuzzy star and travels around the sun in an elliptical orbit. A comet has three parts: a center, which is called the **nucleus**; a hazy cloud around this center, which is called the **coma**; and a stream of dust particles and gas molecules, which always points away from the sun and is called the **tail**. Although some comets appear to be very bright, they do not produce any light of their own. Instead, like our moon, they reflect light from the sun.

| Name | Year in Which It Was First Seen | Name | Year in Which It Was First Seen |
|---|---|---|---|
| Halley's Comet | Before 240 B.C. | Comet Morehouse | 1908 |
| Tycho Brahe's Comet | 1577 | Comet Schwassmann-Wachmann I | 1927 |
| Biela's Comet | 1772 | Comet Humason | 1961 |
| Encke's Comet | 1786 | Comet Ikeya-Seki | 1965 |
| Comet Flaugergues | 1811 | Comet Tago-Sato-Kosaka | 1969 |
| Comet Pons-Winnecke | 1819 | Comet Bennett | 1969 |
| Great Comet of 1843 | 1843 | Comet Kohoutek | 1973 |
| Donati's Comet | 1858 | Comet West | 1976 |

1. Halley's Comet was named for English astronomer Edmond Halley. Do some research to learn where five other comets on this list got their names.

2. The time it takes a comet to make one complete orbit is termed its **period**. Edmond Halley was the first person to recognize that the period for Halley's Comet is approximately seventy-seven years. Using this figure, predict the years in which the next ten sightings of this comet will take place.

3. Because the orbits of comets often take them across the paths of other celestial bodies in the solar system, it would be possible for a comet and a planet to collide. In fact, in 1910, the earth passed unharmed through the edge of Halley's Comet's tail. What would have happened if, instead of passing through the tail, the earth had gone into the coma and collided with the nucleus? Write a science fiction story about how the earth faces the threat of a collision with a comet's nucleus.

# Constellations

A **constellation** is any one of eighty-eight arbitrary groups of stars recognized by astronomers. Ancient observers named forty-eight of these groups according to the pictures made by the stars they contained. All eighty-eight constellations—both ancient and modern—are listed below. Those marked with an asterisk (*) are not visible from midnorthern latitudes.

| Latin Name | English Name | Latin Name | English Name |
| --- | --- | --- | --- |
| Andromeda | Chained Maiden | Cepheus | King |
| Antila | Air Pump | Cetus | Whale |
| Apus* | Bird of Paradise | Chamaeleon* | Chameleon |
| Aquarius | Water Bearer | Circinus* | Compasses |
| Aquila | Eagle | Columba | Dove |
| Ara* | Altar | Coma Berenices | Berenice's Hair |
| Aries | Ram | Corona Australis | Southern Crown |
| Auriga | Charioteer | Corona Borealis | Northern Crown |
| Bootes | Herdsman | Corvus | Crow |
| Caelum | Chisel | Crater | Cup |
| Camelopardalis | Giraffe | Crux* | (Southern) Cross |
| Cancer | Crab | Cygnus | Swan |
| Canes Venatici | Hunting Dogs | Delphinus | Dolphin |
| Canis Major | Great Dog | Dorado* | Swordfish |
| Canis Minor | Small Dog | Draco | Dragon |
| Capricornus | Sea Goat | Equuleus | Little Horse |
| Carina* | Keel | Eridanus | River Eridanus |
| Cassiopeia | Lady in Chair | Fornax | Furnace |
| Centaurus* | Centaur | Gemini | Twins |

# Constellations
## (continued)

| Latin Name | English Name | Latin Name | English Name |
|---|---|---|---|
| Grus* | Crane | Phoenix* | Phoenix |
| Hercules | Hercules | Pictor* | Painter's (Easel) |
| Horologium* | Clock | Pisces | Fishes |
| Hydra | Sea Serpent | Piscis Austrinus | Southern Fish |
| Hydrus* | Water Snake | Puppis | Poop (Stern) |
| Indus* | Indian | Pyxis | Compass |
| Lacerta | Lizard | Reticulum* | Net |
| Leo | Lion | Sagitta | Arrow |
| Leo Minor | Small Lion | Sagittarius | Archer |
| Lepus | Hare | Scorpius | Scorpion |
| Libra | Scales | Sculptor | Sculptor |
| Lupus* | Wolf | Scutum | Shield |
| Lynx | Lynx | Serpens | Serpent |
| Lyra | Lyre | Sextans | Sextant |
| Mensa* | Table (Mountain) | Taurus | Bull |
| Microscopium | Microscope | Telescopium* | Telescope |
| Monoceros | Unicorn | Triangulum | Triangle |
| Musca* | Fly | Triangulum Australe* | Southern Triangle |
| Norma* | Square | Tucana* | Toucan |
| Octans* | Octant | Ursa Major | Great Bear |
| Ophiuchus | Serpent Bearer | Ursa Minor | Small Bear |
| Orion | Hunter | Vela* | Sails |
| Pavo* | Peacock | Virgo | Virgin |
| Pegasus | Pegasus | Volans* | Flying Fish |
| Perseus | Champion | Vulpecula | Fox |

# Moons

A **moon** is a celestial body that orbits another celestial body of larger size. Thus, moons are **satellites**. They are sometimes called **natural satellites** to distinguish them from the **man-made satellites** that have been put into orbit in recent years. As you can see from the list below, most of the planets in our solar system have moons.

| Planet | Moons | |
|---|---|---|
| | Number | Names |
| Mercury | 0 | |
| Venus | 0 | |
| Earth | 1 | Moon (Luna) |
| Mars | 2 | Phobos, Deimos |
| Jupiter | 16 | Metis, Adrastea, Amalthea, Thebe, Io, Europa, Ganymede, Callisto, Leda, Himalia, Lysithea, Elara, Ananke, Carme, Pasiphae, Sinope |
| Saturn | 23 | Titan, Iapetus, Rhea, Dione, Tethys, Enceladus, Mimas, Hyperion, Phoebe, Janus, Epimetheus, 1980 S-6, Telesto, Calypso, Pandora, Prometheus, Atlas, 1980 S-34, 1981 S-7, 1981 S-8, 1981 S-9, 1981 S-10, 1981 S-11 |
| Uranus | 15 | Oberon, Titania, Umbriel, Ariel, Miranda, 1985 U-1, 1986 U-1, 1986 U-2, 1986 U-3, 1986 U-4, 1986 U-5, 1986 U-6, 1986 U-7, 1986 U-8, 1986 U-9 |
| Neptune | 2 | Triton, Nereid |
| Pluto | 1 | Charon |

1. As you can see from the designations given them, nine of the moons that orbit Uranus were discovered in 1986. Do some research to learn why so many moons were discovered in a single year. What event or events made their discovery possible?

2. Many of the moons on this list were named for figures in Greek or Roman mythology. Charon, for example, was the Greek ferryman of the lower world. Do some pleasure reading to learn about the identities and exploits of the deities and creatures for whom moons have been named.

# Planets
## (in order from the sun)

| Planet Name | Diameter, miles | Average Distance from the Sun, miles | Period of Revolution | Known Moons |
|---|---|---|---|---|
| Mercury | 3,100 | 35,960,000 | 88 days | 0 |
| Venus | 7,600 | 67,200,000 | 225 days | 0 |
| Earth | 7,913 | 93,000,000 | 365¼ days | 1 |
| Mars | 4,200 | 141,500,000 | 687 days | 2 |
| Jupiter | 88,000 | 483,400,000 | 11.86 years | 16 |
| Saturn | 71,500 | 886,200,000 | 29.5 years | 23 |
| Uranus | 32,000 | 1,783,000,000 | 84 years | 15 |
| Neptune | 31,000 | 2,794,000,000 | 165 years | 2 |
| Pluto | 1,900 | 3,670,000,000 | 248 years | 1 |

# Solar System Terms

| | | | |
|---|---|---|---|
| aberration | cusps | meteorite | reflection |
| airglow | declination | moon | refraction |
| albedo | dispersion | nadir | regression |
| altitude | diurnal motion | nebula | resolving power |
| apex | Doppler effect | nodes | retrograde motions |
| aphelion | dwarf | nova | right ascension |
| apogee | eccentricity | nutation | revolution |
| aspects | eclipse | oblateness | rotation |
| asteroid | ecliptic | occultations | satellite |
| astronomy | ellipse | orbit | scintillation |
| aurora | emission | parabola | sidereal time |
| axis | ephemeris | parallax | solar time |
| azimuth | equinox | penumbra | solstices |
| black hole | galaxy | perihelion | spectroheliogram |
| chromatic aberration | inclination | phases | spectrum |
| chromosphere | light-year | photosphere | stars |
| comet | lunar | planet | sun |
| conjunction | magnitude | polarity | sunspots |
| constellation | mass | precession | supernova |
| Coriolis effect | mean solar time | prominences | telescope |
| corona | meteor | rays | umbra |
| craters | | | zenith |

Become familiar with the meanings of at least twenty-five of these words, and use them correctly in a space adventure story.

# Spaceflights

| Mission Name | Date(s) | Crew Members |
|---|---|---|
| Vostok 1 | 4/12/61 | Yuri A. Gagarin |
| Mercury-Redstone 3 | 5/5/61 | Alan B. Shepard, Jr. |
| Mercury-Redstone 4 | 7/21/61 | Virgil I. Grissom |
| Vostok 2 | 8/6 to 8/7/61 | Gherman S. Titov |
| Mercury-Atlas 6 | 2/20/62 | John H. Glenn, Jr. |
| Mercury-Atlas 7 | 5/24/62 | M. Scott Carpenter |
| Vostok 3 | 8/11 to 8/15/62 | Andrian G. Nikolayev |
| Vostok 4 | 8/12 to 8/15/62 | Pavel R. Popovich |
| Mercury-Atlas 8 | 10/3/62 | Walter M. Schirra, Jr. |
| Mercury-Atlas 9 | 5/15 to 5/16/63 | L. Gordon Cooper |
| Vostok 5 | 6/14 to 6/19/63 | Valery F. Bykovsky |
| Vostok 6 | 6/16 to 6/19/63 | Valentina V. Tereshkova |
| Voskhod 1 | 10/12/64 | Vladimir M. Komarov |
| | | Konstantin P. Feoktistov |
| | | Boris B. Yegorov |
| Voskhod 2 | 3/18/65 | Pavel I. Belyayev |
| | | Aleksei A. Leonov |
| Gemini-Titan 3 | 3/23/65 | Virgil I. Grissom |
| | | John W. Young |
| Gemini-Titan 4 | 6/3 to 6/7/65 | James A. McDivitt |
| | | Edward H. White, II |
| Gemini-Titan 5 | 8/21 to 8/29/65 | L. Gordon Cooper, Jr. |
| | | Charles Conrad, Jr. |
| Gemini-Titan 7 | 12/4 to 12/18/65 | Frank Borman |
| | | James A. Lovell, Jr. |
| Gemini-Titan 6-A | 12/15 to 12/16/65 | Walter M. Schirra, Jr. |
| | | Thomas P. Stafford |
| Gemini-Titan 8 | 3/16 to 3/17/66 | Neil A. Armstrong |
| | | David R. Scott |
| Gemini-Titan 10 | 7/18 to 7/21/66 | John W. Young |
| | | Michael Collins |
| Gemini-Titan 11 | 9/12 to 9/15/66 | Charles Conrad, Jr. |
| | | Richard F. Gordon, Jr. |
| Gemini-Titan 12 | 11/11 to 11/15/66 | James A. Lovell, Jr. |
| | | Edwin E. Aldrin, Jr. |
| Soyuz 1 | 4/23/67 | Vladimir M. Komarov |

# Spaceflights
## (continued)

| Mission Name | Date(s) | Crew Members |
|---|---|---|
| Apollo-Saturn 7 | 10/11 to 10/22/68 | Walter M. Schirra, Jr.<br>Donn F. Eisele<br>R. Walter Cunningham |
| Soyuz 3 | 10/26 to 10/30/68 | Georgi T. Beregovoi |
| Apollo-Saturn 8 | 12/21 to 12/27/68 | Frank Borman<br>James A. Lovell, Jr.<br>William A. Anders |
| Soyuz 4<br>Soyuz 5 | 1/14 to 1/17/69 | Vladimir A. Shatalov<br>Boris V. Volyanov<br>Aleksei S. Yeliseyev<br>Yevgeny V. Khrunov |
| Apollo-Saturn 9 | 3/3 to 3/13/69 | James A. McDivitt<br>David R. Scott<br>Russell L. Schweickart |
| Apollo-Saturn 10 | 5/18 to 5/26/69 | Thomas P. Stafford<br>Eugene A. Cernan<br>John W. Young |
| Apollo-Saturn 11 | 7/16 to 7/24/69 | Neil A. Armstrong<br>Edwin E. Aldrin, Jr.<br>Michael Collins |
| Soyuz 6 | 10/11 to 10/16/69 | Georgi S. Shonin<br>Valery N. Kubasov |
| Soyuz 7 | 10/12 to 10/17/69 | Anatoly V. Filipchenko<br>Vladislav N. Volkov<br>Viktor V. Gorbatko |
| Apollo-Saturn 12 | 11/14 to 11/24/69 | Charles Conrad, Jr.<br>Richard F. Gordon<br>Alan L. Bean |
| Apollo-Saturn 13 | 4/11 to 4/17/70 | James A. Lovell, Jr.<br>Fred W. Haise, Jr.<br>John L. Swigart, Jr. |
| Apollo-Saturn 14 | 1/31 to 2/9/71 | Alan B. Shepard, Jr.<br>Stuart A. Roosa<br>Edgar D. Mitchell |
| Soyuz 11 | 6/6 to 6/30/71 | Georgi T. Dobrovolsky<br>Vladislav N. Volkov<br>Viktor I. Patsayev |
| Apollo-Saturn 15 | 7/26 to 8/7/71 | David R. Scott<br>Alfred M. Worden<br>James B. Irwin |

# Spaceflights
## (continued)

| Mission Name | Date(s) | Crew Members |
|---|---|---|
| Apollo-Saturn 16 | 4/16 to 4/27/72 | Charles M. Duke, Jr. |
| | | Thomas K. Mattingly, II |
| | | John W. Young |
| Apollo-Saturn 17 | 12/7 to 12/19/72 | Eugene A. Cernan |
| | | Ronald E. Evans |
| | | Harrison Schmitt |
| Skylab 2 | 5/25 to 6/22/73 | Charles Conrad, Jr. |
| | | Joseph P. Kerwin |
| | | Paul J. Weitz |
| Skylab 3 | 7/28 to 9/25/73 | Alan L. Bean |
| | | Jack R. Lousma |
| | | Owen K. Garriott |
| Skylab 4 | 11/16/73 to 2/8/74 | Gerald P. Carr |
| | | Edward G. Gibson |
| | | William Pogue |
| Soyuz 19 | 7/15 to 7/21/75 | Alexi Leonov |
| | | Valeri Kubason |
| Apollo 18 | 7/15 to 7/24/75 | Vance Brand |
| | | Thomas P. Stafford |
| | | Donald K. Slayton |
| Columbia | 4/12 to 4/14/81 | Robert L. Crippen |
| | | John W. Young |
| Columbia | 11/12 to 11/14/81 | Joe Engle |
| | | Richard Truly |
| Columbia | 3/22 to 3/30/82 | Jack R. Lousma |
| | | C. Gordon Fullerton |
| Columbia | 6/27 to 7/4/82 | Thomas K. Mattingly, II |
| | | Henry Hartsfield, Jr. |
| Columbia | 11/11 to 11/16/82 | Vance Brand |
| | | Robert Overmyer |
| | | William Lenoir |
| | | Joseph Allen |
| Challenger | 4/4 to 4/9/83 | Paul J. Weitz |
| | | Karol Bobko |
| | | Story Musgrave |
| | | Donald Peterson |
| Soyuz T-5 | 5/3 to 12/10/83 | Anotoly Berezovnoy |
| | | Valentin Lebedev |
| Challenger | 6/18 to 6/24/83 | Robert L. Crippen |
| | | Norman Thagard |
| | | John Fabian |
| | | Frederick Hauck |
| | | Sally K. Ride |

# Chemical Elements and Compounds

**Elements** are the basic chemical substances from which everything in the universe is made. There are more than one hundred of them. Each element consists of only one kind of atom. Here are the names and symbols for some common elements.

| | | | | | |
|---|---|---|---|---|---|
| aluminum | Al | gold | Au | nickel | Ni |
| barium | Ba | helium | He | nitrogen | N |
| boron | B | hydrogen | H | oxygen | O |
| bromine | Br | iodine | I | potassium | K |
| calcium | Ca | iron | Fe | radium | Ra |
| carbon | C | krypton | Kr | silver | Ag |
| chlorine | Cl | lead | Pb | sodium | Na |
| cobalt | Co | magnesium | Mg | tin | Sn |
| copper | Cu | manganese | Mn | uranium | U |
| fluorine | F | mercury | Hg | zinc | Zn |

A **compound** is a substance made of two or more elements joined into molecules.

| Compound | Common Name | Molecular Formula |
|---|---|---|
| sodium chloride | table salt | NaCl |
| sucrose | table sugar | $C_{12}H_{22}O_{11}$ |
| water | water | $H_2O$ |
| _____ | _____ | _____ |
| _____ | _____ | _____ |
| _____ | _____ | _____ |

1. Write a short story about a super hero who uses at least one of the elements on this list to make himself even stronger.

2. Do some research so that you can add three compounds, their common names, and their chemical formulas to this list.

# Computer Terms

| | |
|---|---|
| **BASIC** | Beginning All-Purpose Symbolic Instruction Code, the computer language designed for education but now used by business |
| **binary system** | a system in which the digits 0 and 1 are used and numbers are grouped by powers of two |
| **bit** | a storage cell in a computer's memory |
| **byte** | a group of bits |
| **cartridge** | box or case that contains a cassette tape |
| **central processing unit (CPU)** | the integrated circuits that form the processing and memory units of a computer |
| **character** | any letter, digit, punctuation mark, or symbol that a programmer uses when processing data |
| **chip** | thumbnail-sized integrated electrical circuit used to build the processing and memory units of today's computers |
| **circuit** | the path of an electric current |
| **COBOL** | Common Business Oriented Language, the computer language used mainly in business |
| **code** | a group of lines, letters, or symbols that can be read and understood by a computer |
| **computer** | a programmable electronic machine that works with numbers |
| **cursor** | a lighted or blinking shape on the video screen which marks the spot where a message will be printed or a symbol or color will appear if a key on the keyboard is pressed |
| **data** | numbers and information that are given to a computer |
| **erase** | to rub out, get rid of, or do away with |
| **floppy disk** | a disk that looks like a 45-rpm record on which programs can be stored |
| **flow chart** | a graphic outline of the steps that are necessary to do a specific job |
| **FORTRAN** | Formula Translation, the computer language used mainly by mathematicians, scientists, and engineers |

# Computer Terms
## (continued)

**graphics**        pictures and colors that can be programmed to appear on a computer's video screen

**hardware**        the working mechanical and electrical parts of a computer, including the video screen, central processing unit, keyboard, disk drive, and printer

**input**        operating step during which information is put into, or given to, a computer; the information that is put into a computer

**keyboard**        the piece of computer hardware that looks like a typewriter and is used to give information to a computer

**memory**        operating step during which a computer stores or recalls data or orders it has been given; the part of the central processing unit in which data are stored; the capacity of a computer to store data

**output**        operating step during which a computer presents its answer, response, or results in usable form; the answer, response, or results presented by a computer

**printer**        the piece of computer hardware that types printed output, or printout

**printout**        computer output that is typed, or printed out, on paper

**processing**        the operating step during which a computer rearranges data, tests them, and uses them to work math problems

**program**        a series or set of instructions given to a computer in a language it can understand

**programmer**        a person who knows at least one computer language and uses it to give instructions to a computer

**software**        any program used on a computer, which may be stored on punched cards, floppy disks, cassette tapes, or reels of tape

**transistor**        a tiny electronic device that acts like a switch and controls the flow of electric current in a chip

**video game**        a game made up of action choices programmed on a tape or disk and played with graphics on a video screen

**video screen**        the piece of computer hardware that looks like a television set and displays symbols, words, numbers, or colors

# Flowers

| | |
|---|---|
| anemone | hyacinth |
| apple blossom | hydrangea |
| aster | iris |
| azalea | jasmine |
| begonia | jonquil |
| black-eyed Susan | lady's slipper |
| bluebell | lantana |
| buttercup | larkspur |
| camellia | lilac |
| carnation | lily of the valley |
| chrysanthemum | marigold |
| coneflower | narcissus |
| cowslip | nasturtium |
| crocus | orchid |
| daffodil | pansy |
| daisy | peach blossom |
| dandelion | peony |
| dogwood | petunia |
| edelweiss | poppy |
| forget-me-not | ranunculus |
| forsythia | rhododendron |
| foxglove | rose |
| freesia | snapdragon |
| fuchsia | sunflower |
| gardenia | sweet pea |
| geranium | thistle |
| gladiolus | tulip |
| goldenrod | violet |
| heather | wisteria |
| hibiscus | yucca |
| hollyhock | zinnia |

# Inventors

| Name | Birth and Death Dates | Nationality | Invention |
|---|---|---|---|
| John Bardeen | 1908- | American | transistor |
| Alexander Graham Bell | 1847-1922 | Scottish-American | telephone |
| Vincent Bendix | 1882-1945 | American | electric self-starter for the automobile |
| Emile Berliner | 1851-1929 | German-American | loose-contact teletransmitter, or microphone |
| Clarence Birdseye | 1886-1956 | American | preserving food by freezing |
| Louis Braille | 1809-1852 | French | system of raised-point writing for literature and music |
| William Seward Burroughs | 1857-1898 | American | key-set recording and adding machine |
| Edmund Cartwright | 1743-1823 | English | power loom |
| George Washington Carver | 1864-1943 | American | agricultural research on the industrial uses of peanuts |
| Samuel Colt | 1814-1862 | American | revolver |
| Peter Cooper | 1791-1883 | American | first American locomotive |
| Glenn Curtiss | 1878-1930 | American | hydroplane |
| Gottlieb Daimler | 1834-1900 | German | high-speed internal combustion automobile engine |
| Lee De Forest | 1873-1961 | American | radio amplifier and radio transmission |
| George Eastman | 1854-1932 | American | the Kodak camera |
| Thomas Alva Edison | 1847-1931 | American | phonograph, incandescent electric lamp, and alkaline rechargeable storage battery |
| Gabriel Daniel Fahrenheit | 1686-1736 | German | mercury thermometer and Fahrenheit scale |
| Alexander Fleming | 1881-1955 | British | penicillin |
| Benjamin Franklin | 1706-1790 | American | bifocal lens, heating stove, and lightning rod |
| Robert Fulton | 1765-1815 | American | steamboat |
| Charles Goodyear | 1800-1860 | American | vulcanization process used to manufacture rubber |
| Johann Gutenberg | ca. 1400-1468 | German | printing from movable type |
| Elias Howe | 1819-1867 | American | sewing machine |

# Inventors
## (continued)

| Name | Birth and Death Dates | Nationality | Invention |
|---|---|---|---|
| Guglielmo Marconi | 1874–1937 | Italian | wireless high-frequency telegraph |
| Ottmar Mergenthaler | 1854–1899 | German-American | Linotype typesetting machine |
| Samuel F. B. Morse | 1791–1872 | American | magnetic telegraph and Morse code |
| Elisha Otis | 1811–1861 | American | steam elevator and elevator brake |
| Blaise Pascal | 1623–1662 | French | adding machine |
| Louis Pasteur | 1822–1895 | French | rabies vaccine and the pasteurization process |
| George Pullman | 1831–1897 | American | Pullman railroad sleeping car with pull-down berths |
| Igor Sikorsky | 1889–1972 | Russian-American | helicopter |
| James Starley | 1830–1881 | English | modern bicycle |
| Edward Teller | 1908– | Hungarian-American | hydrogen bomb |
| George Westinghouse | 1846–1914 | American | air brake |
| Schuyler S. Wheeler | 1860–1923 | American | electric fan |
| Eli Whitney | 1765–1825 | American | cotton gin |
| Orville Wright | 1871–1948 | American | first successful flight in a motor-powered heavier-than-air craft |
| Wilbur Wright | 1867–1912 | American | |
| Linus Yale, Jr. | 1821–1868 | American | cylinder lock |
| Ferdinand von Zeppelin | 1838–1917 | German | rigid dirigible |

··/···‖ ··/–‖ ––/–––/·–/···/· ?
–––/··–‖ ··–/–––/··–/·–/···/·‼

1. Become an inventor. First, straighten a wire coat hanger. Then, bend it into something entirely different. Finally, name your invention and draw a picture or diagram showing how it works or what it can be used to do.

2. Use recycled materials from home to create a unique invention. Display and demonstrate your creation at a classroom **Invention Convention**.

3. Do some research to create a time line on which you show pictures and patent dates for at least ten of these inventions.

# Machines

In physics, **work** is defined as exerting enough force to overcome the resistance of friction, gravity, or inertia so that a mass can be moved through a distance. Strictly speaking, if no movement takes place, no work has been done no matter how much effort or energy has been expended. A **machine** is a device that transmits force so that work can be done. Often, a machine transmits force so as to gain a **mechanical advantage**, meaning that the force which is available for doing the work is greater than the force that was originally applied to the machine. The inclined plane, lever, screw, wedge, and wheel and axle are **simple machines** which offer a mechanical advantage. All complex machines include among their elements one or more of these simple machines.

| | |
|---|---|
| Archimedes' screw | pump |
| battering ram | screw |
| block and tackle | steam shovel |
| catapult | treadmill |
| crane | trip-hammer |
| derrick | turbine |
| electric generator | waterwheel |
| engine | wedge |
| inclined plane | wheel and axle |
| lever | windlass |
| machine tool | windmill |
| pulley | |

1. Select three machines from this list. Draw and label diagrams of these machines to show how they work.

2. Do some research to discover who Archimedes was and why one of these machines is named after him.

3. Archimedes said that he would use a lever to move the earth if someone would give him a place to stand while doing so. Explain what he meant.

# Minerals

A **mineral** is a solid homogenous crystalline chemical element or compound that results from inorganic processes.

| | | |
|---|---|---|
| almandite | greenockite | sard |
| bauxite | hafnium | scandium |
| bentonite | heulandite | smithsonite |
| berkelium | hiddenite | sperrylite |
| boson | holmium | spessartite |
| bronze | idocrase | taconite |
| brookite | iridium | tantalum |
| cairngorm | itacolumite | tanzanite |
| calaverite | kernite | thenardite |
| carnotite | kunzite | titanium |
| chalcedony | lawrencium | tobernite |
| colemanite | magnesia | travertine |
| copper | mendelevium | tremolite |
| cordierite | mercury | troostite |
| covellite | millerite | turquoise |
| dolomite | monzonite | uranium |
| dumortierite | morganite | uvarovite |
| franklinite | niobium | vanadium |
| gadolinite | palladium | willemite |
| gallium | plutonium | witherite |
| garnierite | polonium | wollastonite |
| goethite | promethium | zoisite |
| | samarskite | |

1. **Brookite** was named for the English mineralogist Henry James Brooke, who described thirteen mineral species and first introduced the groups commonly used to classify forms of crystals. **Calaverite** was named for Calaveras County in California, where this mineral was discovered. Select twelve minerals from this list. Do research to discover the origins of their names.

2. Some of the minerals on this list are magnetic, and some of them are radioactive. Choose one of the minerals on the list and pretend that it has unusual characteristics and/or special powers. Write a story set in the future. Have the hero or heroine of the story use these characteristics or powers to rescue someone in distress.

# Nutrition Terms

absorption
alimentary canal
amino acids
assimilation
balanced diet
beriberi
bile
calcium
calorie
carbohydrates
carbon
carnivore
cell
cereals
chew
cholesterol
citrus
complete proteins
dairy products
deficiency
dehydration
diabetes
diet
digestion
empty calories
energy
enzyme

esophagus
fats (or lipids)
fatty acids
fiber
food groups
fruits
gall bladder
glands
glucose
glycerol
glycogen
goiter
grains
gram
herbivore
hormone
hydrogen
hydrolizing enzyme
incomplete proteins
insulin
iodine
iron
lecithin
liver
malnutrition
meats
metabolism
mouth

nitrogen
nourishment
nutrients
nutrition
omnivore
oxygen
pancreas
peristalsis
phosphorus
potassium
proteins
protoplasm
rickets
saliva
salivary amylase
salts
scurvy
small intestine
sphincter muscle
starches
stomach
sugars
swallow
teeth
vegetables
vitamins
water

First, select six of these terms. Next, do some research to learn what each one means. Then, write a paragraph in which you show what these terms have to do with nutrition and how they are related to one another. For example, you might choose **balanced diet**, **carbohydrates**, **fats**, **minerals**, **proteins**, and **water** and show that the latter five are components of the first.

# Plant and Flower Words

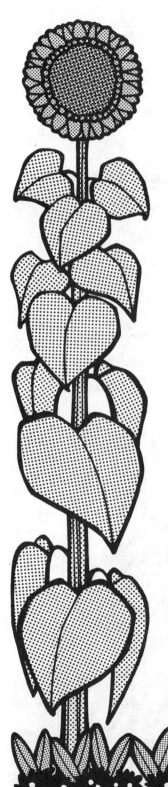
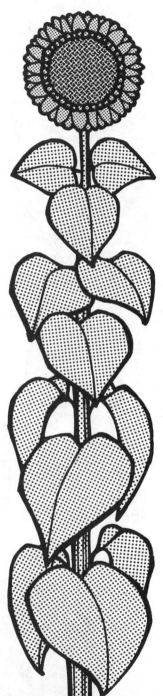

acerate
annual
anther
axil
blade
blossom
bud
bulb
chlorophyll
chloroplast
corm
cotyledons
cross-pollination
cutting
dormant
embryo
endosperm
epicotyl
exfoliate
fern
filament
foliage
fruit
germination
graft
herbaceous
hypocotyl
leaf
lobation
lobe
lobule
megasporangium
megaspore
osmosis
ovary
ovules
palmate

pedate
pedicel
peltate
perennial
petal
phloem
photosynthesis
pinnate
pistil
plumule
pollen
pollination
quinquefoliolate
respiration
rhizome
root
root hairs
root stock
runcinate
seed
sepal
serrate
spore
stalk
stamen
stem
stigma
style
succulent
thorn
transpiration
trifoliolate
tuber
vein
whorl
xylem

# Rocks

Rocks are classified into three major groups according to the way in which they were formed. **Igneous** rocks are volcanic in origin and are formed by the cooling and solidifying of magma. **Metamorphic** rocks are rocks that have been changed by the action of pressure, heat, and/or water to be more compact and more highly crystalline than they were originally. **Sedimentary** rocks are formed of mechanical, chemical, or organic deposits.

| Igneous | Metamorphic | Sedimentary |
|---|---|---|
| basalt | gneiss | breccia |
| gabbro | marble | clay |
| granite | quartzite | coal |
| obsidian | schist | conglomerate |
| peridotite | slate | flint |
| pumice | | limestone |
| rhyolite | | sandstone |
| scoria | | shale |
| svenite | | |

# Science Topics

| | | |
|---|---|---|
| aerodynamics | dinosaurs | hibernation |
| AIDS | disease | horses |
| airplanes | drugs | human body |
| allergies | earth | hurricanes |
| amphibians | earthquakes | immunity |
| anatomy | ecology | insects |
| animal behavior | electricity | inventions |
| astronomy | endangered animals | invertebrates |
| atomic energy | endocrine system | joints |
| atoms | energy | kaleidoscopes |
| automation | engines | light |
| bacteria | fingerprints | lizards |
| birds | first aid | lungs |
| boats | fishes | machines |
| botany | flight | magnetism |
| brain | flowers | mammals |
| cells | fossils | man-made satellites |
| chemistry | fruits | marine life |
| circulatory system | gardening | matter |
| color | genetics | metabolism |
| comets | geodes | meteors |
| computer axial tomography | geology | microscopes |
| computers | gravity | migration |
| conservation | habitats | minerals |
| constellations | heart | molecules |
| digestion | heat | muscular system |

# Science Topics
## (continued)

natural satellites
nervous system
nutrition
oceanography
optical illusions
osmosis
parasites
pest control
photosynthesis
physics
planets
plants
pollution
prehistoric life
public health
quasars

rain forests
recycling
reptiles
respiratory system
robots
rockets
rocks
seeds
senses
shells
snakes
solar energy
solar system
sound
spores
symbiosis

telescopes
terrariums
tides
tornadoes
trees
ultrasound
vaccines
vertebrates
vitamins
volcanoes
water
weather
wetlands
whales
X-rays
zoology

Select a topic from the list for independent study. Decorate the outside of a file folder to go with your topic. Inside the file folder, place the following items: (1) a title page, (2) a table of contents, (3) five pages of information about your topic, (4) illustrations to go with this information, (5) fifteen quiz questions covering your information, (6) a sheet of answers for the questions, and (7) a puzzle, maze, word search, or game based on your topic.

# Trees

| | |
|---|---|
| ailanthus | lime |
| alder | linden |
| almond | locust |
| apple | magnolia |
| ash | mahogany |
| aspen | maple |
| beech | myrtle |
| birch | oak |
| cedar | olive |
| cherry | orange |
| chestnut | palm |
| cycad | palmetto |
| cypress | peach |
| deodar | pear |
| elm | pecan |
| eucalyptus | pine |
| fig | poplar |
| fir | sequoia |
| grapefruit | spruce |
| hazel | sycamore |
| hemlock | walnut |
| hickory | willow |
| lemon | yew |

# Weather Words

altocumulus
altostratus
barometric pressure
Beaufort scale
blizzard
chinook
cirrocumulus
cirrostratus
cirrus
cloud
cloudburst
cold front
cumulocirrus
cumulonimbus
cumulostratus
cumulus
cyclone
dew
drizzle
false cirrus
foehn
fog
front
frost
hail
hailstone
haze
hoarfrost
humidity
hurricane

ice
icicle
lightning
mist
moisture
monsoon
nimbostratus
precipitation
rain
rime
Santa Ana
sleet
smog
snow
snowflakes
snowstorm
squall
stationary front
stratocumulus
stratus
temperature
thunder
thunderbolt
thunderstorm
thunderstorm cirrus
tornado
typhoon
warm front
wind
windstorm

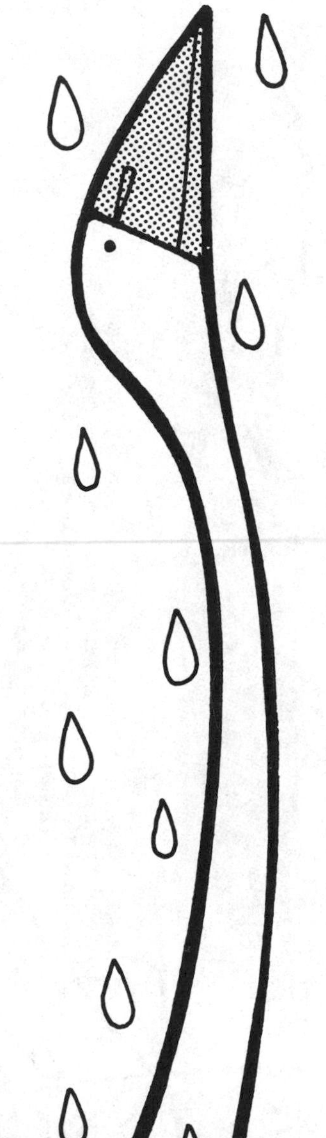

# Bonus Ideas for Science

1. Pick a topic from one of the science lists. Do research on this topic. Make a shoe box diorama depicting your topic, and write a one-page summary of your most important findings.

2. Choose a topic from one of the science lists and research it thoroughly. Wrap a grocery box with colored butcher, construction, or shelf paper. Paste interesting information and pictures about your topic on all six sides of the box.

3. Pick a topic from one of the science lists and research it thoroughly. Use cardboard, clay, papier-mâché, Popsicle sticks, soap, sugar cubes, or other appropriate media to construct a model related to the topic.

4. Choose two dinosaurs from the lists on pages 122 and 123. Do research to learn more about them. Make lists showing ways in which they were alike and ways in which they were different.

5. Select a reptile from the list on page 125. Design a postage stamp in honor of this reptile.

6. After referring to the lists on pages 127 and 128, create a new "itis." Describe its symptoms and tell how doctors will cure it.

7. Pick three constellations from the list on pages 136 and 137. Using gummed stars (available in stationery stores), make the patterns of these constellations on black construction paper and label each one.

Name _____

# Create a Science List

Think of a science-related topic that interests you. On the lines below, create a list that reflects this topic. Illustrate your list, and give it a title.

_____

_____

_____

_____

_____

_____

_____

_____

_____

_____

# Math

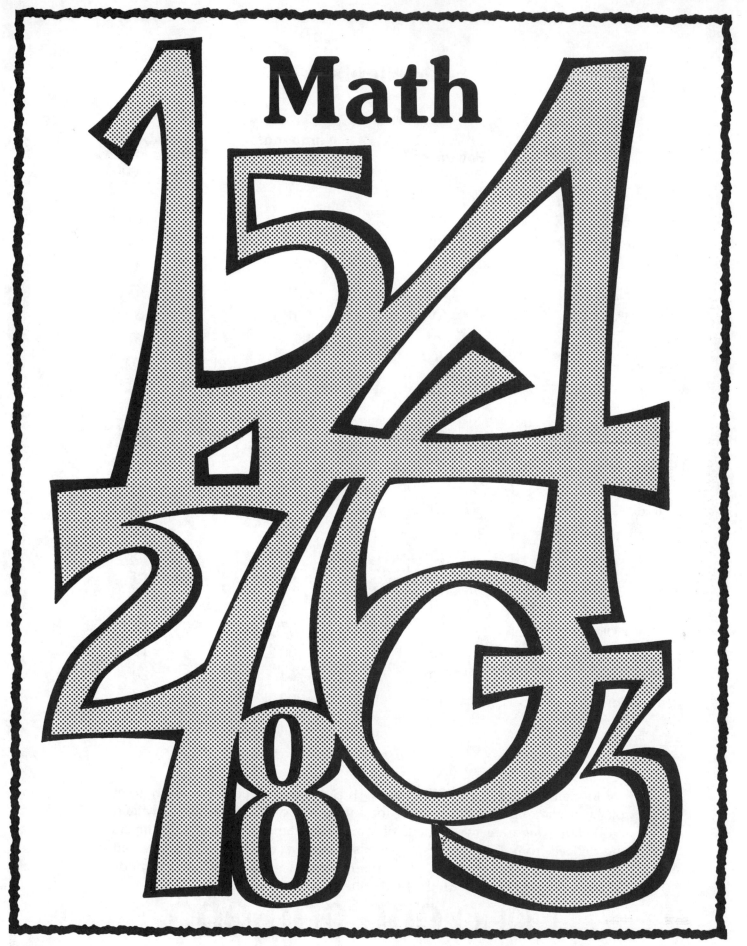

# Big Numbers

| Name | Value in Powers of Ten | Number of Zeros | Number of Periods of Zeros After 1,000* |
|---|---|---|---|
| million | $10^6$ | 6 | 1 |
| billion | $10^9$ | 9 | 2 |
| trillion | $10^{12}$ | 12 | 3 |
| quadrillion | $10^{15}$ | 15 | 4 |
| quintillion | $10^{18}$ | 18 | 5 |
| sextillion | $10^{21}$ | 21 | 6 |
| septillion | $10^{24}$ | 24 | 7 |
| octillion | $10^{27}$ | 27 | 8 |
| nonillion | $10^{30}$ | 30 | 9 |
| decillion | $10^{33}$ | 33 | 10 |
| undecillion | $10^{36}$ | 36 | 11 |
| duodecillion | $10^{39}$ | 39 | 12 |
| tredecillion | $10^{42}$ | 42 | 13 |
| quattuordecillion | $10^{45}$ | 45 | 14 |
| quindecillion | $10^{48}$ | 48 | 15 |
| sexdecillion | $10^{51}$ | 51 | 16 |
| septendecillion | $10^{54}$ | 54 | 17 |
| octodecillion | $10^{57}$ | 57 | 18 |
| novemdecillion | $10^{60}$ | 60 | 19 |
| vigintillion | $10^{63}$ | 63 | 20 |
| centillion | $10^{303}$ | 303 | 100 |

**\*** In mathematics, a **period of zeros** is a group of three zeros which is set off by a comma. For example, in the number one million, which is written 1,000,000, there are two periods of zeros. The names of these big numbers are derived from the numbers of periods of zeros after 1,000 which are used in writing them. For example, the prefix *tri-* means "three," and three periods of zeros after 1,000 are used to write the number one trillion.

1,000,000,000,000

# Math Signs and Symbols

| | | | |
|---|---|---|---|
| + | addition; plus | < | less than |
| ∠ | angle | — | line segment |
| ⌢ | arc | × | multiplication |
| ∷ | as, equal | # | number |
| @ | at | ‖ | parallel |
| ¢ | cent | % | percent |
| △ | change | ⊥ | perpendicular |
| ≅ | congruent | π | pi |
| • | decimal point | → | ray |
| ° | degree | ⌐ | right angle |
| ÷ | division | { } | set |
| $ | dollar | √ | square root |
| ∅ | empty set | − | subtraction |
| = | equal | Σ | summation |
| ≈ | equivalent | ∴ | therefore |
| > | greater than | ≠ | unequal |
| ƒ | function | ≉ | unequivalent |
| ∞ | infinity | ∪ | union (of sets) |
| ∩ | intersection (of sets) | ⇁ | vector |
| ∶ | is to | | |

# Math Terms

| | | |
|---|---|---|
| acute | exponent | percentile |
| addend | factor | perpendicular lines |
| addition | finite | place value |
| algebra | formula | plane |
| angle | fraction | point |
| apothem | geodesic | polynomial |
| arc | geometry | prime factor |
| area | graph | prime number |
| array | grid | probability |
| bi | hypotenuse | quotient |
| binomial | hypothesis | radius |
| bisect | imaginary number | ratio |
| bisector | infinite | real number |
| calculus | integer | reciprocal |
| cardinal number | intercept | remainder |
| chord | intersection | root |
| circumference | interval | secant |
| coefficient | inverse | set |
| concurrent line | line | sine |
| decimal | matrix | square root |
| diameter | minuend | subset |
| divided | multiplication | subtraction |
| division | negative number | symbol |
| element | numeral | tangent |
| equal | obtuse | theorem |
| equidistant | operation | union |
| equivalent | ordinal number | vector |
| expanded notation | parallel | vertices |
| | percent | |

# Metric Measurement

The metric system is a system of weights and measures that proceeds by tens and is based on the meter and the kilogram. In this system, length is measured in meters, weight is measured in grams, and capacity is measured in liters.

### Length
#### (number of meters)

| | | |
|---|---|---|
| myriameter (mym) | = | 10,000 |
| kilometer (km) | = | 1,000 |
| hectometer (hm) | = | 100 |
| dekameter (dam) | = | 10 |
| meter (m) | = | 1 |
| decimeter (dm) | = | 0.1 |
| centimeter (cm) | = | 0.01 |
| millimeter (mm) | = | 0.001 |

### Mass and Weight
#### (number of grams)

| | | |
|---|---|---|
| metric ton (MT) | = | 1,000,000 |
| quintal (q) | = | 100,000 |
| kilogram (kg) | = | 1,000 |
| hectogram (hg) | = | 100 |
| dekagram (dg) | = | 10 |
| gram (g or gm) | = | 1 |
| decigram (dg) | = | 0.1 |
| centigram (cg) | = | 0.01 |
| milligram (mg) | = | 0.001 |

### Capacity
#### (number of liters)

| | | |
|---|---|---|
| kiloliter (kl) | = | 1,000 |
| hectoliter (hl) | = | 100 |
| dekaliter (dal) | = | 10 |
| liter (l) | = | 1 |
| deciliter (dl) | = | 0.1 |
| centiliter (cl) | = | 0.01 |
| milliliter (ml) | = | 0.001 |

1. Use the information given above to fill in the blanks below.

   a. There are _____ millimeters in one centimeter.

   b. There are _____ centimeters in one meter.

   c. There are _____ millimeters in one meter.

   d. There are _____ deciliters in one liter.

   e. There are _____ milliliters in one liter.

2. For the system of weights and measures commonly used in England and the United States, length is measured in feet, yards, and miles; weight is measured in ounces and pounds; and capacity is measured in pints, quarts, and gallons. Make a table of equivalents that will help you convert measurements made in the units of one system to the units of the other system. For example, you might show how meters are related to yards.

# Roman Numerals

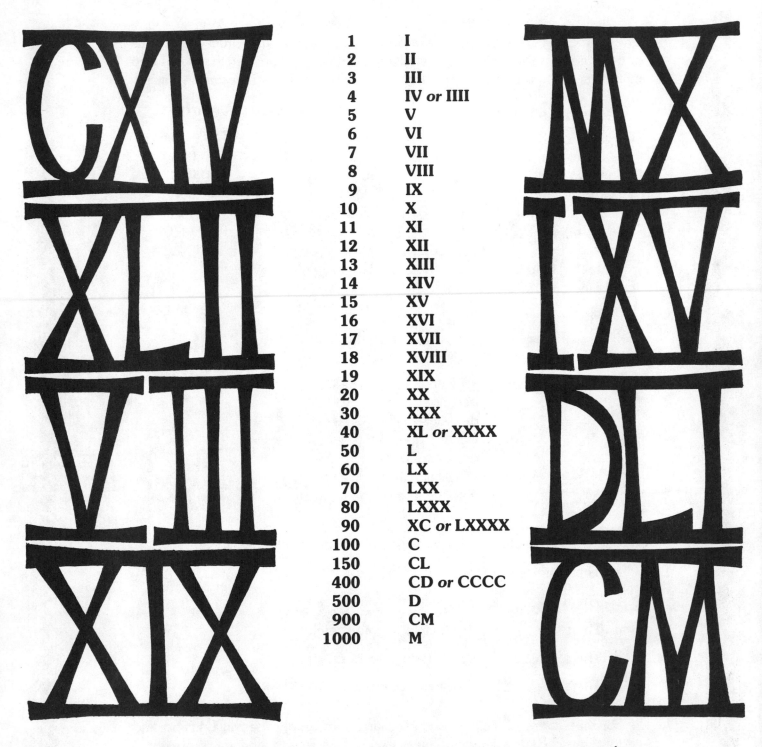

| | |
|---|---|
| 1 | I |
| 2 | II |
| 3 | III |
| 4 | IV *or* IIII |
| 5 | V |
| 6 | VI |
| 7 | VII |
| 8 | VIII |
| 9 | IX |
| 10 | X |
| 11 | XI |
| 12 | XII |
| 13 | XIII |
| 14 | XIV |
| 15 | XV |
| 16 | XVI |
| 17 | XVII |
| 18 | XVIII |
| 19 | XIX |
| 20 | XX |
| 30 | XXX |
| 40 | XL *or* XXXX |
| 50 | L |
| 60 | LX |
| 70 | LXX |
| 80 | LXXX |
| 90 | XC *or* LXXXX |
| 100 | C |
| 150 | CL |
| 400 | CD *or* CCCC |
| 500 | D |
| 900 | CM |
| 1000 | M |

1. Write the year of your birth and the current year in roman numerals.

2. The copyright years for motion pictures are usually written in roman numerals. The next time you watch a movie at home or in a theater, see if you can read this year when it appears on the screen at the beginning or end of the film.

# Shapes

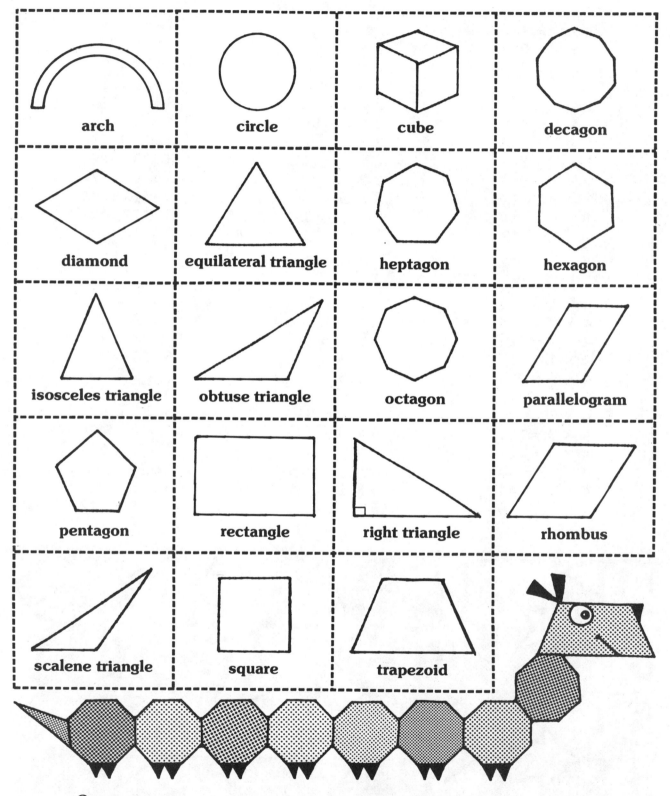

| | | | |
|---|---|---|---|
| arch | circle | cube | decagon |
| diamond | equilateral triangle | heptagon | hexagon |
| isosceles triangle | obtuse triangle | octagon | parallelogram |
| pentagon | rectangle | right triangle | rhombus |
| scalene triangle | square | trapezoid | |

Create a creature using some of the shapes from the list. Add other features such as a mouth, eyes, ears, and a nose.

# Times Tables

| | | |
|---|---|---|
| 1 × 1 = 1 | 2 × 1 = 2 | 3 × 1 = 3 |
| 1 × 2 = 2 | 2 × 2 = 4 | 3 × 2 = 6 |
| 1 × 3 = 3 | 2 × 3 = 6 | 3 × 3 = 9 |
| 1 × 4 = 4 | 2 × 4 = 8 | 3 × 4 = 12 |
| 1 × 5 = 5 | 2 × 5 = 10 | 3 × 5 = 15 |
| 1 × 6 = 6 | 2 × 6 = 12 | 3 × 6 = 18 |
| 1 × 7 = 7 | 2 × 7 = 14 | 3 × 7 = 21 |
| 1 × 8 = 8 | 2 × 8 = 16 | 3 × 8 = 24 |
| 1 × 9 = 9 | 2 × 9 = 18 | 3 × 9 = 27 |
| 1 × 10 = 10 | 2 × 10 = 20 | 3 × 10 = 30 |
| 1 × 11 = 11 | 2 × 11 = 22 | 3 × 11 = 33 |
| 1 × 12 = 12 | 2 × 12 = 24 | 3 × 12 = 36 |

| | | |
|---|---|---|
| 4 × 1 = 4 | 5 × 1 = 5 | 6 × 1 = 6 |
| 4 × 2 = 8 | 5 × 2 = 10 | 6 × 2 = 12 |
| 4 × 3 = 12 | 5 × 3 = 15 | 6 × 3 = 18 |
| 4 × 4 = 16 | 5 × 4 = 20 | 6 × 4 = 24 |
| 4 × 5 = 20 | 5 × 5 = 25 | 6 × 5 = 30 |
| 4 × 6 = 24 | 5 × 6 = 30 | 6 × 6 = 36 |
| 4 × 7 = 28 | 5 × 7 = 35 | 6 × 7 = 42 |
| 4 × 8 = 32 | 5 × 8 = 40 | 6 × 8 = 48 |
| 4 × 9 = 36 | 5 × 9 = 45 | 6 × 9 = 54 |
| 4 × 10 = 40 | 5 × 10 = 50 | 6 × 10 = 60 |
| 4 × 11 = 44 | 5 × 11 = 55 | 6 × 11 = 66 |
| 4 × 12 = 48 | 5 × 12 = 60 | 6 × 12 = 72 |

# Times Tables
## (continued)

| | | |
|---|---|---|
| 7 × 1 = 7 | 8 × 1 = 8 | 9 × 1 = 9 |
| 7 × 2 = 14 | 8 × 2 = 16 | 9 × 2 = 18 |
| 7 × 3 = 21 | 8 × 3 = 24 | 9 × 3 = 27 |
| 7 × 4 = 28 | 8 × 4 = 32 | 9 × 4 = 36 |
| 7 × 5 = 35 | 8 × 5 = 40 | 9 × 5 = 45 |
| 7 × 6 = 42 | 8 × 6 = 48 | 9 × 6 = 54 |
| 7 × 7 = 49 | 8 × 7 = 56 | 9 × 7 = 63 |
| 7 × 8 = 56 | 8 × 8 = 64 | 9 × 8 = 72 |
| 7 × 9 = 63 | 8 × 9 = 72 | 9 × 9 = 81 |
| 7 × 10 = 70 | 8 × 10 = 80 | 9 × 10 = 90 |
| 7 × 11 = 77 | 8 × 11 = 88 | 9 × 11 = 99 |
| 7 × 12 = 84 | 8 × 12 = 96 | 9 × 12 = 108 |

| | | |
|---|---|---|
| 10 × 1 = 10 | 11 × 1 = 11 | 12 × 1 = 12 |
| 10 × 2 = 20 | 11 × 2 = 22 | 12 × 2 = 24 |
| 10 × 3 = 30 | 11 × 3 = 33 | 12 × 3 = 36 |
| 10 × 4 = 40 | 11 × 4 = 44 | 12 × 4 = 48 |
| 10 × 5 = 50 | 11 × 5 = 55 | 12 × 5 = 60 |
| 10 × 6 = 60 | 11 × 6 = 66 | 12 × 6 = 72 |
| 10 × 7 = 70 | 11 × 7 = 77 | 12 × 7 = 84 |
| 10 × 8 = 80 | 11 × 8 = 88 | 12 × 8 = 96 |
| 10 × 9 = 90 | 11 × 9 = 99 | 12 × 9 = 108 |
| 10 × 10 = 100 | 11 × 10 = 110 | 12 × 10 = 120 |
| 10 × 11 = 110 | 11 × 11 = 121 | 12 × 11 = 132 |
| 10 × 12 = 120 | 11 × 12 = 132 | 12 × 12 = 144 |

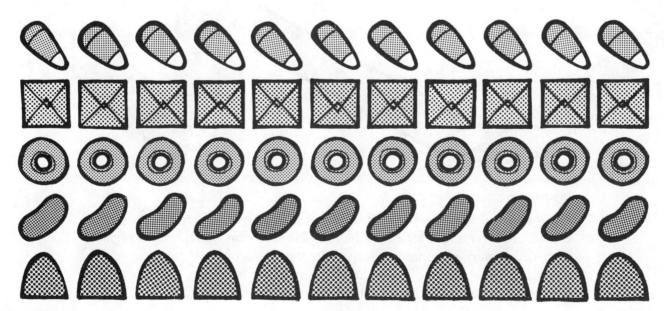

# Units of Measure

acre
ampere
angstrom
bale
barrel
bushel
calorie
cord
coulomb
cycle
decibel
degree
dram
erg
faraday
fathom
furlong
gallon
gill
grain
gram
hectare
hertz
horsepower
joule
karat

kilogram
kilowatt-hour
league
light-year
liter
lumen
meter
micron
mile
minim
minute
mole
peck
pennyweight
pica
pint
point
quire
rad
ream
rod
roentgen
scruple
second
volt
watt

1. Do research to discover what each one of the units on this list is used to measure.

2. The **ampere**, which is the unit in which the intensity of an electric current is measured, is named for André M. Ampère. Ampère was a French physicist who discovered important principles in the fields of both magnetism and electricity. Many units of measure are named for scientists. Do research to find at least five units on this list that were so named.

# Weight, Measurement, and Time

## Linear Measure

| | |
|---|---|
| 12 inches | = 1 foot |
| 3 feet | = 1 yard |
| 5½ yards | = 1 rod |
| 40 rods | = 1 furlong |
| 8 furlongs | = 1 statute mile |

## Square Measure

| | |
|---|---|
| 144 square inches | = 1 square foot |
| 9 square feet | = 1 square yard |
| 30¼ square yards | = 1 square rod |
| 160 square rods | = 1 acre |
| 640 acres | = 1 square mile |

## Liquid Measure

| | |
|---|---|
| 3 teaspoons | = 1 tablespoon |
| 2 tablespoons | = 1 ounce |
| 8 ounces | = 1 cup |
| 2 cups | = 1 pint |
| 2 pints | = 1 quart |
| 4 quarts | = 1 gallon |

## Dry Measure

| | |
|---|---|
| 2 pints | = 1 quart |
| 8 quarts | = 1 peck |
| 4 pecks | = 1 bushel |

## Time Measure

| | |
|---|---|
| 60 seconds | = 1 minute |
| 60 minutes | = 1 hour |
| 24 hours | = 1 day |
| 7 days | = 1 week |
| 4 weeks | = 1 month |
| | (28–31 days) |
| 12 months | = 1 year |
| 10 years | = 1 decade |
| 20 years | = 1 score |
| 100 years | = 1 century |

## Weight

| | |
|---|---|
| 16 ounces | = 1 pound |
| 2,000 pounds | = 1 ton |

1. Use the information given above to fill in the blanks below.

   a. There are _____ feet in a statute mile.

   b. There are _____ yards in a furlong.

   c. There are _____ yards in a statute mile.

   d. There are _____ tablespoons in a cup.

   e. There are _____ pints in a gallon.

2. While there are four weeks in a lunar month, the number of days in a calendar month varies from 28 to 31. If there are 365 days in a year and these days are divided among 12 months, what is the average number of days in a month?

   _____ days

# Who's Who in Math

| | |
|---|---|
| **Niels Henrik Abel** | Norwegian mathematician known for research in the theory of elliptic functions |
| **Howard Aiken** | Harvard University professor who built the first working digital computer in 1944 |
| **Archimedes** | Greek mathematician and inventor who wrote treatises in which he outlined the methods of integral calculus |
| **George Atwood** | English mathematician who wrote many books about math and invented a machine for verifying the laws of acceleration of motion |
| **Charles Babbage** | English mathematician and mechanical genius whose "analytic engine" was the forerunner of present-day calculators and computers |
| **Eugenio Beltrami** | Italian mathematician and physicist known for his work in non-Euclidian geometry |
| **János Bolyai** | Hungarian mathematician who wrote a complete system of geometry at the age of twenty-two |
| **George Boole** | English mathematician and logician who helped develop modern symbolic logic |
| **Vannevar Bush** | American electrical engineer who devised a machine for solving differential equations and, in doing so, built the first modern analog computer |
| **Georg Cantor** | German mathematician known for his work on set theory and on the theory of the infinite |
| **René Descartes** | French scientist, philosopher, and mathematician who is called the "father of modern mathematics" |
| **Euclid** | Greek mathematician who devised the theorems and problems that form a logical system of geometry |
| **Leonhard Euler** | Swiss mathematician and physicist considered to be one of the founders of the science of pure mathematics |
| **Pierre de Fermat** | French mathematician considered to be the founder of the modern theory of numbers and to have invented differential calculus and the calculus of probability |
| **Joseph Fourier** | French geometrician and physicist known for research in the theory of numerical equations |
| **David Hilbert** | German mathematician who reduced geometry to a system of axioms |
| **Howard Kasner** | American mathematician who is known for his work in higher geometry and who coined the terms *googol* and *googolplex* |
| **Pierre Simon de Laplace** | French mathematician who did outstanding work in the fields of celestial mechanics, probability, differential equations, and geodesy |
| **James Clerk Maxwell** | Scottish physicist who developed a mathematical theory to explain electromagnetic activity |
| **John Napier** | Scottish mathematician who invented logarithms and pioneered in the use of the present system of decimal notation |
| **John von Neumann** | American mathematician who wrote a book on the quantum theory and won the Fermi Award for work on the theory, design, and construction of computers |
| **Sir Isaac Newton** | English mathematician credited with the invention of both differential and integral calculus |
| **Blaise Pascal** | French scientist and philosopher who originated, with Fermat, the mathematical theory of probability |

# Bonus Ideas for Math

1. Write a science fiction story using some of the larger numbers from the list on page 162.

2. Brainstorm with your classmates to create a list of ways in which your life would be different if there were no numbers at all. For example, there would be no clocks as we now have, our telephone dialing system would be different, and speedometers on cars would have no meaning. Use this list to write a short story entitled "The Day the Numbers Disappeared."

3. From the list on page 164, select ten math terms that are unfamiliar to you. Use a dictionary or advanced mathematics textbook to discover the meanings of these terms.

4. Referring to the list on page 166, create addition and subtraction problems for a classmate using only Roman numerals.

5. Select a famous mathematician from the list on page 172. Do research to learn more about the life and achievements of this person.

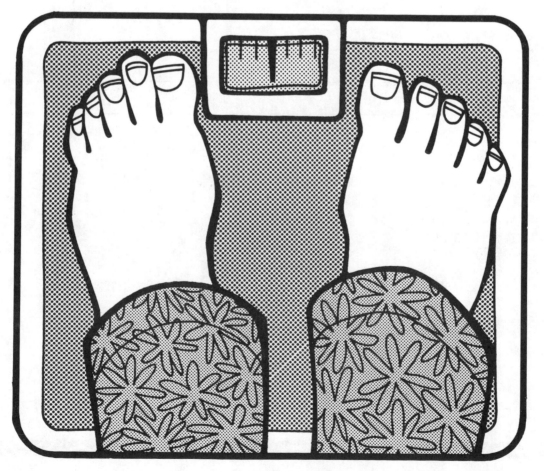

Name _____

# Create a Math List

Think of a math topic that interests you. On the lines below, create a list that reflects this topic. Illustrate your list and give it a title.

_____

_____

_____

_____

_____

_____

_____

_____

_____

# The Arts
# & Sports

# Composers

composer (kəm-pō´-zər), *n.*: a person who writes music

## Baroque Period
*Late 1500s to Middle 1700s*

Johann Sebastian Bach (1685–1750)
Dietrich Buxtehude (*ca.* 1637–1707)
George Frederick Handel (1685–1759)
Jean Baptiste Lully (1632–1687)
Claudio Monteverdi (1567–1643)
Johann Pachelbel (1653–1706)
Henry Purcell (1659–1695)
Alessandro Scarlatti (1659–1725)
Domenico Scarlatti (1685–1757)

## Rococo Period
*Last Thirty to Forty Years of the
Baroque Period*

Karl Philipp Emanuel Bach (1714–1788)
Antonio Vivaldi (*ca.* 1675–1741)

## Classical Period
*Middle 1700s to Early 1800s*

Ludwig van Beethoven (1770–1827)
Muzio Clementi (1752–1832)
Christoph Willibald Gluck (1714–1787)
Joseph Haydn (1732–1809)
Wolfgang Amadeus Mozart (1756–1791)

## Romantic Period
*Early 1800s to Late 1800s*

Vincenzo Bellini (1801–1835)
Hector Berlioz (1803–1869)
Georges Bizet (1838–1875)
Johannes Brahms (1833–1897)
Frédéric Chopin (1810–1849)
Gaetano Donizetti (1797–1848)
Anton Dvořák (1841–1904)
César Auguste Franck (1822–1890)
Edvard Grieg (1843–1907)
Stephen Collins Foster (1826–1864)
Ruggiero Leoncavallo (1858–1919)
Franz Liszt (1811–1886)
Edward MacDowell (1861–1908)
Felix Mendelssohn (1809–1847)
Modest Moussorgsky (1835–1881)
Jacques Offenbach (1819–1880)
Giacomo Puccini (1858–1924)
Nikolai Rimsky-Korsakov (1844–1908)
Gioacchino Rossini (1792–1868)
Camille Saint-Saens (1835–1921)
Franz Schubert (1797–1828)
Robert Schumann (1810–1856)
John Philip Sousa (1854–1932)
Johann Strauss (1825–1899)
Peter Ilyich Tchaikovsky (1840–1893)
Giuseppe Verdi (1813–1901)
Richard Wagner (1813–1886)

# Composers
## (continued)

## Modern Period
*Late 1800s to Middle 1900s*

Béla Bartók (1881-1945)
Irving Berlin (1888-    )
George M. Cohan (1878-1942)
Claude Debussy (1862-1918)
George Gershwin (1898-1937)
Woodrow Wilson ("Woody") Guthrie
   (1912-1967)
Englebert Humperdinck (1854-1921)
Charles Edward Ives (1874-1954)
Scott Joplin (1868-1917)
Jerome Kern (1885-1945)
Cole Porter (1893-1964)
Sergei Prokofiev (1891-1953)
Sergei Rachmaninov (1873-1943)
Maurice Ravel (1875-1937)
Richard Rodgers (1902-1979)
Sigmund Romberg (1887-1951)
Arnold Schoenberg (1874-1951)
Alexander Scriabin (1872-1915)
Jean Sibelius (1865-1957)
Richard Strauss (1864-1949)
Igor Stravinsky (1882-1971)
Jule Styne (1905-    )
Kurt Weill (1900-1950)
Hank Williams (1923-1953)

## Contemporary Period
*Middle 1900s to Present*

Leonard Bernstein (1918-    )
Benjamin Britten (1913-1976)
Aaron Copland (1900-    )
Ferde Grofé (1892-1972)
John Lennon (1940-1980)
Henry Mancini (1924-    )
Lalo Schifrin (1932-    )
Dimitri Shostakovich (1906-1975)
Stephen Sondheim (1930-    )
Dimitri Tiomkin (1894-1979)
Andrew Lloyd Webber (1948-    )
John Towner Williams (1932-    )
Ralph Vaughn Williams (1872-1958)
Meredith Willson (1902-1984)

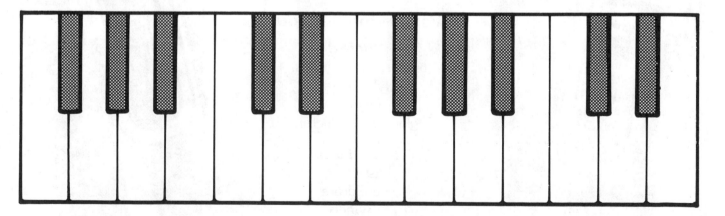

Use this list of composers to write a trivia puzzle for a friend. Study these examples, and then give it a try.

1. Which composer wrote the opera *Hansel and Gretel*?
2. Who wrote the music for *Oklahoma* and *Carousel*?
3. Who wrote the music for *Star Wars*?

# Instruments of an Orchestra

## String Section

violin
viola
cello
double bass
piano
harp

## Woodwind Section

piccolo
flute
oboe
English horn
clarinet
bass clarinet
bassoon
contrabassoon

## Brass Section

trumpet
trombone
French horn
tuba

## Percussion Section

### *Pitched*
timpani (kettledrums)
xylophone
chimes
glockenspiel (bells)

### *Nonpitched*
bass drum
snare drum
castanets
cymbals
gong
tambourine
triangle
woodblocks

# Other Musical Instruments

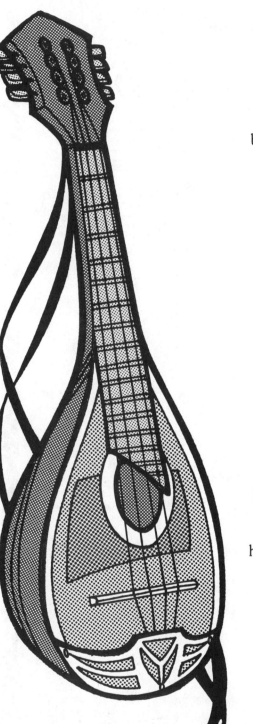

| | |
|---|---|
| accordion | lyre |
| autoharp | mandolin |
| bagpipe | maracas |
| balalaika | marimba |
| bandore | mellophone |
| banjo | monochord |
| barrel organ | ocarina |
| bugle | organ |
| calliope | pandora |
| celesta | panpipe |
| chitarrone | piano accordion |
| clavichord | pibgorn |
| clavier | pipe |
| concertina | psaltery |
| cornet | rebec |
| crwth | recorder |
| dulcimer | saxhorn |
| fife | saxophone |
| flageolet | saxtuba |
| flügelhorn | sitar |
| gamelan | sousaphone |
| gittern | spinet |
| guiro | tabla |
| guitar | tabor |
| harmonica | taboret |
| harpsichord | tamboura |
| helicon | tamburitza |
| hornpipe | tam-tam |
| hurdy-gurdy | timbrel |
| Irish harp | tom-tom |
| Jew's harp | ukulele |
| kantele | vina |
| koto | zither |
| lute | |

# Musical Symbols

| | | | |
|---|---|---|---|
| whole note | 𝅝 | treble clef sign | 𝄞 |
| half note | 𝅗𝅥 | bass clef sign | 𝄢 |
| quarter note | ♩ | staff | |
| eighth note | ♪ | bar | |
| sixteenth note | 𝅘𝅥𝅯 | very loud | *ff* |
| whole rest | 𝄻 | loud (forte) | *f* |
| half rest | 𝄼 | moderately loud | *mf* |
| quarter rest | 𝄽 | moderately soft | *mp* |
| eighth rest | 𝄾 | soft (piano) | *p* |
| sixteenth rest | 𝄿 | very soft | *pp* |
| sharp | ♯ | crescendo (growing louder) | > |
| flat | ♭ | decrescendo (growing softer) | < |

# Musical Terms

| | |
|---|---|
| *adagio* | slowly; in an easy, graceful manner |
| *allegro* | in a brisk, lively manner |
| **bass** | the lower half of the whole vocal or instrumental tonal range |
| **chord** | tones that are sounded together |
| **clef** | a sign placed at the beginning of a musical staff to determine the position of the notes |
| *dolce* | in a soft, smooth, and sweet manner |
| **downbeat** | the first accented beat in a measure |
| *forte* | with strength; in a loud and forceful manner |
| *glissando* | a slide or a passing from one tone to another by a continuous change of pitch |
| **harmony** | the simultaneous combination of musical notes in a chord that is pleasing to the ear |
| **improvise** | to make up melodies while playing without a set plan |
| **interval** | the distance between the pitch of two different tones |
| **key** | scale or system of related tones which are based on, or named by, a key note |
| **key note** | the tone on which a scale or system of related tones is based |
| **key signature** | the sharps or flats placed after a clef to indicate the key in which a musical work has been written and/or is to be played |
| *largo* | in a very slow and broad manner |
| *legato* | in a manner that is smooth and connected |
| *lento* | very slowly |
| **measure** | a group of beats marked off by regularly recurring primary accents |
| *moderato* | at a medium tempo |
| *piano* | in a soft or quiet manner |
| **pitch** | the relation of one tone to another |
| *presto* | at a rapid tempo; very fast |
| **scale** | a graduated series of musical tones ascending or descending in order of pitch and according to a specified scheme of their intervals |
| *staccato* | in a manner that is short, clear-cut, and disconnected |
| **staff** | the lines and spaces on which musical notes are written |
| **tempo** | rate of speed |
| **treble** | the higher half of the whole vocal or instrumental tonal range |
| *vivace* | in a brisk and spirited manner; lively |

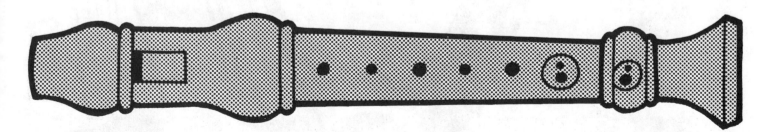

# Sing It

| | |
|---|---|
| a cappella | libretto |
| alto | lullaby |
| aria | lyric |
| ballad | madrigal |
| barbershop | march |
| bass | melody |
| bird song | minstrel |
| blues | note |
| calypso | opera |
| cantata | operetta |
| carol | oratorio |
| cavatina | part-song |
| chanson | pop |
| chant | popular song |
| chantey | quartet |
| chorus | quintet |
| country and western | recitative |
| croon | refrain |
| dirge | rhythm and blues |
| ditty | rock |
| duet | round |
| falsetto | scale |
| folk song | scat |
| glee | soprano |
| harmony | spiritual |
| hum | tenor |
| hymn | trio |
| jazz | troubadour |
| jingle | tune |
| lament | verse |
| lay | yodel |

# Famous Dancers

| | |
|---|---|
| Frederick Ashton | Danny Kaye |
| Fred Astaire | Gene Kelly |
| Mikhail Baryshnikov | Gelsey Kirkland |
| Michael Bennett | Alicia Markova |
| Ray Bolger | Ann Miller |
| Irene Castle | Arthur Murray |
| Vernon Castle | Kathryn Murray |
| Marian Chace | Waslaw Nijinsky |
| Gower Champion | Rudolf Nureyev |
| Marge Champion | Donald O'Connor |
| Cyd Charisse | Anna Pavlova |
| Merce Cunningham | Marius Petipa |
| Agnes De Mille | Juliet Prowse |
| Isadora Duncan | Ginger Rogers |
| Katherine Dunham | Ruth St. Denis |
| Margot Fonteyn | Moira Shearer |
| Bob Fosse | Michael Somes |
| Martha Graham | Maria Tallchief |
| José Greco | Helen Tamiris |
| Beryl Grey | Paul Taylor |
| Joel Grey | Tommy Tune |
| Robert Helpmann | Dick Van Dyke |
| Doris Humphrey | Ben Vereen |
| Gregory Hines | Thommie Walsh |

# Kinds of Dances

| | |
|---|---|
| allemande | mambo |
| ballet | mazurka |
| ballroom dance | minuet |
| belly dance | modern dance |
| bolero | morris |
| bossa nova | pavane |
| break dance | polka |
| bunny hop | polonaise |
| cancan | promenade |
| cha-cha | quadrille |
| Charleston | rag |
| clog dance | reel |
| conga | rhumba |
| cotillion | rigadoon |
| fandango | samba |
| flamenco | saraband |
| folk dance | schottische |
| fox-trot | soft shoe |
| galop | square dance |
| gavotte | stomp |
| hora | swing dance |
| hornpipe | sword dance |
| hula | tango |
| jazz dance | tap dance |
| jig | tarantella |
| jitterbug | twist |
| limbo | two-step |
| lindy | Virginia reel |
| malagueña | waltz |

1. Select ten of these dances and do research to discover when and where each one of them originated.

2. With a friend or partner, learn one of these dances well enough to demonstrate the steps and teach it to someone else.

3. Some dances, such as the **fox trot** and the **bunny hop**, are named for animals. Create and demonstrate a new dance named for an animal. For example, your new dance might be called the "swallow sway" or the "turtle trudge."

# Plays by William Shakespeare

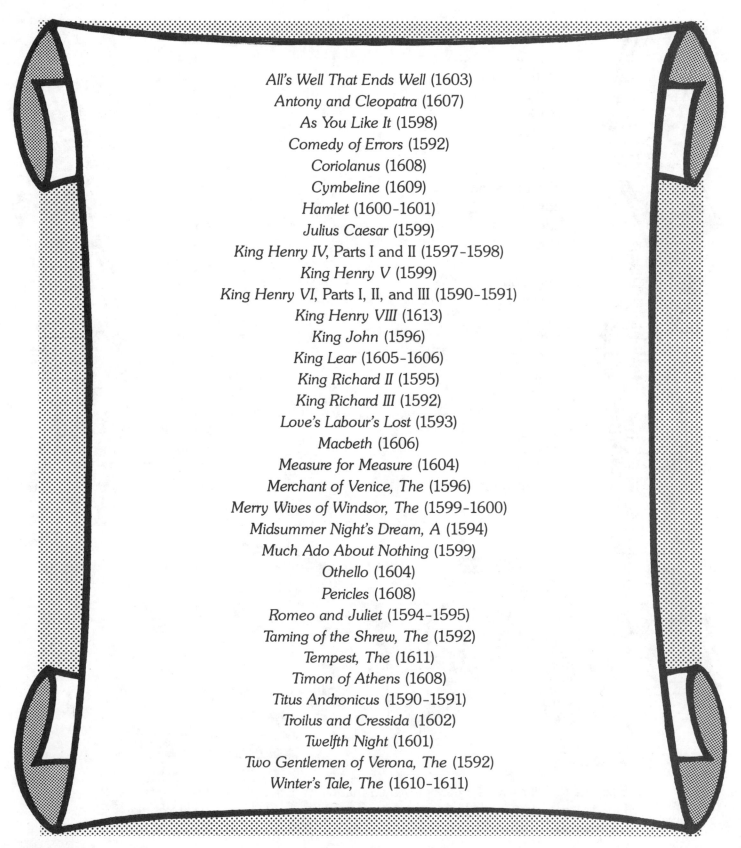

All's Well That Ends Well (1603)
Antony and Cleopatra (1607)
As You Like It (1598)
Comedy of Errors (1592)
Coriolanus (1608)
Cymbeline (1609)
Hamlet (1600-1601)
Julius Caesar (1599)
King Henry IV, Parts I and II (1597-1598)
King Henry V (1599)
King Henry VI, Parts I, II, and III (1590-1591)
King Henry VIII (1613)
King John (1596)
King Lear (1605-1606)
King Richard II (1595)
King Richard III (1592)
Love's Labour's Lost (1593)
Macbeth (1606)
Measure for Measure (1604)
Merchant of Venice, The (1596)
Merry Wives of Windsor, The (1599-1600)
Midsummer Night's Dream, A (1594)
Much Ado About Nothing (1599)
Othello (1604)
Pericles (1608)
Romeo and Juliet (1594-1595)
Taming of the Shrew, The (1592)
Tempest, The (1611)
Timon of Athens (1608)
Titus Andronicus (1590-1591)
Troilus and Cressida (1602)
Twelfth Night (1601)
Two Gentlemen of Verona, The (1592)
Winter's Tale, The (1610-1611)

# Theater Terms

| | |
|---|---|
| ad-lib | offstage |
| applause | onstage |
| arena theater | panel |
| auditorium | pantomime |
| block | playbill |
| borderlight | plot |
| cast | props |
| center stage | punch line |
| choreographer | rehearsal |
| costume | scrim |
| cue | script |
| curtain | set |
| curtain call | soliloquy |
| deadpan | spotlight |
| dialogue | stage |
| diction | stage left |
| dimmer | stage right |
| director | striplight |
| downstage | switchboard |
| drama | theater |
| flat | theater-in-the-round |
| footlights | understudy |
| key lines | upstage |
| makeup | wagon |
| monologue | walk-on |
| narrator | walk-through |

Become familiar with the theater-related meanings of twenty-five of these terms. Use these terms correctly in an original one-act play for which the setting is the theater.

# Architects

| Names | Achievements |
|---|---|
| Max Abramovitz | Avery Fisher Hall, Lincoln Center, New York City |
| Henry Bacon | Lincoln Memorial, Washington, D.C. |
| Marcel Breuer | Whitney Museum of American Art, New York City |
| Callicrates | Collaborated with Ictinus in designing the Parthenon on the Acropolis in Athens, Greece |
| Alexandre Gustave Eiffel | Eiffel Tower, Paris, France |
| R. Buckminster Fuller | U.S. Pavilion, Expo 67, Montreal, Canada |
| Michael Graves | Addition to Whitney Museum of American Art, New York City; Regional Library, San Juan Capistrano, California |
| Walter Gropius | Pan Am Building, New York City |
| James Hoban | The White House, Washington, D.C. |
| Raymond Hood | Rockefeller Center, New York City |
| Ictinus | Parthenon on the Acropolis in Athens, Greece |
| Imhotep | Egyptian creator of the step pyramid |
| Philip C. Johnson | State Theater, Lincoln Center, New York City |
| Louis Le Vau | Parts of the Louvre and the Tuileries in Paris, France; began work on the Palace of Versailles in France |
| Sir Edwin L. Lutyens | New British Embassy, Washington, D.C. |
| Jules Hardouin-Mansart | Completed the Palace of Versailles in France |
| Ludwig Mies van der Rohe | Seagram Building, New York City (with Philip C. Johnson) |
| Robert Mills | Washington Monument, Washington, D.C. |
| Richard J. Neutra | Orange County Courthouse, Santa Ana, California |
| Gyo Obata | National Air and Space Museum, Smithsonian Institution, Washington, D.C. |
| Frederick L. Olmstead | Central Park, New York City |
| William Pereira | Transamerica Building, San Francisco, California |
| John Russell Pope | National Gallery, Washington, D.C. |
| Eero Saarinen | Gateway to the West Arch, St. Louis, Missouri |
| Louis H. Sullivan | Auditorium Building, Chicago, Illinois; Wainwright Building, St. Louis, Missouri |
| Frank Lloyd Wright | Johnson Wax Company, Racine, Wisconsin; Guggenheim Museum, New York City |
| William Wurster | Ghirardelli Square, San Francisco, California |
| Minoru Yamasaki | World Trade Center, New York City |

Above are listed the names of twenty-eight architects with an example of at least one structure designed by each. Select one of these architects and do research to discover the names and locations of at least two additional buildings he designed.

# Artists

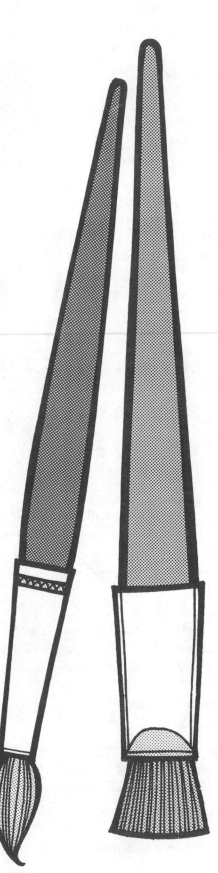

Fra Angelico
John James Audubon
Cicely Barker
George Bellows
Thomas Hart Benton
Sandro Botticelli
Georges Braque
Mary Cassatt
George Catlin
Paul Cézanne
Marc Chagall
Jules Chéret
John Singleton Copley
Gustave Courbet
Henri Edmond Cross
Nathaniel Currier
Salvador Dali
Honoré Daumier
Jacques Louis David
Hilaire Germain Edgar Degas
Marcel Duchamp
Raoul Dufy
Albrecht Dürer
Thomas Eakins
Jan van Eyck
Jean Honoré Fragonard
Thomas Gainsborough
Paul Gauguin
Giotto
Vincent van Gogh
El Greco
William Hogarth
Winslow Homer
Jean Auguste Dominique Ingres
James M. Ives
Vasily Kandinsky
Paul Klee
Leonardo da Vinci
Edouard Manet
Reginald Marsh
Henri Matisse
Michelangelo Buonarroti
Jean François Millet

# Artists
## (continued)

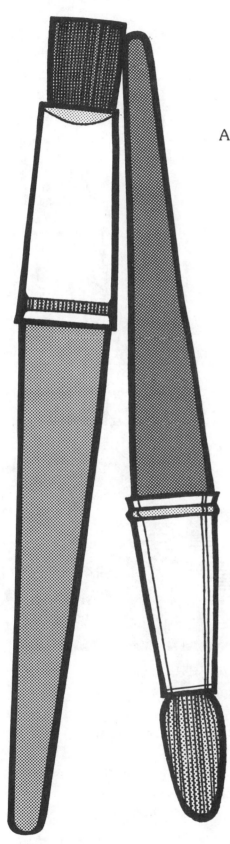

Joan Miró
Amedeo Modigliani
Piet Mondrian
Claude Monet
Berthe Morisot
Anne Mary Roberts ("Grandma") Moses
Alphonse Mucha
Edvard Munch
John Nieto
Georgia O'Keefe
José Clemente Orozco
Pablo Picasso
Camille Jacob Pissarro
Jackson Pollack
Edward Henry Potthast
Maurice B. Prendergast
Raphael
Rembrandt van Rijn
Frederic Remington
Pierre Auguste Renoir
Joshua Reynolds
Diego Rivera
Georges Rouault
Henri Rousseau
Peter Paul Rubens
John Singer Sargent
Georges Pierre Seurat
David Alfaro Siqueiros
John Sloan
Sally Strand
Gilbert Stuart
Tintoretto
Titian
Henri de Toulouse-Lautrec
Maurice Utrillo
Andy Warhol
Benjamin West
James Abbott McNeill Whistler
Carl Wimar
Grant Wood
C. L. Woodhouse
Andrew Wyeth
N. C. Wyeth

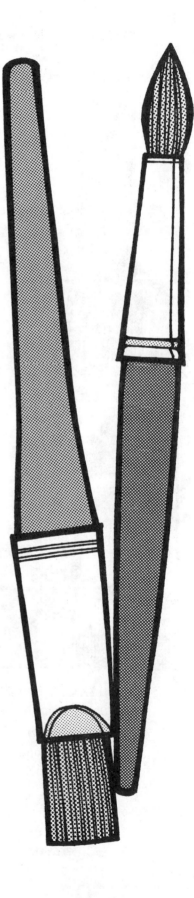

# Arts and Crafts

| | |
|---|---|
| acrylics | fashion design |
| batik | graphic design |
| block printing | jewelry making |
| book binding | knitting |
| calligraphy | macramé |
| candle making | model building |
| carpentry | needlepoint |
| cartooning | oil painting |
| carving | origami |
| ceramics | paper making |
| champlevé | photography |
| china painting | printmaking |
| cloisonné | puppet making |
| crewelwork | quilting |
| crocheting | rug making |
| decoupage | sculpting |
| doodle art | sewing |
| dough art | silk-screening |
| drawing | textile design |
| embroidery | tie dying |
| enameling | watercolor painting |
| etching | weaving |
| fabric painting | woodcraft |

1. Collect pictures or actual examples of objects created or decorated by means of some of these arts or crafts and display them in a **Classroom Crafts Corner**.

2. Add books containing step-by-step instructions or patterns to this special corner.

3. Learn enough about one of these arts or crafts to demonstrate it for classmates. As a part of your demonstration, show and/or explain tools and materials that are needed, and acquaint class members with the terminology that is peculiar to this art or craft.

# Famous Sculptors

Robert Aitken
Louis Amateis
Thomas Ball
Frédéric Auguste Bartholdi
Gianlorenzo Bernini
Gutzon Borglum
Constantin Brancusi
Alexander Calder
Benvenuto Cellini
Donatello
John Joseph Earley
Jacob Epstein
Erté
Rudolph Evans
James Earle Fraser
Laura Gardin Fraser
Daniel Chester French
Harriet Whitney Frishmuth
Lorenzo Ghiberti
Alberto Giacometti
Jean-Robert Ipousteguy
Carl Paul Jennewein
Walter Linck
Jacques Lipchitz
William M. McVey

Aristide Maillol
Paul Manship
Michelangelo Buonarroti
Carl Milles
Clark Mills
Henry Moore
Louise Nevelson
Constantino Nivola
Brenda Putnam
Andre Ramseyer
Frederic Remington
José de Rivera
François Auguste René Rodin
Augustus Saint-Gaudens
Johann Gottfried Schadow
Henry Merwin Shrady
Franklin Simmons
David Smith
Andrea del Verrocchio
John Quincy Adams Ward
George Frederic Watts
Sidney Waugh
Adolph Alexander Weinman
Felix W. de Weldon
Ossip Zadkine

# Authors

An **author** is someone who has written a literary work. This work may take any one of several forms. For example, it may be a book, an essay, a novel, a play, a poem, or a short story.

## Past

Below are listed the names of some authors from the past and the title of at least one literary work by each.

| Name | Birth and Death Dates | Title |
|------|------------------------|-------|
| Louisa May Alcott | 1832–1888 | *Little Women; Little Men* |
| Hans Christian Andersen | 1805–1875 | Fairy tales: "The Ugly Duckling" |
| James M. Barrie | 1860–1937 | *Peter Pan* |
| L. Frank Baum | 1856–1919 | Wizard of Oz series |
| Pearl S. Buck | 1892–1973 | *The Good Earth* |
| Edgar Rice Burroughs | 1875–1950 | *Tarzan of the Apes* |
| Lewis Carroll | 1832–1898 | Poetry: "The Jabberwocky" Short stories: *Alice's Adventures in Wonderland* |
| Agatha Christie | 1891–1976 | *And Then There Were None; Murder on the Orient Express* |
| James Fenimore Cooper | 1789–1851 | Leatherstocking series |
| Charles Dickens | 1812–1870 | *A Christmas Carol; The Cricket on the Hearth; A Tale of Two Cities* |
| Arthur Conan Doyle | 1859–1930 | Sherlock Holmes series |
| Robert Frost | 1874–1963 | Poetry: "Departmental"; "Fire and Ice"; "Mending Wall"; "Provide, Provide"; "The Road Not Taken"; "Stopping by Woods on a Snowy Evening" |
| Erle Stanley Gardner | 1889–1970 | Perry Mason series |
| Jakob Grimm | 1785–1863 | *Grimm's Fairy Tales* |
| Wilhelm Grimm | 1786–1859 | *Grimm's Fairy Tales* |
| Bret Harte | 1836–1902 | *The Luck of Roaring Camp* |
| Nathaniel Hawthorne | 1804–1864 | *The House of Seven Gables; The Scarlet Letter* |
| O. Henry | 1862–1910 | Short stories: "The Gift of the Magi"; "Ransom for Red Chief" |
| Washington Irving | 1783–1859 | "The Legend of Sleepy Hollow" |
| Mackinlay Kantor | 1904–1977 | *The Voice of Bugle Ann* |
| Rudyard Kipling | 1865–1936 | *The Jungle Book* |
| Hugh Lofting | 1886–1947 | Dr. Dolittle series |
| Jack London | 1876–1916 | *Call of the Wild* |

# Authors
## (continued)

| Name | Birth and Death Dates | Title |
|---|---|---|
| Herman Melville | 1819-1891 | *Moby Dick* |
| A. A. Milne | 1882-1956 | *Winnie-the-Pooh* |
| Clement C. Moore | 1779-1863 | "A Visit from Saint Nicholas" |
| Ogden Nash | 1902-1971 | Humorous verse: *I'm a Stranger Here Myself* |
| Edgar Allan Poe | 1809-1849 | Poetry: "The Raven" Short stories: "The Fall of the House of Usher"; "The Murders in the Rue Morgue"; "The Tell-Tale Heart" |
| Carl Sandburg | 1878-1967 | Poetry: *Chicago Poems*; "Chicago"; "Fog" |
| Antoine de Saint-Exupéry | 1900-1944 | *Le Petit Prince* ("The Little Prince") |
| Robert Louis Stevenson | 1850-1894 | *Treasure Island* |
| James Thurber | 1894-1961 | *The Owl in the Attic* |
| Mark Twain | 1835-1910 | *The Adventures of Tom Sawyer; The Adventures of Huckleberry Finn* |
| Jules Verne | 1828-1905 | *Twenty Thousand Leagues Under the Sea* |
| Thornton Wilder | 1897-1975 | Plays: *Our Town; The Skin of Our Teeth* |

## Present

Isaac Asimov
Judy Blume
Ray Bradbury
Beverly Cleary
Roald Dahl
Joan Didion
Theodore Geisel
Elizabeth Forsythe Hailey
P. D. James
Garrison Keillor

Stephen King
Robert Ludlum
Lance Morrow
Joyce Carol Oates
Carl Sagan
Richard Scarry
Maurice Sendak
Shel Silverstein
Neil Simon

Isaac Bashevis Singer
Louis Thomas
John Updike
Leon Uris
Gore Vidal
Judith Viorst
Robert Penn Warren
Eudora Welty
E. B. White

1. Choose five authors from the past and read at least one work by each.

2. The English word **pseudonym** comes from the Greek word **pseudonymos**, meaning "bearing a false name." A pseudonym is a fictitious name, especially one used by an author to hide his or her real identity. **Lewis Carroll, O. Henry**, and **Mark Twain** are pseudonyms. Do some research to discover the real names of these authors and to learn the pseudonyms used by Charles Dickens and Theodore Geisel.

3. Invent a pseudonym, or pen name, for yourself.

# Caldecott Medal Winners

The **Caldecott Medal** is awarded each year by the American Library Association to the illustrator of the most distinguished picture book for children published in the United States of America. This medal is named for Randolph Caldecott (1846-1886), an English artist who is famous for his charming and humorous illustrations.

| Year | Title | Illustrator |
|---|---|---|
| 1938 | *Animals of the Bible* | Dorothy P. Lathrop |
| 1939 | *Mei Li* | Thomas Handforth |
| 1940 | *Abraham Lincoln* | Ingri and Edgar Parin Aulaire |
| 1941 | *They Were Strong and Good* | Robert Lawson |
| 1942 | *Make Way for Ducklings* | Robert McCloskey |
| 1943 | *The Little House* | Virginia Lee Burton |
| 1944 | *Many Moons* | Louis Slobodkin |
| 1945 | *Prayer for a Child* | Elizabeth Orton Jones |
| 1946 | *The Rooster Crows* | Maud and Miska Petersham |
| 1947 | *The Little Island* | Leonard Weisgard |
| 1948 | *White Snow, Bright Snow* | Roger Duvoisin |
| 1949 | *The Big Snow* | Berta and Elmer Hader |
| 1950 | *Song of the Swallows* | Leo Politi |
| 1951 | *The Egg Tree* | Katherine Milhous |
| 1952 | *Finders Keepers* | Nicolas Mordvinoff |

# Caldecott Medal Winners
## (continued)

| Year | Title | Illustrator |
|------|-------|-------------|
| 1953 | *The Biggest Bear* | Lynd K. Ward |
| 1954 | *Madeline's Rescue* | Ludwig Bemelmans |
| 1955 | *Cinderella; or The Little Glass Slipper* | Marcia Brown |
| 1956 | *Frog Went A-Courtin'* | Feodor Rojankovsky |
| 1957 | *A Tree Is Nice* | Marc Simont |
| 1958 | *Time of Wonder* | Robert McCloskey |
| 1959 | *Chanticleer and the Fox* | Barbara Cooney |
| 1960 | *Nine Days to Christmas* | Marie Hall Ets |
| 1961 | *Baboushka and the Three Kings* | Nicolas Sidjakov |
| 1962 | *Once a Mouse* | Marcia Brown |
| 1963 | *The Snowy Day* | Ezra Jack Keats |
| 1964 | *Where the Wild Things Are* | Maurice Sendak |
| 1965 | *May I Bring a Friend?* | Beni Montresor |
| 1966 | *Always Room for One More* | Nonny Hogrogian |
| 1967 | *Sam, Bangs, and Moonshine* | Evaline Ness |
| 1968 | *Drummer Hoff* | Ed Emberley |
| 1969 | *The Fool of the World and the Flying Ship* | Uri Shulevitz |
| 1970 | *Sylvester and the Magic Pebble* | William Steig |

# Caldecott Medal Winners
## (continued)

| Year | Title | Illustrator |
|------|-------|-------------|
| 1971 | *A Story—A Story* | Gail E. Haley |
| 1972 | *One Fine Day* | Nonny Hogrogian |
| 1973 | *The Funny Little Woman* | Blair Lent |
| 1974 | *Duffy and the Devil* | Margot Zemach |
| 1975 | *Arrow to the Sun: A Pueblo Indian Tale* | Gerald McDermott |
| 1976 | *Why Mosquitoes Buzz in People's Ears: A West African Tale* | Leo and Diane Dillon |
| 1977 | *Ashanti to Zulu: African Traditions* | Leo and Diane Dillon |
| 1978 | *Noah's Ark* | Peter Spier |
| 1979 | *The Girl Who Loved Wild Horses* | Paul Goble |
| 1980 | *Ox-Cart Man* | Barbara Cooney |
| 1981 | *Fables* | Arnold Lobel |
| 1982 | *Jumanji* | Chris Van Allsburg |
| 1983 | *Shadow* | Marcia Brown |
| 1984 | *The Glorious Flight: Across the Channel with Louis Blériot* | Alice and Martin Provensen |
| 1985 | *Saint George and the Dragon* | Trina Schart Hyman |
| 1986 | *The Polar Express* | Chris Van Allsburg |
| 1987 | *Hey, Al* | Richard Egielski |

# Newbery Medal Winners

The **Newbery Medal** is awarded each year by the American Library Association to the American author of the most distinguished contribution to literature for children. This medal is named for John Newbery (1713-1767), an English publisher and bookseller.

| Year | Title | Author |
|------|-------|--------|
| 1922 | *The Story of Mankind* | Hendrik Van Loon |
| 1923 | *The Voyages of Doctor Dolittle* | Hugh Lofting |
| 1924 | *The Dark Frigate* | Charles Hawes |
| 1925 | *Tales from Silver Lands* | Charles Finger |
| 1926 | *Shen of the Sea* | Arthur Chrisman |
| 1927 | *Smoky* | Will James |
| 1928 | *Gay-Neck, the Story of a Pigeon* | Dhan Gopal Mukerji |
| 1929 | *The Trumpeter of Krakow* | Eric P. Kelly |
| 1930 | *Hitty, Her First Hundred Years* | Rachel Field |
| 1931 | *The Cat Who Went to Heaven* | Elizabeth Coatsworth |
| 1932 | *Waterless Mountain* | Laura Adams Armer |
| 1933 | *Young Fu of the Upper Yangtze* | Elizabeth Lewis |
| 1934 | *Invincible Louisa* | Cornelia Meigs |
| 1935 | *Dobry* | Monica Shannon |
| 1936 | *Caddie Woodlawn* | Carol Brink |
| 1937 | *Roller Skates* | Ruth Sawyer |
| 1938 | *The White Stag* | Kate Seredy |
| 1939 | *Thimble Summer* | Elizabeth Enright |
| 1940 | *Daniel Boone* | James Daugherty |
| 1941 | *Call It Courage* | Armstrong Sperry |

# Newbery Medal Winners
## (continued)

| Year | Title | Author |
|------|-------|--------|
| 1942 | *The Matchlock Gun* | Walter D. Edmonds |
| 1943 | *Adam of the Road* | Elizabeth Janet Gray |
| 1944 | *Johnny Tremain* | Esther Forbes |
| 1945 | *Rabbit Hill* | Robert Lawson |
| 1946 | *Strawberry Girl* | Lois Lenski |
| 1947 | *Miss Hickory* | Carolyn Sherwin Bailey |
| 1948 | *The Twenty-One Balloons* | William Pene du Bois |
| 1949 | *King of the Wind* | Marguerite Henry |
| 1950 | *The Door in the Wall* | Marguerite de Angeli |
| 1951 | *Amos Fortune, Free Man* | Elizabeth Yates |
| 1952 | *Ginger Pye* | Eleanor Estes |
| 1953 | *Secret of the Andes* | Ann Nolan Clark |
| 1954 | *. . . And Now Miguel* | Joseph Krumgold |
| 1955 | *The Wheel on the School* | Meindert DeJong |
| 1956 | *Carry On, Mr. Bowditch* | Jean Lee Latham |
| 1957 | *Miracles on Maple Hill* | Virginia Sorensen |
| 1958 | *Rifles for Watie* | Harold V. Keith |
| 1959 | *The Witch of Blackbird Pond* | Elizabeth George Speare |
| 1960 | *Onion John* | Joseph Krumgold |
| 1961 | *Island of the Blue Dolphins* | Scott O'Dell |
| 1962 | *The Bronze Bow* | Elizabeth George Speare |
| 1963 | *A Wrinkle in Time* | Madeleine L'Engle |
| 1964 | *It's Like This Cat* | Emily Neville |

# Newbery Medal Winners
## (continued)

| Year | Title | Author |
|------|-------|--------|
| 1965 | *Shadow of a Bull* | Maia Wojciechowska |
| 1966 | *I, Juan de Pareja* | Elizabeth Borton de Treviño |
| 1967 | *Up a Road Slowly* | Irene Hunt |
| 1968 | *From the Mixed-Up Files of Mrs. Basil E. Frankweiler* | Elaine Konigsburg |
| 1969 | *The High King* | Lloyd Alexander |
| 1970 | *Sounder* | William H. Armstrong |
| 1971 | *The Summer of the Swans* | Betsy Byars |
| 1972 | *Mrs. Frisby and the Rats of NIMH* | Robert C. O'Brien |
| 1973 | *Julie of the Wolves* | Jean Craighead George |
| 1974 | *The Slave Dancer* | Paula Fox |
| 1975 | *M. C. Higgins, the Great* | Virginia Hamilton |
| 1976 | *The Grey King* | Susan Cooper |
| 1977 | *Roll of Thunder, Hear My Cry* | Mildred D. Taylor |
| 1978 | *Bridge to Terabithia* | Katherine Paterson |
| 1979 | *The Westing Game* | Ellen Raskin |
| 1980 | *A Gathering of Days: A New England Girl's Journal* | Joan Blos |
| 1981 | *Jacob Have I Loved* | Katherine Paterson |
| 1982 | *A Visit to William Blake's Inn* | Nancy Willard |
| 1983 | *Dicey's Song* | Cynthia Voight |
| 1984 | *Dear Mr. Henshaw* | Beverly Cleary |
| 1985 | *The Hero and the Crown* | Robin McKinley |
| 1986 | *Sara, Plain and Tall* | Patricia MacLachlan |
| 1987 | *The Whipping Boy* | Sid Fleischman |

# Men in Sports

Henry Aaron
Kareem Abdul-Jabbar
Muhammad Ali
Lance Alworth
Mario Andretti
Eddie Arcaro
Arthur Ashe
Roger Bannister
Elgin Baylor
Bob Beamon
Boris Becker
Johnny Bench
Yogi Berra
Larry Bird
George Blanda
Brian Boitano
Bjorn Borg
Andrei Bukin
Dick Butkus
Dick Button
Roy Campanella
Billy Casper
Wilt Chamberlain
Roberto Clemente
Ty Cobb
Jimmy Connors
Pete Dawkins
Joe DiMaggio
Julius Erving
Whitey Ford
Dick Fosbury
A. J. Foyt

Mitch Gaylord
Lou Gehrig
Bob Gibson
Wayne Gretzky
Scott Hamilton
John Havlicek
Eric Heiden
Paul Hornung
Gordie Howe
Bobby Hull
Reggie Jackson
Bruce Jenner
Earvin "Magic" Johnson
Rafer Johnson
Duke Kahanamoku
Jean-Claude Killy
Sandy Koufax
Rod Laver
Carl Lewis
Greg Louganis
Joe Louis
Bob McAdoo
John McEnroe
Mickey Mantle
Juan Marichal
Roger Maris
Bob Mathias
Willie Mays
Edwin Moses
Stan Musial
John Nabor
Joe Namath

# Men in Sports
## (continued)

| | |
|---|---|
| John Newcombe | Willie Shoemaker |
| Jack Nicklaus | Frank Shorter |
| Ray Nitschke | O. J. Simpson |
| Sondre Norheim | Sam Snead |
| Matti Nykaenen | Warren Spahn |
| Al Oerter | Mark Spitz |
| Merlin Olsen | Amos Alonzo Stagg |
| Bobby Orr | Bart Starr |
| Steve Owen | Roger Staubach |
| Jesse Owens | Casey Stengel |
| Satchel Paige | Ingemar Stenmark |
| Arnold Palmer | Fran Tarkenton |
| Axel Paulsen | Daley Thompson |
| Walter Payton | Jim Thorpe |
| Pelé | Bill Tilden |
| Bob Pettit | Y. A. Tittle |
| Richard Petty | Lee Trevino |
| Laffit Pincay, Jr. | Gene Tunney |
| Gary Player | Johnny Unitas |
| Oscar Robertson | Al Unser |
| Jackie Robinson | Bobby Unser |
| Bill Rodgers | Fernando Valenzuela |
| Pete Rose | Peter Vidmar |
| Bill Russell | Bill Walton |
| Babe Ruth | Johnny Weissmuller |
| Nolan Ryan | Jerry West |
| Jim Ryun | Ted Williams |
| Ulrich Salchow | Carl Yastrzemski |
| Gale Sayers | Cy Young |
| Tom Seaver | Pirmin Zurbriggen |

1. From this list, select twenty names that are unfamiliar to you. Using these names, create a chart on which you list the athlete, the country in which he was born, and the sport or sports in which he has excelled.

2. Many of these men set world records, won Olympic medals, won a particular series of competitions (such as the grand slam in tennis), or were first to perform particular feats. Do some research to learn more about the truly outstanding achievements of at least ten of these athletes.

# Modern Olympic Game Sites

| Year | Summer Games | Winter Games |
|------|--------------|--------------|
| 1896 | Athens, Greece | |
| 1900 | Paris, France | |
| 1904 | St. Louis, Missouri, USA | |
| 1906 | Athens, Greece | |
| 1908 | London, England | |
| 1912 | Stockholm, Sweden | |
| 1920 | Antwerp, Belgium | |
| 1924 | Paris, France | Chamonix, France |
| 1928 | Amsterdam, Netherlands | St. Moritz, Switzerland |
| 1932 | Los Angeles, California, USA | Lake Placid, New York, USA |
| 1936 | Berlin, Germany | Garmisch-Partenkirchen, Germany |
| 1948 | London, England | St. Moritz, Switzerland |
| 1952 | Helsinki, Finland | Oslo, Norway |
| 1956 | Melbourne, Australia | Cortina d'Ampezzo, Italy |
| 1960 | Rome, Italy | Squaw Valley, California, USA |
| 1964 | Tokyo, Japan | Innsbruck, Austria |
| 1968 | Mexico City, Mexico | Grenoble, France |
| 1972 | Munich, Federal Republic of Germany | Sapporo, Japan |
| 1976 | Montreal, Canada | Innsbruck, Austria |
| 1980 | Moscow, USSR | Lake Placid, New York, USA |
| 1984 | Los Angeles, California, USA | Sarajevo, Yugoslavia |
| 1988 | Seoul, Korea | Calgary, Canada |

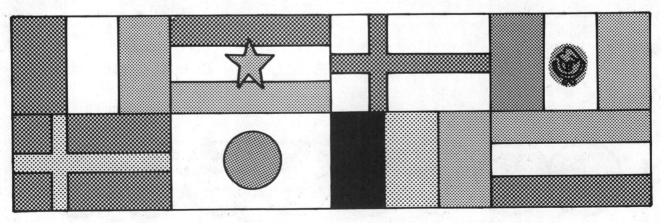

1. Locate these former Olympic sites on a world map or globe.

2. Select three new locations for future games and tell why you chose each one.

3. In general, the Olympic Games have been held every four years since 1896, but there are some notable exceptions. For example, the games were held in 1906, and they were not held in either 1916, 1940, or 1944. Do some research to learn the reasons for these exceptions to the Olympic quadrennial pattern.

# Olympic Events
## Summer Games

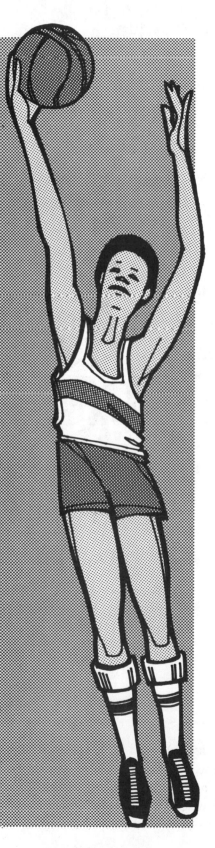

**archery**

**basketball**

**boxing**

**canoeing**

**cycling**

**diving**
   platform
   springboard

**equestrian events**
   dressage
   grand prix jumping
   three-day event

**fencing**
   épée
   foil
   sabre

**gymnastics, artistic**
   *men*
      floor exercise
      horizontal bar
      parallel bars
      pommel horse
      rings
      vault
   *women*
      balance beam
      floor exercise
      uneven parallel bars
      vault

**gymnastics, rhythmic**

**handball**

**hockey**

**judo**

**pentathlon**

**rowing**

**shooting**
   pistol
   rifle
   shotgun

**soccer**

**swimming**
   backstroke
   breaststroke
   butterfly
   freestyle
   medley
   synchronized

**tennis**

**track and field**
   decathlon
   discus throw
   heptathlon
   high jump
   javelin throw
   long jump
   running events
      100 meters
      200 meters
      400 meters
      800 meters
      1,500 meters
      3,000 meters
      hurdles
      marathon
      relays
      steeplechase
   shot put
   walking events

**volleyball**

**water polo**

**weight lifting**

**wrestling**

**yachting**

# Olympic Events
## Winter Games

**Alpine skiing**
downhill
slalom
giant slalom
Super G slalom
combined downhill and slalom

**biathlon**
10 kilometers
20 kilometers
40-kilometer relay

**bobsledding**
two-man
four-man

**cross-country (Nordic) skiing**
*men*
15 kilometers (9.3 miles)
30 kilometers (18.6 miles)
50 kilometers (31.0 miles)
40-kilometer relay
*women*
5 kilometers (3.1 miles)
10 kilometers (6.2 miles)
15-kilometer relay

**curling**

**disabled skiing**

**figure skating**
men's singles
women's singles
pairs
ice dancing

**freestyle skiing**
aerials
ballet
moguls

**ice hockey**

**luge**
*men*
singles
doubles
*women*
singles

**ski jumping**
70 meters
90 meters

**speed skating**
*men*
500 meters
1,000 meters
1,500 meters
5,000 meters
10,000 meters
*women*
500 meters
1,000 meters
1,500 meters
3,000 meters
5,000 meters

From the lists on pages 203 and 204, select an Olympic event with which you are unfamiliar and find out about it. For example, you might select the **biathlon**, **curling**, **equestrian events**, **fencing**, **freestyle skiing**, or the **pentathlon**. Discover when and where this event originated, when it became a part of the Olympics, how it is done, and how the winner is determined.

# Sports and Athletic Activities

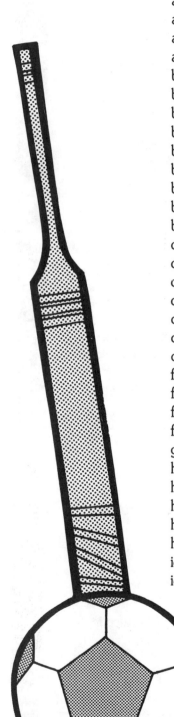

aerobics
alpine skiing
archery
artistic gymnastics
auto racing
badminton
baseball
basketball
bicycling
billiards
boating
bobsledding
bowling
boxing
canoeing
cricket
croquet
cross-country skiing
darts
deck tennis
diving
fencing
field hockey
fishing
football
golf
handball
hiking
horseback riding
horseshoes
hunting
ice hockey
ice skating

jai alai
jogging
judo
jumping rope
karate
kickball
lacrosse
mountain climbing
paddle tennis
polo
racquetball
rhythmic gymnastics
roller skating
rugby
running
sailing
shuffleboard
skate boarding
sledding
soccer
softball
squash
surfing
swimming
table tennis
tennis
tetherball
volleyball
walking
water skiing
wrestling
yoga

# Sports Teams
## Baseball

### National League

Atlanta Braves
Chicago Cubs
Cincinatti Reds
Houston Astros

Los Angeles Dodgers
Montreal Expos
New York Mets
Philadelphia Phillies

Pittsburgh Pirates
St. Louis Cardinals
San Diego Padres
San Francisco Giants

### American League

Baltimore Orioles
Boston Red Sox
California Angels
Chicago White Sox
Cleveland Indians

Detroit Tigers
Kansas City Royals
Milwaukee Brewers
Minnesota Twins

New York Yankees
Oakland A's
Seattle Mariners
Texas Rangers
Toronto Blue Jays

## National Basketball Association

Atlanta Hawks
Boston Celtics
Chicago Bulls
Cleveland Cavaliers
Dallas Mavericks
Denver Nuggets
Detroit Pistons
Golden State Warriors

Houston Rockets
Indiana Pacers
Los Angeles Clippers
Los Angeles Lakers
Milwaukee Bucks
New Jersey Nets
New York Knickerbockers

Philadelphia 76ers
Phoenix Suns
Portland Trail Blazers
Sacramento Kings
San Antonio Spurs
Seattle SuperSonics
Utah Jazz
Washington Bullets

## National Football League

Atlanta Falcons
Baltimore Colts
Buffalo Bills
Chicago Bears
Cincinnati Bengals
Cleveland Browns
Dallas Cowboys
Denver Broncos
Detroit Lions

Green Bay Packers
Houston Oilers
Kansas City Chiefs
Los Angeles Raiders
Los Angeles Rams
Miami Dolphins
Minnesota Vikings
New England Patriots
New Orleans Saints
New York Giants

New York Jets
Philadelphia Eagles
Pittsburgh Steelers
St. Louis Cardinals
San Diego Chargers
San Francisco 49ers
Seattle Seahawks
Tampa Bay Buccaneers
Washington Redkins

1. Select five of these teams and do research to discover how they got their names.
2. Find out the colors, logo, and mascot (if any) for each of the five teams you selected.
3. Choose one team whose name you feel is inappropriate and rename it. Select different colors and design a new logo to go with the new name.

# Sports Terms

### Baseball
at bat
base hit
bunt
diamond
fly
foul
glove
homer
inning
mitt
pitch
strike
walk

### Basketball
air ball
backboard
basket
charging
court
dribble
free throw
guard
hoop
jump shot
key
rebound
slam dunk

### Football
block
down
fair catch
gridiron
huddle
kickoff
offside
pass
punt
quarter
safety
tackle
touchdown

### Ice Hockey
assist
face-off
goalie
hat trick
high-sticking
icing
offside
pass
power-play goal
puck
shorthanded goal
Stanley Cup
stick

### Soccer
chip
dribble
free kick
kickoff
match
offside
pass
pitch
rebound
save
screen
tackle
throw-in

### Miscellaneous
alley
Axel
birdie
bogey
chip
gait
love
mogul
parry
putt
rack
schuss
shuttlecock
telemark

1. Often, when the same terms are used in different sports, they have different meanings. Choose two terms (for example, **dribble** and **pitch**) that are used in reference to at least two sports (that is, basketball and soccer, and baseball and soccer). Show that you understand these terms by drawing a picture of each one.

2. Identify the words in the miscellaneous column by matching each one to at least one sport. When you think of sports, don't forget badminton, bowling, fencing, golf, horseback riding, skiing, and tennis.

3. Sometimes, words that are associated with one sport rhyme with words that are associated with another sport (for example, **bunt** and **punt**, **glove** and **love**, **kick** and **stick**). Write a poem in which you make use of some of these rhymes.

# Women in Sports

Tenley Albright
Laura Baugh
Joan Benoit
Patty Berg
Bonnie Blair
Susan Butcher
Evonne Goolagong Cawley
Nadia Comaneci
Maureen Connolly
Judy Cook
Patty Costello
Margaret Smith Court
Mary Decker
Donna de Varona
Gertrude Ederle
Peggy Fleming
Dawn Fraser
Linda Fratianne
Althea Gibson
Janet Guthrey
Dorothy Hamill
Carol Heiss
Sonja Henie
Karin Kania
Billie Jean King

Micki King
Olga Korbut
Chris Evert Lloyd
Patricia McCormick
Julianne McNamara
Elizabeth Manley
Debby Mason
Debbie Meyer
Annemarie Proell Moser
Shirley Muldowney
Martina Navratilova
Mary Lou Retton
Kathy Rigby
Wilma Rudolph
Mary Scharff
Melanie Smith
Robyn Smith
Debi Thomas
Wyomia Tyus
Grete Waitz
Kathy Whitworth
Helen Wills
Katarina Witte
Sheila Young
Babe Didrikson Zaharias

1. From this list, select ten names that are unfamiliar to you. Using these names, create a chart on which you list the athlete, the country in which she was born, and the sport or sports in which she has excelled.

2. Many of these women set world records, won Olympic medals, won a particular series of competitions (such as the grand slam in tennis), or were first to perform particular feats. Do some research to learn about the truly outstanding achievements of at least five of these athletes.

# Bonus Ideas for the Arts and Sports

1. Create a new list related to the arts or to sports. For example, your list might be of
   a. books about dogs
   b. cartoon characters
   c. choreographers
   d. famous cartoonists
   e. famous paintings of people
   f. folk songs

2. Make a poster about a famous architect, artist, author, composer, dancer, sculptor, or athlete whose name appears on one of the lists in this section. Your poster should include a picture of this person and six or more fascinating facts about him or her.

3. Write a letter to one of the people listed in this section. In your letter, tell this person what you most admire about his or her work and achievements. In addition, ask six questions that you would like to have this person answer. If the person is alive and you are able to locate his or her address, mail your letter and see if you receive a reply. If the person is not alive or you are unable to locate his or her address, exhange letters with a friend, and each write a reply to the other's letter.

4. Pick two instruments from the list on pages 178 and 179. Do research to learn what these instruments look like, how they sound, and how they are played.

5. Choose two dances from the list on page 184. Do research to learn the countries in which these dances originated, the celebrations or festivals with which they are associated, and the special clothing or costumes that are worn by dancers who perform them.

6. Select a sport or athletic activity from the list on page 205. Create a list of terms associated with this sport or activity. For example, if you choose baseball, you might list some or all of the following terms:

| | |
|---|---|
| balk | grounder |
| bunt | homer |
| curve | knuckle ball |
| dugout | out |
| fly | safe |
| foul | strike |

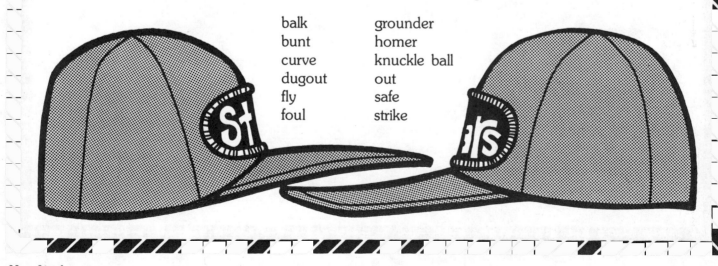

Name _____

# Create an Arts or Sports List

Think of a topic in the arts or sports which interests you. On the lines below, create a list that reflects this topic. Illustrate your list and give it a title.

_____

# Just for Fun

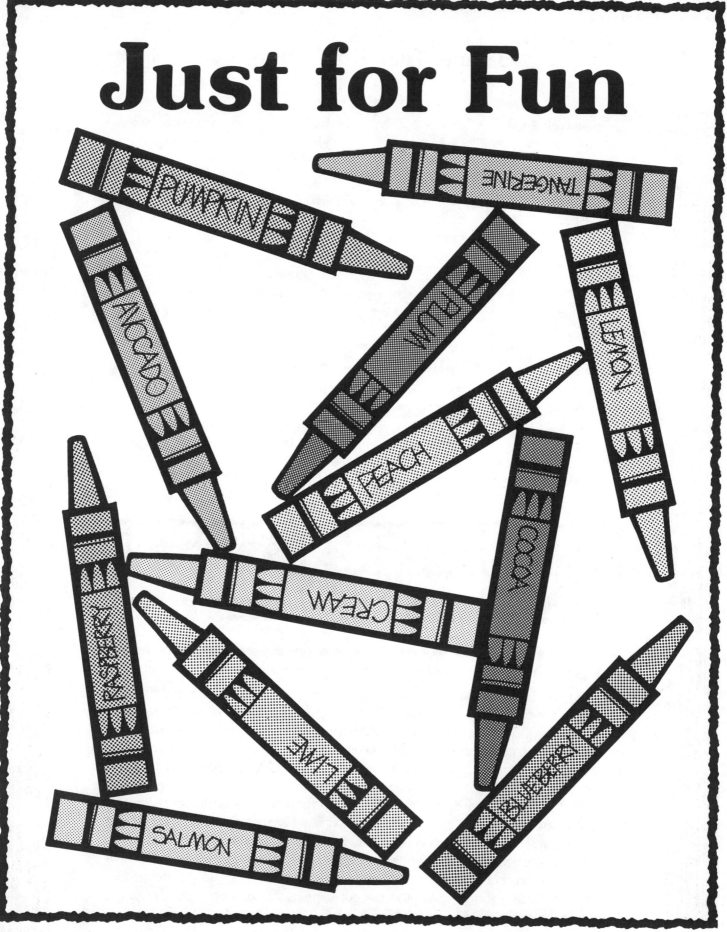

# Things That Hold Things

| | | | |
|---|---|---|---|
| alembic | case | hod | saucepan |
| amphora | cask | jar | scoup |
| bag | casket | jigger | scuttle |
| barrel | chalice | jug | skillet |
| basin | cistern | keg | stoup |
| basket | coffer | kettle | tank |
| bassinet | cradle | krater | tankard |
| bottle | crate | ladle | test tube |
| bowl | crock | lecythus | tin |
| box | cruet | magnum | tray |
| bucket | cruse | mug | trough |
| caddy | cup | pail | tub |
| cage | decanter | pan | tumbler |
| caisson | demijohn | pitcher | tun |
| caldron | ewer | plate | tureen |
| can | flagon | pot | urn |
| canister | flask | punch bowl | vase |
| canteen | glass | puncheon | vat |
| carafe | goblet | rack | vessel |
| carboy | hamper | retort | vial |

1. From this list, select ten words that are unfamiliar to you. Look up the meanings of these words in a dictionary. Then, draw and label a picture of each one.

2. Many of these containers are designed to hold either solids or liquids. Some of them can be used equally well to hold both. Turn these facts into a game. Obtain eighty plain index cards. Print one word from this list in black on one side of each card. On the other side, print in red the word **liquids**, **solids**, or **both**, depending on what that container is designed to hold. Shuffle the cards. Show them one at a time to a friend or classmate, whose task it is to respond by saying whether the named container holds liquids, solids, or both. Set a timer. Allow only a few seconds for each card. Place those cards that are identified correctly in one pile and those that are unidentified or are identified incorrectly in another pile. When all eighty cards have been shown, count the number of cards in the "correct pile" to determine an individual score and/or the overall winner. To increase the challenge, decrease the time allowed for each card.

# Things That Measure

| | | |
|---|---|---|
| accelerometer | electric meter | range finder |
| altimeter | Fathometer | scale |
| ammeter | galvanometer | sextant |
| anemometer | hourglass | speedometer |
| atomic clock | hydrometer | spirometer |
| balance | hygrometer | sundial |
| barometer | light meter | tachometer |
| caliper | manometer | theodolite |
| chronometer | micrometer | thermometer |
| clepsydra | odometer | voltmeter |
| clock | pedometer | watch |
| divider | potentiometer | water clock |
| | quadrant | |

1. More than twenty of the terms listed above contain the word **meter**. Why? Where did this word come from? What does it mean?

2. From this list, select five measuring devices with which you are unfamiliar. Do research to learn what they measure and how they work. Then, draw and label pictures or a series of diagrams which will acquaint friends or classmates with these devices.

3. Use at least twenty of these words to create a game in which classmates draw lines or arrange cards to match the name of each device with the name of the thing it is designed to measure.

# Things to Celebrate

### January

1    New Year's Day
6    Sherlock Holmes's Birthday
15   Martin Luther King, Jr.'s, Birthday
27   Wolfgang Amadeus Mozart's Birthday

### February

1    National Freedom Day
2    Groundhog Day
4    Boy Scouts of America's Birthday*
     Charles Lindbergh's Birthday
11   National Inventors' Day
     Thomas Alva Edison's Birthday
12   Abraham Lincoln's Birthday
14   Valentine's Day
15   Susan B. Anthony Day
22   George Washington's Birthday
29   Leap Year Day
     Mardi Gras**
     Shrove Tuesday**
     Ash Wednesday**

### March

3    Alexander Graham Bell's Birthday
11   Johnny Appleseed Day
12   Girl Scout Day
15   The Ides of March
17   Saint Patrick's Day
     Girl Scout Week*
     Vernal Equinox*
     Palm Sunday**

### April

1    April Fool's Day
7    World Health Day
13   Thomas Jefferson's Birthday
14   Pan American Day
23   William Shakespeare's Birthday
     Arbor Day*
     Good Friday**
     Easter**
     Passover**
     National Volunteer Week*
     National Library Week*

### May

1    May Day
4    Holocaust Day
5    Cinco de Mayo
22   National Maritime Day
30   Memorial Day
     Armed Forces Day*
     Mother's Day*
     National Music Week*
     National Be Kind to Animals Week*

### June

14   Flag Day
27   Helen Keller's Birthday
     Father's Day*
     Summer Solstice*

---

* Date or dates may vary within the indicated month.
** Both month and date may vary.

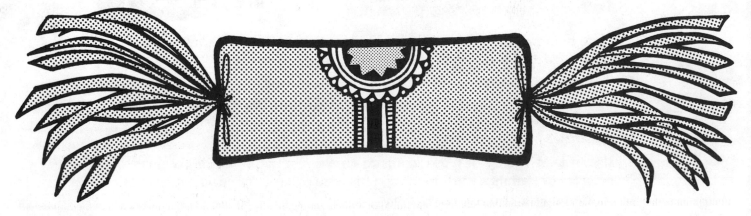

# Things to Celebrate
## (continued)

### July

1   Canada Day
4   Independence Day
14  Bastille Day in France
24  Amelia Earhart's Birthday

### August

12  Ponce de León Day in Puerto Rico
    Good Nutrition Month

### September

17  Citizenship Day
    Labor Day*
    Grandparents' Day*
    Autumnal Equinox*
    American Indian Day*
    Rosh Hashanah**
    Yom Kippur**

---

*Date or dates may vary within the indicated month.
**Both month and date may vary.

### October

12  Columbus Day
24  United Nations Day
31  National UNICEF Day
31  Halloween
    Thanksgiving Day in Canada*
    National Fire Prevention Week*
    National Employ the Handicapped
        Week*

### November

5   Guy Fawkes Day in England
11  Veterans' Day
29  Louisa May Alcott's Birthday
    Election Day*
    Thanksgiving Day*
    American Education Week*
    National Children's Book Week*

### December

7   Pearl Harbor Day
15  Bill of Rights Day
17  Wright Brothers Day
25  Christmas
31  New Year's Eve
    Hanukkah*
    Winter Solstice*
    Boxing Day in the British
        Commonwealth of Nations*

# Things to Collect

antique toys
arrowheads
art
autographs
baseball cards
baskets
bells
books
bottle caps
bottles
bumper stickers
buttons
cartoons
coins
decorated eggs
dolls
fans
feathers
flowers
football cards
fossils
insects
jokes
keys
leaves

marbles
matchbooks
model cars
pennants
photographs
pins
plates
playbills
postcards
posters
postmarks
programs
puppets
riddles
rocks
seeds
shells
stamps
stickers
stuffed animals
tapes
thimbles
ticket stubs
tropical fishes
wind-up toys

# Things to Do to Food

When most people think of preparing food, they think of cooking. Below is a list that will broaden your thinking about what to do to food.

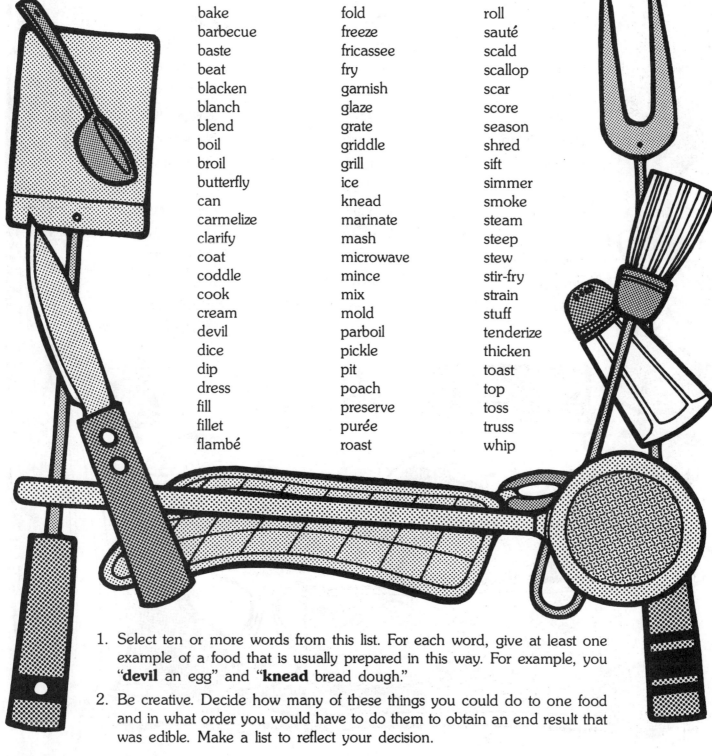

| | | |
|---|---|---|
| bake | fold | roll |
| barbecue | freeze | sauté |
| baste | fricassee | scald |
| beat | fry | scallop |
| blacken | garnish | scar |
| blanch | glaze | score |
| blend | grate | season |
| boil | griddle | shred |
| broil | grill | sift |
| butterfly | ice | simmer |
| can | knead | smoke |
| carmelize | marinate | steam |
| clarify | mash | steep |
| coat | microwave | stew |
| coddle | mince | stir-fry |
| cook | mix | strain |
| cream | mold | stuff |
| devil | parboil | tenderize |
| dice | pickle | thicken |
| dip | pit | toast |
| dress | poach | top |
| fill | preserve | toss |
| fillet | purée | truss |
| flambé | roast | whip |

1. Select ten or more words from this list. For each word, give at least one example of a food that is usually prepared in this way. For example, you **"devil** an egg" and **"knead** bread dough."

2. Be creative. Decide how many of these things you could do to one food and in what order you would have to do them to obtain an end result that was edible. Make a list to reflect your decision.

# Things to Eat

| | | |
|---|---|---|
| ambrosia | endive | napoleon |
| anise | escargot | nougat |
| baklava | fennel | piccalilli |
| béarnaise | filbert | pippin |
| béchamel | flan | quiche |
| brittle | frangipane | rosemary |
| casaba | gherkin | rutabaga |
| ceviche | giblet | sapodilla |
| chateaubriand | goulash | soursop |
| chorizo | kiss | stroganoff |
| codling | kohlrabi | strudel |
| compote | kreplach | succotash |
| costard | kumquat | syllabub |
| couscous | leek | thyme |
| crumpet | madeleine | tofu |
| daikon | marzipan | vichyssoise |
| damson | mousse | whey |

# Things to Read

| | | |
|---|---|---|
| advertisement | formula | poem |
| agreement | graffiti | portfolio |
| almanac | greeting card | postcard |
| anecdote | handbook | poster |
| anthology | horoscope | program |
| application | instructions | proposal |
| atlas | invitation | questionnaire |
| bill | journal | receipt |
| billboard | label | recipe |
| book | letter | register |
| brochure | limerick | report |
| bulletin | list | review |
| bumper sticker | log | riddle |
| cartoon | magazine | script |
| catalog | manual | sentence |
| chart | map | sign |
| circular | marquee | skywriting |
| clue | memo | speech |
| contract | menu | statement |
| critique | newspaper | story |
| diary | note | summary |
| dictionary | notebook | tabloid |
| digest | obituary | telegram |
| directory | palindrome | test |
| encyclopedia | pamphlet | textbook |
| epigram | paragraph | thesaurus |
| epigraph | periodical | transcript |
| epitaph | placard | verdict |
| essay | play | verse |
| flier | playbill | will |

# Things to Wear on Your Body

ascot
balmacaan
bolero
camisole
cardigan
chesterfield
cloak
cravat
cummerbund
dickey
djellaba
farthingale
furbelow
garibaldi
greatcoat
guernsey
jabot
jersey
jodhpurs
joseph
kimono
knickers
Macfarlane
mackinaw
mackintosh
mantle
mantua
palatine
peignoir
polonaise
puttee
rabato
raglan
roquelaure
sari
sarong
smallclothes
tabard
toga
tunic
ulster
waistcoat

Select fifteen things to wear from this list and do research to learn more about the people and places for which these things were named.

# Things to Wear on Your Feet

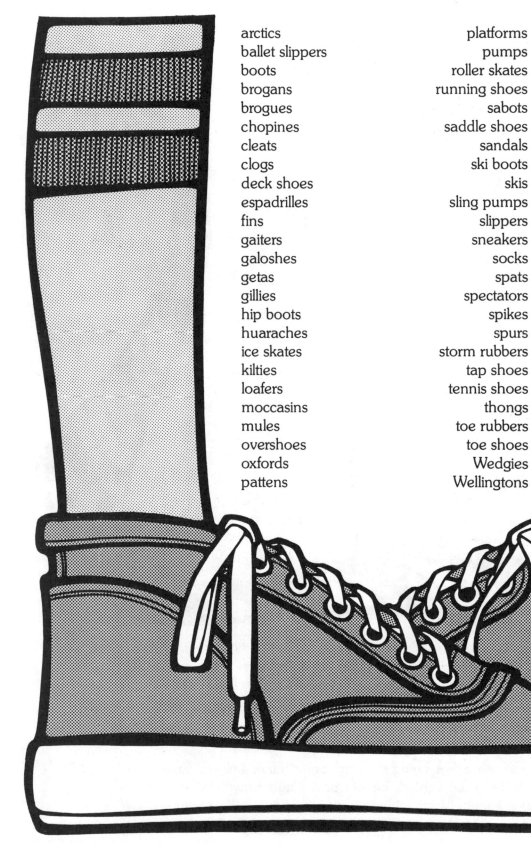

| | |
|---|---|
| arctics | platforms |
| ballet slippers | pumps |
| boots | roller skates |
| brogans | running shoes |
| brogues | sabots |
| chopines | saddle shoes |
| cleats | sandals |
| clogs | ski boots |
| deck shoes | skis |
| espadrilles | sling pumps |
| fins | slippers |
| gaiters | sneakers |
| galoshes | socks |
| getas | spats |
| gillies | spectators |
| hip boots | spikes |
| huaraches | spurs |
| ice skates | storm rubbers |
| kilties | tap shoes |
| loafers | tennis shoes |
| moccasins | thongs |
| mules | toe rubbers |
| overshoes | toe shoes |
| oxfords | Wedgies |
| pattens | Wellingtons |

# Things to Wear on Your Head

| | |
|---|---|
| balaclava | mantilla |
| Balmoral | miter |
| bangkok | mortarboard |
| bathing cap | opera hat |
| beanie | Panama hat |
| beret | peruke |
| biretta | pith helmet |
| bonnet | pixie |
| bowler | porkpie |
| busby | sallet |
| calot | scarf |
| cap | shako |
| chapeau | shower cap |
| cloche | skullcap |
| cowboy hat | snood |
| crown | sombrero |
| derby | Stetson |
| fedora | stocking cap |
| fez | tam-o'-shanter |
| gibus | tiara |
| Glengarry | top hat |
| hard hat | toque |
| havelock | turban |
| helmet | visor |
| homburg | wig |
| Jinnah cap | yarmulke |
| kepi | zucchetto |

1. Design a hat to be worn by all people who share a particular occupation or profession, such as computer programmers or doctors. Make a detailed drawing of your design and label the various special features and parts. Give your design a name.

2. Make a montage using pictures of hats found in magazine ads. See how many different kinds of hats you can find and include.

3. Pretend that you are a hat sitting on someone's head. For example, you might choose to be a fire fighter's helmet or a king's crown. Write a diary entry or narrative about all of the things that happen to you and your wearer during one twenty-four-hour period.

# Things to Write About
## Animal Stories

1. Watson, the Worm
2. Horse Fever
3. The Blue Ribbon Pet
4. Puppy Power
5. A Turtle in Trouble
6. The Baboon That Loved Bubble Gum
7. The Empty Cage
8. Pet Problems
9. The Burglar and the Bear
10. The Pet Store Window
11. The Goofy Gopher
12. A Skunk in the Trunk
13. Rhino on the Run
14. A Visit to the Zoo
15. Pick of the Litter
16. The Laughing Lion
17. One Puppy Too Many
18. Horace, the Roller-Skating Hippo
19. Tale of the Giant Gorilla
20. Cat in the Candy Store
21. Fido to the Rescue
22. Noah, the Boa
23. How the Dalmatian Got Its Spots
24. Monkey Business
25. Mrs. Rich and the Rhino

# Things to Write About
## Just for Fun

1. Giggling Gus of Gatorville
2. The Magical Mirror
3. An Ingenious Invention
4. Mummy on the Loose
5. Wish upon a Unicorn
6. The Whistling Wopperbopper
7. When Numbers Disappeared
8. A Glimpse of the Future
9. The Tri-Eyed Slitherwart
10. The Secret Formula of Dr. Ficklepickle
11. A Ride on the Rainbow
12. The Practical Joke
13. Backwards Day
14. The Blue Balloon Escape
15. The Purple House on Murple Street
16. Miss Mandy and the Candy Machine
17. A Cow on the Roof
18. The Surprise Package
19. The Chocolate Chip Gang
20. The Kid with the Green Face
21. The Popcorn That Wouldn't Stop Popping
22. The Bubble Gum Disaster
23. The Magical Lollipop Tree
24. How the Toad Got Its Tongue
25. The Time Machine

# Things to Write About
## Miscellaneous

1. Decisions, Decisions
2. Lost at Sea
3. A Special Secret
4. Conquer the Waves
5. To the Rescue
6. Wally, the Wizard
7. When the Sun Disappeared
8. A Kid in Trouble
9. The Spider That Grew and Grew
10. A Narrow Escape
11. Climb to the Peak
12. Without a Warning
13. On the Island of Goochie-Geechie
14. The Happiest Day
15. Trapped
16. The Hot-Air Balloon Ride
17. A Skunk in My Tub
18. Was I Ever Mad!
19. The Magical Ladder to Nowhere
20. Visitor from Another Planet
21. Mable in Muddville
22. All in a Day's Work
23. A Friend in Need
24. Stranded in the Desert
25. A Day I'll Never Forget

# Things to Write About
## Mysteries

1. The Fortune Cookie Caper
2. Super Spy for the FBI
3. Revenge of the Raven
4. A Scream in the Night
5. The Creature of Willow Creek
6. Up from the Deep
7. The Secret of Timber Tunnel
8. The Groaning Ghost
9. The Phone Booth Mystery
10. The Empty Room
11. Swamp Creature
12. The Monster That Took over the Earth
13. Happenings in the Haunted House
14. The Creepy Claw
15. The Nightmare
16. Not a Second Too Soon!
17. The Cave of the Dragon
18. The Case of the Stolen Key
19. Schoolroom Mystery
20. The Vanishing Footprints
21. The Howl of the Hound
22. The Mysterious Mirror
23. Detective Donna Solves the Mystery
24. Night of the Fog
25. The Ghost in the Attic

# Things to Write About
## Sports Stories

1. The Tryouts
2. My Turn to Bat
3. When the Crowds Went Wild
4. Scoring Secrets
5. Tops on the Team
6. How I Saved the Game
7. Slugger Strikes Out
8. The Day of the Championships
9. The Winning Goal
10. Super Stars
11. Bessie of Baseball Fame
12. Touchdown Troubles
13. On the Run
14. The Champ
15. The Soccer Star
16. The Stringers Meet the Wingers
17. The Play that Changed the Game
18. Race Against the Clock
19. How I Survived My Rookie Year
20. Newcomer to the Team
21. A Crack at the Bat
22. Wrestlemania
23. The Volleyball Victory
24. My Basketball Blunder
25. The Hockey Hoax

# Things with Holes

bagels
balloons
basketball hoops
beads
beanshooters
belts
bowling balls
button-down collars
buttons
chicken wire
chimneys
collanders
computer paper
doughnuts
drains
electrical outlets
eyedroppers
faucets
floppy disks
funnels
golf courses
graters
handcuffs
hollow logs
honeycombs
hoops
inner tubes
laces
lace-up-shoes
life preservers
Life Saver candies
locks

macaroni
needles
nets
noses
nozzles
nuts
pegboards
pencil sharpeners
pierced ears
pipes
records
rings
rubber bands
salt and pepper shakers
scissors
screen doors
sieves
sifters
socks
spigots
sponges
spools
spouts
squirt guns
strainers
straws
swiss cheese
teeth (sometimes)
tennis rackets
washers
wind instruments
window screens

# Braille Alphabet

Louis Braille was a French organist and teacher of the blind. He developed a system of raised-dot writing for literature and music. This remarkable system, called the Braille alphabet, makes it possible for people who cannot see to read with their fingertips.

The Braille alphabet is based on a rectangle made up of six dot positions. By changing the number of dots used and varying their positions within the rectangle, Louis Braille was able to come up with enough variations to represent twenty-six letters, ten numerals, and all needed punctuation marks.

Within the rectangle, each dot position has a number. Different combinations of these positions represent different letters, numerals, and punctuation marks, and even indicate when a letter should be capitalized. For example, a dot in position 1 represents the letter **a**. A combination of dots in positions 2, 5, and 6 stands for a period. A dot in position 6 *before* a letter indicates that the letter should be capitalized.

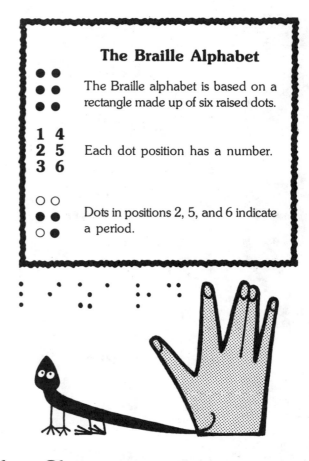

### The Braille Alphabet

The Braille alphabet is based on a rectangle made up of six raised dots.

Each dot position has a number.

Dots in positions 2, 5, and 6 indicate a period.

## Braille Alphabet Chart

| a | b | c | d | e | f | g | h | i | j | k | l | m |
|---|---|---|---|---|---|---|---|---|---|---|---|---|

| n | o | p | q | r | s | t | u | v | w | x | y | z |
|---|---|---|---|---|---|---|---|---|---|---|---|---|

# Greek Alphabet

| | | | | |
|---|---|---|---|---|
| A α | alpha | | N ν | nu |
| B β | beta | | Ξ ξ | xi |
| Γ γ | gamma | | O o | omicron |
| Δ δ | delta | | Π π | pi |
| E ε | epsilon | | P ϱ | rhō |
| Z ξ | zēta | | Σ σ ς | sigma |
| H η | ēta | | T τ | tau |
| Θ θ | thēta | | Y υ | upsilon |
| I ι | iota | | Φ φ | phi |
| K ϰ | kappa | | X χ | chi |
| Λ λ | lambda | | Ψ ψ | psi |
| M μ | mu | | Ω ω | ōmega |

# International Morse Code

## Letters

| | | | |
|---|---|---|---|
| A • — | G — — • | N — • | U • • — |
| B — • • • | H • • • • | O — — — | V • • • — |
| C — • — • | I • • | P • — — • | W • — — |
| D — • • | J • — — — | Q — — • — | X — • • — |
| E • | K — • — | R • — • | Y — • — — |
| F • • — • | L • — • • | S • • • | Z — — • • |
| | M — — | T — | |

## Numbers

| | |
|---|---|
| 0 — — — — — | 5 • • • • • |
| 1 • — — — — | 6 — • • • • |
| 2 • • — — — | 7 — — • • • |
| 3 • • • — — | 8 — — — • • |
| 4 • • • • — | 9 — — — — • |

## Punctuation Marks

| | | | |
|---|---|---|---|
| period (.) | • — • — • — | semicolon (;) | — • — • — • |
| comma (,) | — — • • — — | colon (:) | — — — • • • |
| question mark (?) | • • — — • • | apostrophe (') | • — — — — • |
| hyphen (-) | — • • • • — | | |

Because it can be difficult to tell where one Morse code letter ends and another begins, people writing in this code often place a single slash (/) between letters and a double slash (//) between words.

# Manual Alphabet

Some people who cannot hear learn to spell and speak with their fingers. The alphabet for finger spelling is called the manual alphabet. It is pictured below. Use this alphabet to spell your name, a greeting, and a word that names a feeling.

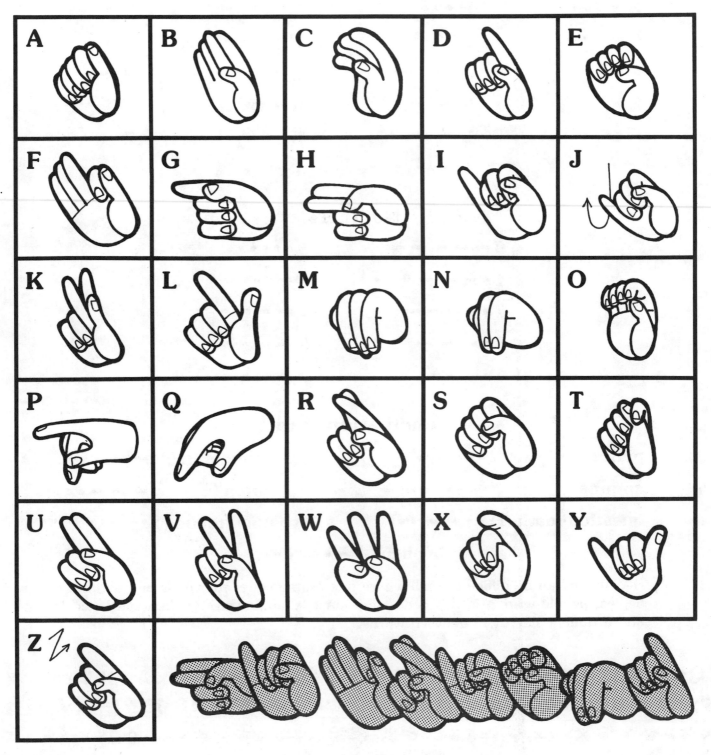

# Map Symbols

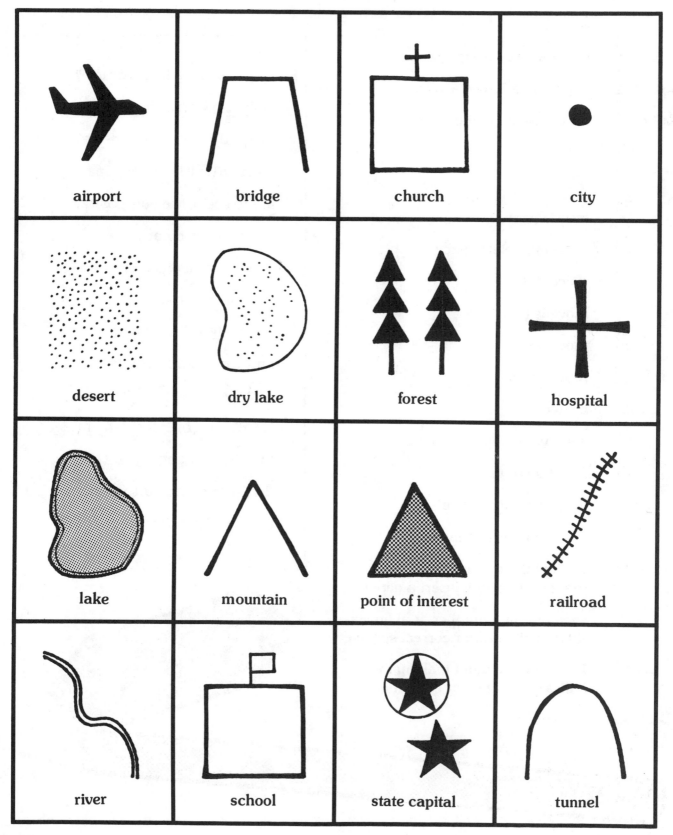

| | | | |
|---|---|---|---|
| airport | bridge | church | city |
| desert | dry lake | forest | hospital |
| lake | mountain | point of interest | railroad |
| river | school | state capital | tunnel |

# Proofreaders' Symbols

| | |
|---|---|
| ¶ | begin a new paragraph |
| *cap* or ≡ | capitalize a lowercase letter |
| *lc* or / | lowercase a capital letter |
| ℌ | delete |
| ∧ | insert |
| # | insert space |
| ⌒ | close up; delete space |
| ⏋ | move right |
| ⌐ | move left |
| ⊓ | move up |
| ⊔ | move down |
| ⊐⊏ | center |
| ‖ | align vertically |
| ⋏ | insert a comma |
| ⋎ | insert an apostrophe |
| ⋎⋎ | insert quotation marks |
| ⊙ | change the existing punctuation mark to a period; insert a period |
| *sp* | spell out (of a number or abbreviation); verify and/or correct spelling |
| *stet* | let it stand without making the indicated change or correction |
| *tr* or ⌒⌒ | transpose |

¶ Proof reading is a tedius *sp* task a proofreader must carefully compare type set material with the original (MS) to see if the compositer has "followed copy. He or she must also determine if the correct type face, size and weight have been used and if the column width matches the (specs.) These things can only be determined by loking carefully at the designer's and editors marks on the edited manuscript.

# Sports Symbols
## Basketball

Holding

Pushing

Traveling

Personal Foul

Player Control Foul

Technical Foul

Illegal Dribble

Illegal Use of Hands

Time Out

Cancel Score

# Sports Symbols
## Football

Dead Ball    Time Out    Start the Clock    First Down    Safety    Touchdown or Field Goal

Offside    Illegal Procedure    Illegal Motion    Illegally Passing or Handing Ball Forward    Illegal Use of Hands and Arms

Ineligible Receiver Down Field on Pass    Forward Pass or Kick-Catching Interference    Intentional Grounding    Ball Illegally Touched, Kicked, or Batted    Incomplete Forward Pass, Penalty Declined, No Play, or No Score

Clipping    Unsportsmanlike Conduct    Personal Foul    Roughing the Kicker

# Weather Symbols

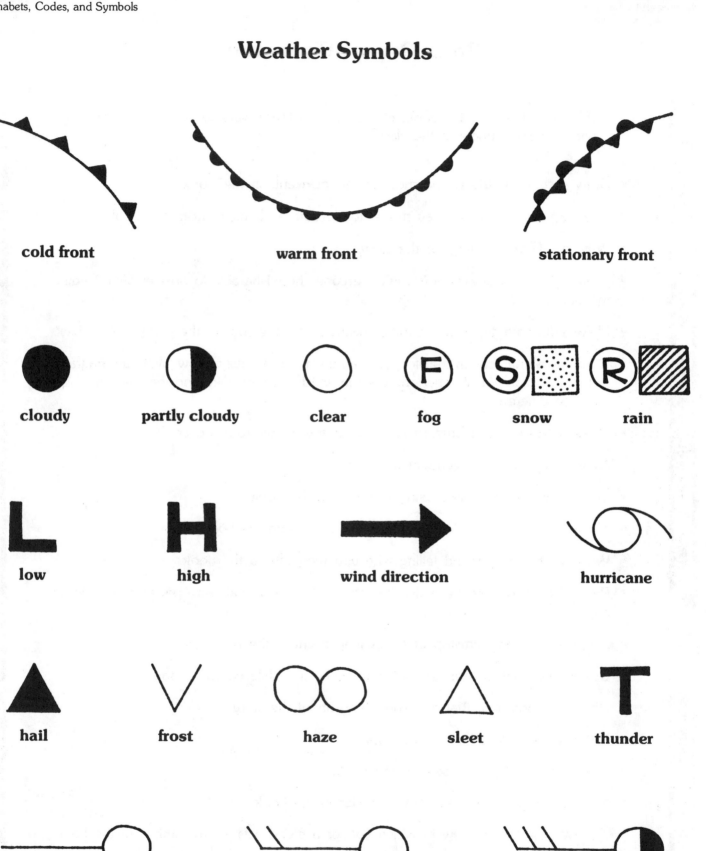

cold front

warm front

stationary front

cloudy

partly cloudy

clear

fog

snow

rain

low

high

wind direction

hurricane

hail

frost

haze

sleet

thunder

wind (1-4 mph)

wind (15-20 mph)

partly cloudy
wind (21-31 mph)

# Book Report Brainstorms

After you have read a book, choose one of these ways to share your book with other members of the class.

- Draw a cartoon strip of the most important events in the story.

- Make a soap, wood, or clay model to illustrate a character from the book.

- Write a different ending for the story.

- Make a list of questions you think everyone should be able to answer after reading the book.

- Make a diorama depicting the most exciting part of the book or the part you liked best.

- Compare a character in the story with a person you actually know. Write a paragraph or two in which you describe the ways in which they are alike and the ways in which they are different.

- Make a word search puzzle using vocabulary words from the book.

- Make a time line of events in the story.

- Make a crossword puzzle using words from the book.

- Make a stitchery sampler to illustrate a scene from the book.

- Write a letter to a friend telling why you recommend the book.

- Pretend that you are the main character and write several diary pages describing an important event in the book.

- Make a shoe box filmstrip of an exciting event in the story.

- Use a wire coat hanger and string to make a mobile based on the book.

- Design a bookmark that tells something about the story.

- Make a poster to advertise the book.

- Write a one-act play based on the book.

- Make a puppet to represent a character in the book.

- Tape-record an interview in which you or a friend acts as the author of the book.

- Write a review of the book for a magazine or newspaper.

# Children's Periodicals

*Bananas*
Scholastic, Inc.
730 Broadway
New York, New York    10003

*Boys' Life*
Boy Scouts of America
1325 Walnut Hill Lane
Irving, Texas    75038-3096

*Chickadee Magazine*
(For young children from *Owl*)
The Young Naturalist Foundation
56 The Esplanade, Suite 306
Toronto, Ontario    M5E 1A7
Canada

*Child Life*
Children's Better Health Institute
1100 Waterway Boulevard, Box 567
Indianapolis, Indiana    46206

*The Children's Album*
(Stories, plays, poetry, crafts)
EGW Publishing Company
Box 6086
Concord, California    94524

*Children's Digest*
Children's Better Health Institute
1100 Waterway Boulevard, Box 567
Indianapolis, Indiana    46206

*Children's Playmate*
Children's Better Health Institute
1100 Waterway Boulevard, Box 567
Indianapolis, Indiana    46206

*Cobblestone*
(American history for ages 8-14)
Cobblestone Publishing, Inc.
20 Grove Street
Peterborough, New Hampshire 03458

*Cricket*
Open Court Publishing Company
315 Fifth Street
Peru, Illinois    61354

*The Dolphin Log*
The Cousteau Society
8440 Santa Monica Boulevard
Los Angeles, California    90069

*Ebony Jr.*
820 South Michigan Avenue
Chicago, Illinois    60605

*The Electric Company Magazine*
Children's Television Workshop
One Lincoln Plaza
New York, New York    10023

*Highlights for Children*
803 Church Street
Honesdale, Pennsylvania    18431

*Humpty Dumpty's Magazine*
Childen's Health Publications
1100 Waterway Boulevard, Box 567
Indianapolis, Indiana    46206

*Jack and Jill*
Children's Health Publications
1100 Waterway Boulevard, Box 567
Indianapolis, Indiana    46206

*MAD*
E. C. Publications
485 MADison Avenue
New York, New York    10022

*Muppet Magazine*
475 Park Avenue South
New York, New York    10016

# Children's Periodicals
## (continued)

*National Geographic World*
National Geographic Society
17th and M Streets, N.W.
Washington, D.C.    20036

*Noah's Ark*
(A monthly newspaper about Jewish history,
     holidays, and laws)
7726 Portal
Houston, Texas    77071

*Odyssey*
(Emphasizes astronomy and outer space for
     ages 8–12)
Kalmbach Publishing Company
1027 N. Seventh Street
Milwaukee, Wisconsin    53233

*Owl Magazine*
(discovery magazine for children)
The Young Naturalist Foundation
56 The Esplanade, Suite 306
Toronto, Ontario    M5E 1A7
Canada

*Penny Power*
(A *Consumer Reports* publication for young
     people)
256 Washington Street
Mount Vernon, New York    10550

*Pennywhistle Press*
(Weekly tabloid newspaper supplement)
Gannett Company, Inc.
Box 500-P
Washington, D.C.    20044

*Ranger Rick*
National Wildlife Federation
1412 Sixteenth Street, N.W.
Washington, D.C.    20036

*Sports Illustrated*
Time, Inc.
Time and Life Building
New York, New York    10020

*'Teen Magazine*
6715 Sunset Boulevard
Box 3297
Los Angeles, California    90028

*3-2-1 Contact*
Children's Television Workshop
One Lincoln Plaza
New York, New York    10023

*U.S. Kids*
4343 Equity Drive
Columbus, Ohio    43216

*Wow*
Scholastic, Inc.
730 Broadway
New York, New York    10003

*Young American*
(Newspaper for kids)
Young American Publishing Company
Box 12409
Portland, Oregon    97212

*Young Author's Magazine*
(Features work of gifted kids)
Theraplan, Incorporated
3015 Woodsdale Boulevard
Lincoln, Nebraska    68502

*Zoobooks*
930 W. Washington, Suite 6
San Diego, California    92103

# Clubs and Organizations for Kids

Entries for this list are based on information contained in the *Encyclopedia of Associations* (21st ed.; Detroit, Mich.: Gale Research Company, 1987). This three-volume guide includes the names, addresses, and brief descriptions of more than 23,000 national and international organizations. These organizations are listed in alphabetical order in the index and then by category in the encyclopedia itself. Among the categories are Agricultural, Athletic and Sports, Business and Commercial, Educational, Hobby and Avocational, and Scientific and Technical. If you have a special interest that is not included among the organizations listed on pages 241–242 and you want to know if there is a club or organization for people who share this interest, consult the *Encyclopedia of Associations* in the research section of your public library.

Academy of Model Aeronautics (AMA)
1810 Samuel Morse Drive
Reston, Virginia   22090
*Phone:* 202-347-2751

Amateur Athletic Union of the
   United States (AAU)
3400 West 86th Street
Indianapolis, Indiana   46268
*Phone:* 317-872-2900

American Youth Hostels (AYH)
P.O. Box 37613
Washington, D.C.   20013
*Phone:* 202-783-6161

American Youth Soccer Organization
   (AYSO)
P.O. Box 5045
Peter Burnett Building
5403 West 138th Street
Hawthorne, California   90251
*Phone:* 213-643-6455

Boys Clubs of America (BCA)
771 First Avenue
New York, New York   10017
*Phone:* 212-557-7755

Boy Scouts of America (BSA)
1325 Walnut Hill Lane
Irving, Texas   75038
*Phone:* 214-659-2000

Camp Fire, Inc. (CFI)
4601 Madison Avenue
Kansas City, Missouri   64112
*Phone:* 816-756-1950

4-H Program
Extension Service
U.S. Department of Agriculture
Washington, D.C.   20250
*Phone:* 202-447-5853

Future Farmers of America (FFA)
National FFA Center
Box 15160
5632 Mount Vernon Memorial Highway
Alexandria, Virginia   22309
*Phone:* 703-360-3600

Girls Clubs of America (GCA)
205 Lexington Avenue
New York, New York   10016
*Phone:* 212-689-3700

# Clubs and Organizations for Kids
## (continued)

Girl Scouts of the U.S.A. (GSUSA)
830 Third Avenue and 51st Street
New York, New York   10022
*Phone:* 212-940-7500

International Friendship League
Beacon Hill
55 Mount Vernon Street
Boston, Massachusetts   02108
*Phone:* 617-523-4273

International Soap Box Derby, Inc.
P. O. Box 7233
Akron, Ohio   44306
*Phone:* 216-733-8723

Junior Philatelists of America
c/o Central Office
P. O. Box 15329
San Antonio, Texas   78212

Little League Baseball (LLB)
Williamsport, Pennsylvania   17701
*Phone:* 717-326-1921

National Association of Girls Clubs
5808 16th Street, N.W.
Washington, D.C.   20011
*Phone:* 202-726-2044

National Association of Rocketry
182 Madison Drive
Elizabeth, Pennsylvania   15037
*Phone:* 412-384-6490

National Audubon Society (NAS)
950 Third Avenue
New York, New York   10022
*Phone:* 212-832-3200

National Campers and Hikers
   Association (NCHA)
7172 Transit Road
Buffalo, New York   14221
*Phone:* 716-634-5433

Pop Warner Football (PWF)
1315 Walnut Street, Suite 606
Philadelphia, Pennsylvania   19107
*Phone:* 215-735-1450

Puppeteers of America (PA)
Five Cricklewood Path
Pasadena, California   91107

Ranger Rick's Nature Club
Children's Division of the
   National Wildlife Federation
1412 16th Street, N.W.
Washington, D.C.   20036
*Phone:* 703-790-4000

Special Olympics, Inc.
1701 K Street, N.W., Suite 203
Washington, D.C.   20006

Student Letter Exchange
910 Fourth Street, S.E.
Austin, Minnesota   55912
*Phone:* 507-433-4389

World Pen Pals
1690 Como Avenue
St. Paul, Minnesota   55108
*Phone:* 612-647-0191

YMCA
291 Broadway
New York, New York   10007

# Dewey Decimal Classification
## The One Hundred Divisions

**000 Generalities**
010 Bibliography
020 Library and information sciences
030 General encyclopedic works
040 [unassigned]
050 General serial publications
060 General organizations and museology
070 Journalism, publishing, newspapers
080 General collections
090 Manuscripts and book rarities

**100 Philosophy**
110 Metaphysics
120 Epistemology, causation, humankind
130 Paranormal phenomena and arts
140 Specific philosophical viewpoints
150 Psychology
160 Logic
170 Ethics (Moral philosophy)
180 Ancient, medieval, Oriental
190 Modern Western philosophy

**200 Religion**
210 Natural religion
220 Bible
230 Christian theology
240 Christian moral and devotional theology
250 Local church and religious orders
260 Social and ecclesiastical theology
270 History and geography of church
280 Christian denominations and sects
290 Other and comparative religions

**300 Social Sciences**
310 Statistics
320 Political science
330 Economics
340 Law
350 Public administration
360 Social problems and services
370 Education
380 Commerce (Trade)
390 Customs, etiquette, folklore

**400 Language**
410 Linguistics
420 English and Anglo-Saxon languages
430 Germanic languages—German
440 Romance languages—French
450 Italian and Romanian languages
460 Spanish and Portuguese languages
470 Italic languages—Latin
480 Hellenic languages—Greek
490 Other languages

**500 Pure Sciences**
510 Mathematics
520 Astronomy and allied sciences
530 Physics
540 Chemistry and allied sciences
550 Sciences of the earth and other worlds
560 Paleontology
570 Life sciences
580 Botanical sciences
590 Zoological sciences

**600 Technology (Applied Sciences)**
610 Medical sciences—Medicine
620 Engineering and allied operations
630 Agriculture and related technologies
640 Home economics and family living
650 Management and auxiliary services
660 Chemical and related technologies
670 Manufactures
680 Manufacture for specific uses
690 Buildings

**700 The Arts**
710 Civic and landscape art
720 Architecture
730 Plastic arts—Sculpture
740 Drawing, decorative and minor arts
750 Painting and paintings
760 Graphic arts—Prints
770 Photography and photographs
780 Music
790 Recreational and performing arts

**800 Literature (Belles-Lettres)**
810 American literature in English
820 English and Anglo-Saxon literatures
830 Literatures of Germanic languages
840 Literatures of Romance languages
850 Italian and Romanian literatures
860 Spanish and Portuguese literatures
870 Italic literatures—Latin
880 Hellenic literatures—Greek
890 Literatures of other languages

**900 General Geography and History**
910 General geography—Travel
920 General biography and genealogy
930 General history of ancient world
940 General history of Europe
950 General history of Asia
960 General history of Africa
970 General history of North America
980 General history of South America
990 General history of other areas

# The Parts of a Book

| | |
|---|---|
| **half-title page** | The first printed page in a book and the page on which only the main part of the book title is listed. Both the subtitle and the author's name are omitted from this page. |
| **title page** | The second printed page in a book and the page on which the full title of the book, the name of the author, the name of the illustrator, and the name of the publisher are listed. |

**author**       the person who wrote the book
**illustrator**  the person who drew the pictures
**publisher**    the company that printed the book

| | |
|---|---|
| **copyright page** | Usually the back of the title page, this page includes the copyright notice, the name of the person or publishing company holding the copyright, and the year in which the book was copyrighted. |
| **dedication page** | Page that carries a brief statement in which the author inscribes or addresses his book to someone as a way of recognizing or complimenting that person. |
| **table of contents** | A list of the significant parts of a book by title and page number in the order in which they appear. It is usually near the front of the book and includes the introduction, all chapter titles, the bibliography, and the index (if there is one). |
| **preface** | A statement by the author telling how or why he or she wrote the book and acknowledging any help he or she had in doing so. |
| **introduction** | An essay that sets the scene for the book, explains the subject or format of the book, or tells how to use the book. |
| **body or text** | The main part of the book. |
| **notes** | Additional explanatory information about facts in the text or about the sources from which they have been gathered. |
| **glossary** | An alphabetical listing of the difficult, special, or technical words used in a book with their definitions and, sometimes, their pronunciations. |
| **bibliography** | A list of articles and other works referred to in the book or used by the author in writing it, or a list of writings relating to the same subject as the text. The works in a bibliography are usually arranged in alphabetical order based on the authors' last names. |
| **index** | An alphabetical list of the names or topics covered in a book, together with the numbers of the pages on which they are defined, explained, or discussed. The index usually appears at the end of the book. |

# A Hundred Holiday Words

### Valentine's Day

- arrow
- bow
- candy
- cards
- caring
- cookies
- cupid
- February
- flowers
- hearts
- lace
- love
- red
- sweetheart
- valentines

### Halloween

- apples
- bats
- black
- broom
- candy
- cats
- costumes
- ghosts
- goblins
- jack-o'-lanterns
- makeup
- masks
- monsters
- night
- October
- orange
- pumpkins
- skeletons
- spooky
- treats
- tricks
- witch

### Thanksgiving

- corn
- cornucopia
- cranberries
- fall
- feast
- football
- gathering
- gravy
- harvest
- Indians
- *Mayflower*
- November
- Pilgrims
- Plymouth Rock
- pumpkin
- pumpkin pie
- stuffing
- turkey

### Hanukkah

- candles
- dreidel
- eight
- festival
- gelt
- Hanukkah
- latkes
- lights
- Maccabees
- menorah
- miracle
- oil
- presents
- songs
- temple

### Christmas

- angel
- bells
- candles
- candy canes
- carols
- chestnuts
- crèche
- December
- elf
- gifts
- green
- holly
- lights
- mistletoe
- ornaments

- parades
- popcorn
- red
- reindeer
- Rudolph
- Santa Claus
- shopping
- sleigh
- snow
- stockings
- toys
- tree
- wassail
- winter
- wreath

Use some of the words on this list and the grid on page 264 to create a crossword puzzle or a word search for a family member for one of these holidays.

# Colors

| | | | |
|---|---|---|---|
| alabaster | canary | crow | lake |
| amber | carmine | cyan | lapis lazuli |
| amethyst | celadon | damask | lavender |
| apricot | cerise | delft | lemon |
| aquamarine | cerulean | drab | lilac |
| aubergine | champagne | dun | lime |
| auburn | charcoal | ebony | madder |
| avocado | chartreuse | ecru | magenta |
| azure | cherry | emerald | mahogany |
| bay | chestnut | fawn | malachite |
| beet | chocolate | fuchsia | maroon |
| beige | cinnabar | gold | mauve |
| bice blue | cinnamon | gray | navy |
| bice green | coal | green | ocher |
| black | cobalt | hazel | olive |
| blood | cocoa | heliotrope | orange |
| blue | coffee | henna | orchid |
| brick | copen | indigo | peach |
| bronze | copper | ink | peacock |
| brown | coral | ivory | pearl |
| buff | cream | jet | periwinkle |
| cadmium | crimson | khaki | pink |

# Colors
## (continued)

| | | | |
|---|---|---|---|
| pitch | russet | soot | ultramarine |
| plum | sable | sorrel | umber |
| puce | saffron | spice | vermilion |
| purple | salmon | tan | vert |
| red | sapphire | tangerine | violet |
| rhodamine | scarlet | taupe | walnut |
| rose | sepia | tawny | white |
| royal blue | sienna | teal | xanthic |
| royal purple | silver | titian | yellow |
| ruby | slate | turquoise | |

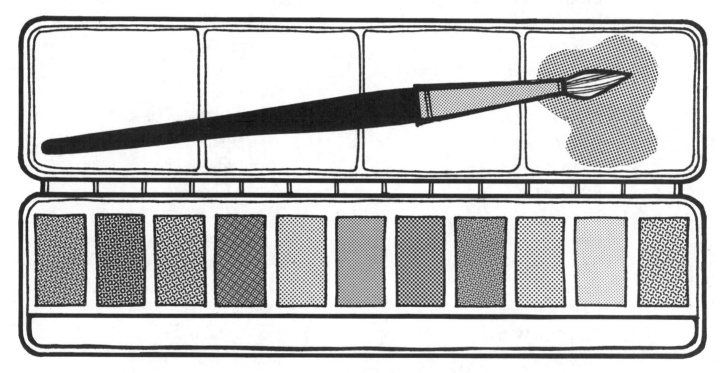

1. Make a chart on which you classify these colors as either **reds**, **oranges**, **yellows**, **greens**, **blues**, **purples**, **browns**, **blacks**, or **whites**.

2. Use crayons, marking pens, or paints to show subtle differences in shade within a single color classification, such as reds or blues.

3. Write a descriptive poem or paragraph in which you use some of the color words from this list.

4. Pick ten of the color words on this list which are new to you. Use a dictionary to discover where these words came from and to write descriptions of the colors to which they refer.

5. Many compound words contain the names of colors. Examples are *blackmail*, *blueprint*, *greenhorn*, *silverware*, and *Yellowstone*. See how many color compounds you can add to this list.

# Famous Detectives in Fiction

| Detective or Agent | Author |
| --- | --- |
| Lew Archer | Ross Macdonald |
| Mack Bolan | Don Pendleton |
| Inspector Napoleon Bonaparte | Arthur W. Upfield |
| James Bond | Ian Fleming |
| Encyclopedia Brown | Donald Sobol |
| Nick Carter | John Coryell |
| Charlie Chan | Earl Derr Biggers |
| Nancy Drew | Carolyn Keene |
| Peter Gunn | Henry Kane |
| Mike Hammer | Mickey Spillane |
| Joe Hardy | Frank Dixon |
| Sherlock Holmes | Sir Arthur Conan Doyle |
| Travis McGee | John D. MacDonald |
| Phillip Marlowe | Raymond Chandler |
| Jane Marple | Agatha Christie |
| Hercule Poirot | Agatha Christie |
| Horace Rumpole | John Mortimer |
| Sam Spade | Dashiell Hammett |
| Spenser | Robert B. Parker |
| Dick Tracy | Chester Gould |
| Lord Peter Whimsey | Dorothy Sayers |
| Nero Wolfe | Rex Stout |

# Famous Pairs

Abbott and Costello

Adam and Eve

Alfredo and Violetta

Amos and Andy

Antony and Cleopatra

Elizabeth Barrett and Robert Browning

Batman and Robin

Beauty and the Beast

Bonnie and Clyde

Archie and Edith Bunker

George Burns and Gracie Allen

Rhett Butler and Scarlett O'Hara

Calvin and Hobbes

Cheech and Chong

Cyrano and Roxane

Dagwood and Blondie

Dick and Jane

Donald and Daisy Duck

Don Quixote and Dulcinea del Toboso

Nelson Eddy and Jeannette MacDonald

Fred and Wilma Flintstone

Gilbert and Sullivan

Hansel and Gretel

# Famous Pairs
## (continued)

Henry Higgins and Eliza Doolittle

Jack and Jill

Kermit and Miss Piggy

Lady and the Tramp

Laurel and Hardy

Lerner and Lowe

Lucy and Desi

Mickey and Minnie Mouse

Napoleon and Josephine

Othello and Desdemona

Ozzie and Harriet

Radames and Aïda

Robin Hood and Maid Marian

Rodgers and Hammerstein

Rodgers and Hart

Romeo and Juliet

Franklin and Eleanor Roosevelt

Sonny and Cher

Superman and Lois Lane

Tarzan and Jane

Tristan and Isolde

# Hobbies and Occupations

| Field | Person | Subject of Study or Interest |
|---|---|---|
| agronomy | agronomist | soil |
| anthropology | anthropologist | man |
| archaeology | archaeologist | ancient civilizations |
| astronomy | astronomer | celestial bodies |
| audiology | audiologist | hearing |
| biology | biologist | living organisms, both plant and animal |
| botany | botanist | plants |
| cardiology | cardiologist | heart |
| conchology | conchologist | shells |
| criminology | criminologist | crime |
| dermatology | dermatologist | skin |
| endocrinology | endocrinologist | glands |
| entomology | entomologist | insects |
| etymology | etymologist | word origins and histories |
| genealogy | genealogist | families and ancestors |
| geology | geologist | rocks |
| geophysics | geophysicist | earth |
| graphology | graphologist | handwriting |
| helminthology | helminthologist | parasitic worms |
| hematology | hematologist | blood and blood-forming organs |
| herpetology | herpetologist | amphibians and reptiles |

# Hobbies and Occupations
## (continued)

| Field | Person | Subject of Study or Interest |
|-------|--------|------------------------------|
| horticulture | horticulturist | growth and cultivation of fruits, vegetables, flowers, or ornamental plants |
| hydrology | hydrologist | water |
| ichthyology | icthyologist | fish |
| malacology | malacologist | mollusks |
| mammalogy | mammalogist | mammals |
| numerology | numerologist | numbers |
| numismatics | numismatist | coins, tokens, medals, and paper money |
| ophthalmology | ophthalmologist | eye |
| ornithology | ornithologist | birds |
| osteology | osteologist | bones |
| otology | otologist | ears |
| paleontology | paleontologist | fossils |
| pathology | pathologist | diseased tissues |
| philately | philatelist | stamps |
| philology | philologist | literature or linguistics |
| phrenology | phrenologist | skulls |
| podiatry | podiatrist | feet |
| psychology | psychologist | mind; mental processes and activities |
| zoology | zoologist | animals |

# Interview Questions

## Early Years

1. Where were you born?
2. Do you have any brothers or sisters?
3. Did you have a pet as a child? If so, what kind?
4. What special memories do you have of your childhood?
5. What was your favorite toy?
6. Did you collect anything as a child? If so, what?
7. Who were your close friends while you were growing up?
8. What things did you and your family enjoy doing together?

## Education and Career

1. Where did you go to school?
2. What was your favorite subject in school?
3. What person influenced your life the most?
4. How old were you when you started your career?
5. What made you choose your present vocation?
6. What special training and/or education is needed for your job?
7. Describe a typical day on your job.
8. What do you like most about your work?
9. What do you like least about your work?
10. What is the most exciting or gratifying thing that's happened to you on your job?

## Special Interests

1. What hobbies and special interests do you enjoy in your spare time?
2. What is the best book you've ever read?
3. What is your favorite food?
4. What three words best describe you?
5. What is one thing you would like to change about yourself?
6. What is one thing you would do differently if you could start over?

# Monsters and Creatures

| | |
|---|---|
| Abominable Snowman | Hydra |
| Argus | kraken |
| basilisk | manticore |
| Big Foot | Medusa |
| centaur | Minotaur |
| Cerberus | Nessie (or Loch Ness monster) |
| Chimera | Nessus |
| Cyclops | phoenix |
| Dracula | roc |
| dragon | Sasquatch |
| Frankenstein | Sphinx |
| gargoyle | Titans |
| giant | vampire |
| Gorgons | werewolf |
| griffin | wyvern |
| Harpies | yeti |

1. Design a poster advertising one of these monsters or creatures for sale.

2. Make a monster mobile using six or more of the creatures listed.

3. Read some of the Greek epics or myths in which many of these monsters appear.

4. Use some of the creatures on this list and the grid on page 264 to create a crossword puzzle or a word search.

# Movie Stars from A to Z

| | | |
|---|---|---|
| F. Murray Abraham | Joan Crawford | Ava Gardner |
| Alan Alda | Hume Cronyn | Judy Garland |
| Woody Allen | Bing Crosby | Teri Garr |
| Julie Andrews | Tom Cruise | Greer Garson |
| Ann-Margaret | Tony Curtis | Janet Gaynor |
| Fred Astaire | Doris Day | Mitzi Gaynor |
| Lauren Bacall | Yvonne De Carlo | Lillian Gish |
| Anne Bancroft | Olivia de Havilland | Louis Gossett, Jr. |
| Brigitte Bardot | Catherine Deneuve | Elliott Gould |
| Lionel Barrymore | Robert De Niro | Betty Grable |
| Warren Beatty | John Derek | Farley Granger |
| Candice Bergen | Marlene Dietrich | Stewart Granger |
| Ingrid Bergman | Kirk Douglas | Cary Grant |
| Jacqueline Bisset | Michael Douglas | Lee Grant |
| Linda Blair | Richard Dreyfuss | Kathryn Grayson |
| Humphrey Bogart | Faye Dunaway | Alec Guinness |
| Shirley Booth | Clint Eastwood | Mark Hamill |
| Ernest Borgnine | Buddy Ebsen | Rex Harrison |
| Marlon Brando | Samantha Eggar | Goldie Hawn |
| Charles Bronson | Anita Ekberg | Rita Hayworth |
| Yul Brynner | Linda Evans | Audrey Hepburn |
| George Burns | Douglas Fairbanks | Katharine Hepburn |
| Ellen Burstyn | Douglas Fairbanks, Jr. | Charlton Heston |
| Richard Burton | Peter Falk | Dustin Hoffman |
| James Cagney | Mia Farrow | William Holden |
| Michael Caine | Barbara Feldon | Celeste Holm |
| Dyan Cannon | Sally Field | Bob Hope |
| Leslie Caron | W. C. Fields | Anthony Hopkins |
| Charles Chaplin | Peter Finch | Ron Howard |
| Cyd Charisse | Carrie Fisher | Rock Hudson |
| Maurice Chevalier | Nina Foch | John Hurt |
| Julie Christie | Henry Fonda | William Hurt |
| Claudette Colbert | Glenn Ford | Angelica Huston |
| Ronald Colman | Harrison Ford | Betty Hutton |
| Sean Connery | Michael J. Fox | Glenda Jackson |
| Gary Cooper | Clark Gable | Derek Jacobi |
| Bill Cosby | Eva Gabor | James Earl Jones |
| Joseph Cotten | Zsa Zsa Gabor | Jennifer Jones |
| Jeanne Crain | Greta Garbo | Louis Jourdan |

# Movie Stars from A to Z
## (continued)

| | | |
|---|---|---|
| Danny Kaye | David Niven | Talia Shire |
| Diane Keaton | Donald O'Connor | Simone Signoret |
| Howard Keel | Laurence Olivier | Jean Simmons |
| Gene Kelly | Ryan O'Neal | Frank Sinatra |
| Grace Kelly | Tatum O'Neal | Maggie Smith |
| Deborah Kerr | Jennifer O'Neill | Elke Sommer |
| Jack Klugman | Peter O'Toole | Ann Sothern |
| Alan Ladd | Al Pacino | Sylvester Stallone |
| Dorothy Lamour | Geraldine Page | Barbara Stanwyck |
| Burt Lancaster | Gregory Peck | Rod Steiger |
| Jessica Lange | Anthony Perkins | Jimmy Stewart |
| Angela Lansbury | River Phoenix | Meryl Streep |
| Charles Laughton | Mary Pickford | Jessica Tandy |
| Peter Lawford | Suzanne Pleshette | Elizabeth Taylor |
| Janet Leigh | Sidney Poitier | Shirley Temple |
| Vivien Leigh | Jane Powell | Gene Tierney |
| Jack Lemmon | Stefanie Powers | Lily Tomlin |
| Jerry Lewis | Anthony Quinn | Spencer Tracy |
| Sophia Loren | Luise Rainer | John Travolta |
| Rob Lowe | Tony Randall | Kathleen Turner |
| Kelly McGillis | Robert Redford | Liv Ullmann |
| Shirley MacLaine | Christopher Reeve | Peter Ustinov |
| Dean Martin | Lee Remick | Dick Van Dyke |
| Lee Marvin | Burt Reynolds | Jon Voight |
| James Mason | Debbie Reynolds | Lindsay Wagner |
| Marlee Matlin | Diana Rigg | Robert Wagner |
| Walter Matthau | Molly Ringwald | John Wayne |
| Victor Mature | Cliff Robertson | Raquel Welch |
| Bette Midler | Ginger Rogers | Richard Widmark |
| Ray Milland | Mickey Rooney | Cornell Wilde |
| Ann Miller | Katherine Ross | Gene Wilder |
| Liza Minnelli | Jane Russell | Robin Williams |
| Demi Moore | Eva Marie Saint | Shelley Winters |
| Dudley Moore | Roy Scheider | Joanne Woodward |
| Mary Tyler Moore | Paul Scofield | Keenan Wynn |
| Roger Moore | George C. Scott | Susannah York |
| Patricia Neal | Randolph Scott | Gig Young |
| Paul Newman | Omar Sharif | Loretta Young |
| Olivia Newton-John | Brooke Shields | Efrem Zimbalist, Jr. |
| Jack Nicholson | | |

# Mythological Gods and Goddesses

| Greek Deity | Description or Area of Responsibility | Roman Deity |
|---|---|---|
| Gaea | Earth (or Mother Earth) | Tellus |
| Uranus | Heaven (or Father Heaven); husband of Gaea | |
| Cronos | son of Uranus and Gaea; youngest of the Titans | Saturn |
| Rhea | daughter of Uranus and Gaea; wife of Cronos; mother of Demeter, Hades, Hera, Hestia, Poseidon, and Zeus; goddess of the earth | Ops |
| Zeus | son of Cronos and Rhea; ruler of heaven; god of rain; king of the gods | Jupiter |
| Hera | daughter of Cronos and Rhea; sister and wife of Zeus; mother of Ares, Hebe, and Hephaestus; goddess of marriage and womanhood; queen of the gods | Juno |
| Aphrodite | created from the remains of Uranus, which had been thrown into the sea; goddess of love and beauty; patroness of seafarers and of war; most beautiful of all the goddesses; had the power to grant irresistible beauty to mortals | Venus |
| Athena | sprang forth fully grown and in complete armor from the forehead of Zeus; goddess of truth and wisdom, justice and war; defender of Athens; patroness of the arts and trades | Minerva |
| Poseidon | son of Cronos and Rhea; husband of Gaea (Mother Earth); originally lord of earthquakes and freshwater streams; later god of the sea and of horses and horse racing | Neptune |
| Hades | son of Cronos and Rhea; husband of Persephone; king of the lower world; giver of all blessings that come from within the earth, including both crops and precious metals; god of wealth; also called Aides, Aidoneus, Orcus, Tartarus, and Pluto | Dis *or* Dis Pater |
| Demeter | daughter of Cronos and Rhea; sister of Zeus; mother of Persephone; goddess of the earth's fruits, especially corn | Ceres |
| Apollo | son of Zeus and Leda; twin brother of Artemis; patron of archery, music, and medicine; protector of law and defender of the social order; closely associated with the sun | Apollo |
| Artemis | daughter of Zeus and Leda; twin sister of Apollo; originally associated with birth and care of the young; later viewed as protector of maidens and goddess of the hunt; often represented by a bear or bow; closely associated with the moon | Diana |
| Ares | son of Zeus and Hera; handsome but savage god of the warlike spirit | Mars |
| Hermes | son of Zeus and Maia; herald of Zeus; messenger of the gods; god of eloquence, prudence, and cleverness; inventor of the alphabet, astronomy, gymnastics, weights, measures, and the lyre; god of the roads; protector of travelers | Mercury |
| Hephaestus | son of Zeus and Hera; god of fire; skilled worker in metals who made armor, weapons, and ornaments for the gods | Vulcan |
| Hestia | daughter of Cronos and Rhea; sister of Zeus; maiden goddess of the fire burning on the hearth and of domestic life in general | Vesta |
| Hebe | daughter of Zeus and Hera; goddess of youth; waited upon the gods, filling their cups with nectar; had the power to make old people young again | Juventas |

# Palindromes

The English word **palindrome** comes from the Greek word *palindromos*, meaning "running back again." A palindrome is a word or group of words that reads the same both forward and backward. Examples of palindromes are listed below.

| | | | |
|---|---|---|---|
| bib | gag | pop | rotor |
| bob | level | pup | sees |
| civic | mom | race car | solos |
| dad | noon | radar | toot |
| did | not a ton | refer | we sew |
| eve | peep | repaper | wet stew |

Able I was ere I saw Elba.

A dog—a panic in a pagoda!

A man, a plan, a canal—Panama!

Madam, I'm Adam.

Too hot to hoot.

Was it a cat I saw?

**WET STEW**

1. Add to this list of palindromes.

2. According to the *Guinness Book of World Records*, Edward Benbow of Bewdley, England, invented the longest English palindrome. Containing 65,000 words, it begins with the words "Rae hits Eb, sire . . . " and ends with the words "Beer is best, I hear." See how long a palindrome you can invent.

3. Words are not the only palindromes. Numbers can be palindromes, also. For example, in every year there is one day whose date is a palindrome. In 1987, this day was July 8—7/8/87. Discover and write the palindrome dates for the current year, the year in which you were born, and the year in which your school building was constructed.

# Proverbs

A **proverb** is a brief saying that states a universal truth or expresses a choice morsel of folk wisdom.

A bird in the hand is worth two in the bush.

A fool and his money are soon parted.

All that glitters is not gold.

An apple a day keeps the doctor away.

A rolling stone gathers no moss.

As the twig is bent, so grows the tree.

A stitch in time saves nine.

A thing of beauty is a joy forever.

A watched pot never boils.

Be it ever so humble, there's no place like home.

Better late than never.

Better safe than sorry.

Don't count your chickens before they're hatched.

Don't cross the bridge until you come to it.

Don't cry over spilt milk.

Don't judge a book by its cover.

Don't look a gift horse in the mouth.

Don't put all of your eggs in one basket.

Early to bed, early to rise, makes a man healthy, wealthy, and wise.

Half a loaf is better than none.

Haste makes waste.

Look before you leap.

Love is blind.

Make hay while the sun shines.

Necessity is the mother of invention.

Never leave 'till tomorrow what you can do today.

Nothing is certain but death and taxes.

Nothing succeeds like success.

One bad apple doesn't spoil the bunch.

One picture is worth more than ten thousand words.

On the day of victory, no one is tired.

Pride goeth before a fall.

The pen is mightier than the sword.

Variety is the spice of life.

Whatever is worth doing at all is worth doing well.

When poverty comes in at the door, love flies out the window.

# Water Words

| | | |
|---|---|---|
| water | waterfowl | water-repellent |
| water balance | waterfront | water-resistant |
| water ballet | water gap | watershed |
| waterbed | water gas | waterside |
| water beetle | water gate | water ski |
| water biscuit | water glass | waterspout |
| water blister | water hole | water strider |
| waterborne | water lily | water system |
| water boy | waterline | water table |
| waterbuck | waterlogged | watertight |
| water buffalo | waterloo | water tower |
| water chestnut | water main | water turkey |
| water closet | watermark | water vapor |
| watercolor | watermelon | water wagon |
| water cooler | water moccasin | waterway |
| watercourse | water ouzel | waterwheel |
| watercraft | water pipe | water wings |
| watercress | water polo | water witch |
| waterfall | waterpower | waterworks |
| | waterproof | |

Use some of these words and their definitions to create a matching game. In **Column A**, list at least twelve words from this list. In **Column B**, write simple definitions for these words in random order. Follow the form and format of the example below. When you have finished creating your puzzle, ask a friend to match the words with their definitions by writing the correct letter on each line.

| **Column A** | **Column B** |
|---|---|
| _____ 1. water biscuit | A. an aquatic bird |
| _____ 2. water closet | B. a design pressed in paper |
| _____ 3. waterfowl | C. a bathroom |
| _____ 4. watermark | D. a cracker |
| _____ 5. water strider | E. a long-legged bug that moves about on the surface of the water |

# What's Up?

The versatile word **up** can be a noun, a verb, an adjective, an adverb, or a preposition, depending on how it is used. Here is a list of words that begin with **up**.

| | | |
|---|---|---|
| up-and-coming | upon | upshot |
| up-and-down | upper | upside |
| up-and-up | uppercase | upside down |
| upbeat | upper class | upstage |
| upbraid | upper crust | upstairs |
| upbringing | uppercut | upstart |
| update | upper hand | upstate |
| upend | uppermost | upstream |
| upgrade | uppity | upstroke |
| upheaval | upraise | upswing |
| uphill | upright | uptake |
| uphold | uprising | uptight |
| upholster | uproar | up-to-date |
| upkeep | uproot | up-to-the-minute |
| upland | ups and downs | uptown |
| uplift | upscale | upturn |
| upmost | upset | upwind |
| | upshift | |

1. Write a humorous story using as many of these **up** words as possible.

2. Pick one of the following words and use it to create your own list like the one above: **day**, **double**, **down**, or **ice**.

# Bonus Ideas Just for Fun

1. Select six unusual objects from the Things That Hold Things list on page 212. Do research to discover what these objects look like. Draw and label a picture of each one.

2. From the list on pages 214 and 215, choose a holiday you would like to learn more about. Do research to discover the origin of this holiday and the specific foods and customs associated with its celebration.

3. Select a creative writing title from one of the lists on pages 223 through 227. Working with a partner, write and illustrate a short story inspired by the title you have selected.

4. Exchange creative writing papers with a classmate and each proofread the other's work. Where appropriate, use the symbols listed on page 234.

5. Select one thing from the list of Things with Holes on page 228. On a sheet of white art paper, draw a picture of this thing. Cut out the hole. Color your picture. Write a paragraph describing this thing. Pretend that you are describing it to a person who has never seen one. Tell what it is made of, how big it is, and what it is used for.

6. A proverb is a brief saying that states a universal truth or expresses a choice morsel of folk wisdom in words that are simple and easy to understand. Select a proverb from the list on page 259. Using a thesaurus, rewrite this proverb to make it sound much more complex. For example, you might rewrite *Don't cry over spilt milk* to be *Refrain from engaging in lacrimation in response to the inadvertent wasting of a dairy product.*

7. Using a sheet of lined paper or the form on page 263, create a list of your own. For example, you might list
   a. board games,
   b. candy bars,
   c. famous animals on television or in the movies,
   d. ice cream flavors,
   e. kinds of shelters,
   f. nursery rhymes,
   g. things that are a particular color, such as red,
   h. things that are round,
   i. things that are sold in tubes, or
   j. words with the word *down* in them.

# Create a Just-for-Fun List

Think of a just-for-fun topic that interests you. On the lines below, create a list that reflects this topic. Illustrate your list and give it a title.

_____

_____

_____

_____

_____

_____

_____

_____

_____

_____

# Create a Puzzle

Use this grid to create a crossword puzzle or a word search based on one of the lists in this book. Print the title of your puzzle on the line below. On the back of this page, write instructions, clues and definitions, and/or a list of words for which students are to search. On a separate sheet of paper, provide an answer key.

_____

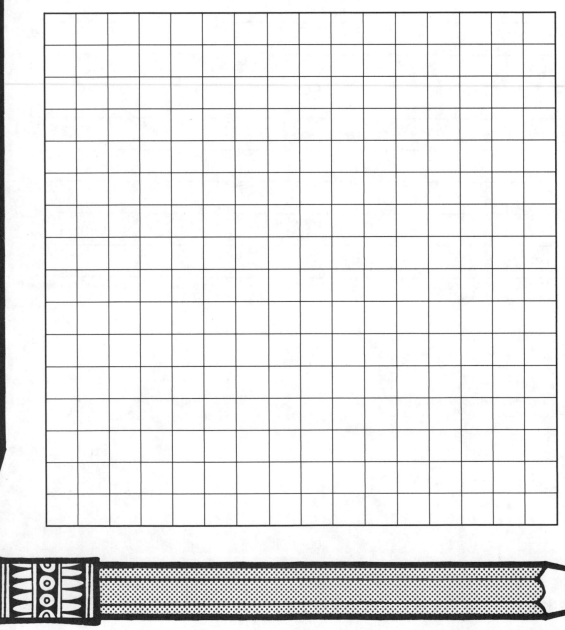